My Defence

MY DEFENCE

My Defence

Winning, losing, scandals
and the drama of Germany 2006

Ashley Cole

with Steve Dennis

headline

First published in 2006
by HEADLINE PUBLISHING GROUP

1

A CIP catalogue record for this title is available from the British Library

0 7553 1540 5 (ISBN-10)
978 0 7553 1540 6 (ISBN-13)

Text design by
Ben Cracknell Studios

Typeset in Palatino Light by Avon DataSet Ltd,
Bidford on Avon, Warwickshire

Printed and bound in Great Britain by
Mackays of Chatham plc, Chatham, Kent

Headline's policy is to use papers that are natural, renewable and recyclable
products and made from wood grown in sustainable forests. The logging and
manufacturing processes are expected to conform to the environmental
regulations of the country of origin.

HEADLINE PUBLISHING GROUP
A division of Hachette Livre UK Ltd
338 Euston Road
London NW1 3BH

www.headline.co.uk
www.hodderheadline.com

**To my two biggest supporters in life –
my mum and my wife.**

Acknowledgements

Getting a book published is a team effort, and the team behind *My Defence* has been 'immaculate' – slick, tight, well-organised and in a league of its own. I'd like to thank: everyone at team Headline, especially the 'manager' David Wilson; Steve Dennis – you've shown good skills, we linked up well and I couldn't have done it without you; my agents Jonathan Barnett and David Manesseh – you made this book happen, and I'm indebted to you both for your friendship, advice and endless support; my lawyer Graham Shear – you're always there and your defensive work is rock solid.

A big up to all my boys: brother Mattie, Jermaine Wynters, Paulo Vernazza, Jon Fortune, Cecil Talian – your friendship not only matters to me but it's been massive through the good and not so good, and huge thanks to all my other friends who've cheered me on – you know who you are.

I don't know how to thank the one person I owe my life to – Mum – because 'thank you' don't seem enough. She's the best, has always been there for me, and I'd have been lost if she hadn't been behind me every step of the way.

And finally to Cheryl, I knew you were for me from the moment we met. You're my best friend, my huge support and my reason to be happy. Oh yes, and now you're my wife – and I'm liking the sound of that!

Ashley

August 2006

Contents

Ashley . . . has everything it takes to be to Arsenal what Paolo

Maldini has been to AC Milan: a player so strongly linked to a

club that he will be forever associated with it, and come to

symbolise it. Ashley is the future for Arsenal, and they should make

sure they are aware of it.

Patrick Vieira
My Autobiography, Orion, 2005

Introduction

Okay, from the off, this is not an autobiography.
I'm too young for all that life-story stuff.

This is my journey to Germany 2006, with all the twists, turns and controversy along the way; then it's the story of what happened to England when we were there; and then there's my account of an uncertain summer and what the newspapers called 'the most tortuous transfer saga in Premiership history' – and they don't know the half of it.

So see this book as more of an 18-months-in-the-life-of story; the best and worst of times on and off the pitch. I've been called all the names under the sun, been both back page 'sport' and front page 'scandal' headline news, enjoyed the biggest highs of my career, and met and married the woman of my dreams.

So much has been written about me, and so many people think

they know me and what's *really* gone on, that there comes a time when enough is enough, and you have to speak up for yourself. Before people question my loyalty, they need to know the club politics and the betrayal I felt in the first place. And then they can pass judgement.

That's why it seemed right to tell my side of the story. Not Arsenal's. Not the FA Premier League's. Mine. And it's a story the Arsenal board would prefer the Arsenal fans not to read.

All I hope is that the football fan hears me out and looks at the overall picture before rushing to judgement on my infamous 'tapping-up scandal' with Chelsea, and this summer's transfer dealings.

All I ask is that you read my account and then make up your own mind because so many fans – especially at Arsenal – condemned me based on the outcome of the FA Premier League tribunal and what the newspapers said.

In the process, I hope you learn more about football behind-the-scenes: in the dressing room, in the boardroom, in the spotlight, in the Premiership, in the Champions League and in the World Cup.

So please read on because whether it's about life in the Arsenal or England back four, life in the witness stand, or life in the middle of a summer transfer saga, this is 'my defence'.

Thank you for listening.

Dreamland

I'm looking for Mum in the jubilant crowd, trying to pick her out, trying to see through the glare of the sun and the tangle of streamers falling from the sky. She's up there in the stand, in her usual seat at Highbury, behind the directors' box. She'll be cheering and singing and clapping with the best of them, feeling as ecstatic as the other 36,000 fans as the sun beats down on the pitch, as it snows red and white confetti, as the champagne creates a wet mist in front of me.

She'll be there cheering me on as she has from day one, feeling just as proud about this moment as I do. I can't pick her out in all the mayhem, with all the din, but I raise an arm and wave anyway. She'll have her eye on me even though I can't see her. She'll know I'm saluting her because it's something I've done at the start and end of every Arsenal game since making my senior debut in November 1999.

The importance of this occasion is massive because she has just witnessed, and I have just been a part of, a very special and historic match. It's shortly after five o'clock in the afternoon on 15 May 2004, and the digital orange letters on the scoreboard no longer tell the result of our final game of the season: 'Arsenal 2 Leicester 1'. Instead, it reads 'Congratulations!' and it keeps flashing, like an amber warning to the rest of football. Highbury is rocking, and the fans are singing their hearts out: 'We are un-beat-able . . . say we are un-beat-able!'

We're in the middle of the sweetest of parties, in the middle of our favourite arena with a noise so loud it's like being surrounded on all four sides by the loudest of speakers, pumping up the volume. I'm looking around, trying to take it all in, desperate to find Mum's face. Still can't see her. Streamers and confetti fall and settle around us. I turn away from the spray of bubbly that Sylvain Wiltord has let off in front of the lads, all huddled and jumping in celebration on the blue podium which reads 'Arsenal: Barclaycard Champions 2003–2004'. We've done more than just win the Premiership title. We've become 'The Invincibles', unbeaten for every one of our 38 league games; the first side since Preston North End in 1888–89 to pull it off. Played 38. Won 26. Drawn 12. Lost 0. History will remember this as 'the immaculate season', and none of us will forget this moment for as long as we live.

Each player is ecstatic and hoarse from yelling and screaming. None of us can grasp the scale of what we've done, how mentally strong we've had to be. I'm looking at the lads' faces as we pose up for the bank of press photographers: Lauren is singing, Sol's got his finger in the air, saluting us all as 'Number One', Gilberto looks choked, Patrick is bent down, cheering in my ear, and I've got this smile on my face which will last all summer. Arsene Wenger, the boss, in his blue shirt and suit trousers, will be somewhere tucked out of the limelight, letting us milk it. Football don't get much better than this: stood on this pitch, at this home, in front of this family of team-mates, staff and fans.

There is no better time to be an Arsenal player; no better time to be an Arsenal fan.

And the fans were still there the next day, singing and cheering, when we went in an open-top, double-decker bus procession through Islington. A quarter of a million Gooners lined the streets, and north London was a mass of red and white and yellow as our bus trundled through the crowds. As a player, when you're stood there looking down on the smiling faces, seeing thousands of clapping hands held high above thousands of heads, it is an incredible feeling. It is a joy you know is being shared between players and fans, and that's what binds a club together.

That endless celebration crowned an incredible season where we clicked like the slickest of machines. Every player in every department was on the same wavelength, and we were a team connected by unity, desire, hunger, spirit and instinct. We'd gone into each match believing we could not be beaten. Our belief was a twelfth man running around in a red and white shirt, and other teams were scared of us; frightened and backing off.

We'd secured the title four matches earlier: clinching it in an away game at Spurs. And what better place could there have been to win it. Every Arsenal player and fan wanted to do it at White Hart Lane. I've friends who are players at Spurs, but the north London rivalry made us all want to be crowned champions under their noses, on their turf. And it was all going well right up to the 90th minute as we led 2–1 and got ready to jump around.

It was then that our keeper Jens Lehmann had one of his mad moments when Robbie Keane trod on his toes in the box. Jens shoved him over. Penalty. 2–2. The champagne was on ice. Or so we thought. Until Alan Shearer secured the title for us. We didn't realise until the final whistle that his Newcastle goal, a belter of a curler into the top corner, had left Chelsea unable to catch us. It was time to celebrate.

Sol, because he was ex-Spurs, was a gentleman, and walked off the pitch and into the dressing room because he didn't want to wind up his former supporters. Not me, though. I was off and running, doing a lap of honour with Thierry, in his vest, swinging his shirt. We stood there at the corner flag, singing and dancing with the Arsenal fans and the rest of the team. There was a massive banner saying 'ARSENAL: CHAMPIONS' STAND' at White Hart Lane. Talk about rubbing it in, but I liked their style!

That's when we noticed a number of fake, plastic Premiership trophies dancing around above all those heads in the stand. A supporter tossed one down to the team and, one by one, roared on by the fans, each player held it up in the air with both hands as if it was the real thing. Then came my turn. I was the last one to do it. That's when the thought came to me: to go and plonk this 'trophy' slap bang at the heart of White Hart Lane.

I turned from the corner flag and ran, pelting across the pitch as the fans cheered. Thierry and Ray Parlour followed. I got to the centre circle and stood there, right next to the big white blob of the centre spot. I raised the trophy high above my head and brought it down like I was sinking a flag into enemy territory, slamming it down on the spot. It was like someone had scored a goal. The Arsenal fans went crazy. It was the best moment. There's a picture of me with Thierry, him draped in a Gunners flag and me draped in a blue Champions flag, posing with the trophy in that exact spot; capturing the nerve of it all. Nothing beats putting our 'trophy' in the middle of that pitch. Nothing tops 38 games unbeaten. I was celebrating the best times of my life with a club I adored, in front of fans who had sang my name all season long.

I'm in Gunners dreamland, and the future seems as certain as the fact that my life is going to be spent at Highbury and then the new Emirates Stadium. This is my club, my life, and always has been. And it is the same for my mum, Sue. Despite growing up in a QPR household, she's a Gunner through and through. She's been behind me every step of the way since I was a kid, and we've both got our lives mapped out at Avenell Road and then Ashburton Grove. The future remains full of dreams and goals in a red and white shirt.

I want to hammer Manchester United into submission umpteen more times. I want the title over and over again. I want to make history and break more club and league records. I want to be Tony Adams and Patrick Vieira and become the next captain and hold as many trophies aloft as possible. Real ones, not plastic ones. I want to stay on at Arsenal and break David O'Leary's 555 league appearances. Even beat John Lukic as the oldest player, running out until I am 40. I want to do so much.

Around the corner, there is the 2004 Euro Championships in Portugal. I'm now part of Sven-Goran Eriksson's England future, too. My form for the club has put me right up there on the international stage, and I want to be part of a national team that becomes the best in Europe and then the best in the world. Germany 2006 is on the horizon. My second World Cup. England's chance to prove ourselves.

Life couldn't be much sweeter. This is the stuff of dreams for the kid from Puma FC in east London. I felt like I was in the land of make-believe when I walked through the famous Marble Hall to sign up for Arsenal aged nine. Now I'm touching the dream as much as I'm touching the Premiership trophy.

I'm so happy, it's not true.

Nothing, but nothing, could possibly go wrong.

1

A Matter of Honour

As soon as my foot struck the ball, I knew it meant trouble, but there weren't no stopping it. There's nothing like the feeling of a sweet connection, when you hit the ball just right and it's heading towards goal. Only this ball, my tennis ball, weren't bound for any net, and I was only six years old.

This yellow blur arched towards Mum's precious picture frame in the lounge of our fourth-floor flat in Poplar, east London. It was like one of those slow-motion moments showing a howler on *Match of the Day*. Only Mum weren't as measured as Alan Hansen with her analysis. She went absolutely crazy because that treasured wooden frame housed her best photos of me and my brother Mattie, then aged five. When the ball hit it, the frame dropped, smashing the glass and splintering the wood. With the whalloping that followed – because I, as the footballer, carried the can – I learned from an early age never to play ball in the lounge again. I also learned that once something is broke, it's permanently knackered. Mum got new glass and managed to glue the frame into some state of repair, but she always banged on about how she could still see the cracks and the join. I'd never had anything that important or precious. Nothing of any material worth anyhow. Not at that age. What I treasured most was the only dream I had: to one day play for the Arsenal.

I didn't care whether I was a striker or defender, a Kenny Sansom or an Ian Wright. Or any other Gunner I'd watched on our little portable television in the flat: Kevin Campbell, Paul Davis, David Rocastle, Tony Adams, Perry Groves, Anders Limpar or Dennis Bergkamp. Little did I know back then that I would have the honour and privilege of playing alongside a few of them. So when I walked into Highbury three years later and signed up, I suddenly found something that was precious: the chance to play for one of the finest, most brilliant, most powerful teams in the world.

And no-one was going to smash that dream into pieces.

Though my dream was not something that could be hung on a wall, it was more precious than any family picture frame. It was the start of a special relationship because I would become a 'home-grown' player with Arsenal FC, putting me among a unique group of names that grew up at the club, climbed through the apprentice ranks and made it to the first team: names such as that darling of the North Bank, Charlie George, Frank Stapleton, David O'Leary, Liam Brady – now head of youth development – Tony Adams, Martin Keown, David Rocastle, George Armstrong and the current assistant manager Pat Rice, to name but a few.

I can't begin to tell you how it felt to be an Arsenal player, pulling that famous red and white strip over my head for my debut as a sub against Middlesbrough in 1999, winning that coveted No. 3 shirt and running out in front of the Arsenal fans. Mum was dead proud. Her son, the one who had perched on the edge of her bed in her room watching highlights on the box, had become a fully fledged Gunner. I'd always wanted her to be proud of me. That stuff matters to me. When I had a loan spell away from Highbury with Crystal Palace she followed me home and away. She even followed me to Grimsby of all places. Even now, after every game, it's her opinion I check out after the boss has said his bit. If she says I've had a good game, then that's good. But she never shies away from telling me if I've been crap, and has often hammered my performances. Most footballers grew up having dads on the touch-line. I grew up with an Arsenal-mad mum shouting and yelling encouragement. She, of all people, knew how important Arsenal was to me. Just walking into Highbury you sense the history, the glory and the tradition. Each time I played, sat on the bench or trained, I never lost that feeling of being blessed, of being the luckiest lad from east London.

As a fan, I remember the memorable games like everyone else: from the tears of losing 3–1 to Spurs in the 1991 FA Cup, to the breathless joy in 1989 when Michael Thomas scored that second goal against Liverpool at Anfield to secure the league title for the first time in 18 years.

As a player, under Arsene Wenger, I was lucky enough to be part of his continental revolution; part of a dream team that carved its name in history with the 2002 FA Cup and Premiership double, and then with that 'invincible' league run which, ultimately, became 49 unbeaten matches on the trot. They were immense, unforgettable years that will leave the cheers of many ghosts echoing around Highbury, long after the pitch, seats and tiers have been ripped out to make way for flats. It is an irony that Highbury is going to be turned into flats, because for many of the players, staff and fans, it's been a home away from home since hosting its first game in 1913. So it's not just the East and West Stand facades being kept during development. The memories will also linger in those Marble Halls.

It is these memories, whether you're a fan or player, which tie you in knots to a club. If, like me, you have been a fan since childhood, that passion only gets deeper. I've heard that passion swell the boundaries of that compact stadium when I've been in the middle of that pitch. First the noisy lot in the Clock End, then the North Bank and, before you know it, the chanting is bouncing around the place; bouncing and swaying, rising and falling. I've thrived on the back of that support. My spine has tingled even when I've stepped off the team coach and the fans have been outside cheering us off, one by one. My heart and soul was tied to Arsenal with a fisherman's knot. I don't think even Houdini could have unravelled it. Not for one minute did I see myself leaving. There was only ever one club in England, let alone London, and that was the Arsenal.

Well, that was then. That was before the 2004–05 season. That was before something precious was smashed into tiny pieces.

I know what was said. As do the directors sat in the Arsenal FC board meeting. Arsene Wenger was backing me and doing his best from the start. He said my salary was behind the other players in the team and should be reviewed. That would have been not long after the Leicester game at the end of the storming 2003–04 season. The party was over, but the boss wanted certain players to be rewarded; me chief among them. For the manager to speak up for me like that was typical of the fairness that runs through him. He doesn't wait for players to moan or agents to haggle. He saw an imbalance and wanted it corrected, and so he took it to the top.

David Dein, the vice-chairman, and to me the face of the Arsenal board, would lead renegotiations. Now, I had heard stories about Arsenal's, and other clubs', decision-makers not knowing how to treat leading players. Tales like that wafted around the dressing room like a bad smell. Even in the Arsenal youth team, rumours about the club being tight with the cash flew around; tight in the context of football, anyway. As a first-teamer, you quickly wise up to the ruthless business that is football generally, and realise that loyalty is sometimes a poor relation to profit and cold business. I've read reports before suggesting players are all about cash and couldn't even spell 'loyalty'. That's bullshit. There might be some players whose hearts are probably more into their bank balances than their clubs. But don't tell me that loyalty isn't paramount to the likes of Robbie Fowler with Liverpool, Ryan Giggs with Manchester United or John Terry and Frank Lampard with Chelsea. I'd like to think my association with Arsenal was once viewed the same way.

But players swap stories and we get to hear on the grapevine when one player hasn't been treated right or gets handed a deal that doesn't reflect his talent or service. I got the feeling the board hadn't wanted to fight for the contracts of the likes of Martin Keown, Kanu or Sylvain Wiltord; it seems Edu was not offered the contract he deserved so he took that insult and left. We all knew when world-class legend Patrick Vieira, whose French blood had long been transfused with the blood of red and white, had got a phone call from Mr Dein telling him negotiations had been going on with Juventus and the board's stance was 'neutral' as to whether he stayed or left. Not surprisingly, he left. Then Arsenal wonders why a big hole was blown out of the team and the dressing room.

I remember, during the 2002 World Cup in Japan and South Korea, that David Seaman was in talks over a new club contract, and there had already been a rumour whizzing round the dressing room that Arsenal – represented by David Dein who was at the tournament in his role as a member of the FA International Committee – was being difficult. Seaman, the greatest keeper in Arsenal's history, was a true legend and a brilliant servant to the club, and everyone but the board, it looked to me, wanted him to finish his career at the club. During that World Cup we played a lot on the computers, and Seaman was addicted to a fishing game. Mr Dein would be sat there talking away while Seaman played, and I wondered to myself, 'Who isn't listening to whom?' Both probably.

After the tournament, David was still the best goalie around, but it looks like the deal he was offered to stay on weren't the right one, and many in the dressing room felt he weren't treated right. I always felt that had to be one of the reasons why David ended up going to Manchester City – also so he could get first-team football. It was hard to see him leave.

I'd signed my first senior contract with Arsenal aged 19. I remember pinching myself at landing a £25,000-a-week deal. No-one, least of all me, could have predicted how rapidly I'd become an ever-present feature of both the Arsenal and England teams. I played out of my skin and my aunt's scrapbook filled up with articles saying good things about me.

As I've said, by the end of our unbeaten championship season, it was clear the boss felt my salary was not a true reflection of my position within the team and that's why he set out to improve my existing contract. There was also a lot of newspaper talk about the likes of Sol Campbell, Patrick Vieira and Thierry Henry being on contracts worth between £80,000 and £100,000 a week. The newspapers, for once, were not far wrong. When you look at figures like that, you can understand why agents are involved. It's people like my agents Jonathan Barnett and David Manasseh, who have been like protective uncles to me, who negotiate with the clubs and make sure the player is getting a fair deal and, more importantly, is getting what he's *worth*. I can't sit here and write about how footballers deserve such wages when there are nurses, policemen and firemen out there doing much more important jobs. Footballers will always be on a sticky wicket discussing cash, but the industry where my skills are employed is awash with stupid money. The market, thanks to television and sponsorship and the odd Russian billionaire, has risen to meet that demand.

Footballers are like houses: only worth what people will pay for them. And clubs and owners are currently paying sky-high to achieve supreme teams, whether it was Jack Walker at Blackburn or Roman Abramovich at Chelsea. Whatever industry someone is in, it's only right they get paid fairly, in line with the rest of the workforce. It's about fairness not greed, and I'm not a greedy person. I had enough of a grounded, working-class upbringing in east London to understand the value of money, and I have friends who have normal, manual, not very well-paid jobs. So there is not a day goes by when I don't realise how exceptionally lucky I am to enjoy the life I now have.

It's because I appreciate this that I've never once moaned during contract negotiations, never made a fuss, and my pen has been across that paper within 20 minutes of a contract being put before me. No-one could ever call me a prima donna. Playing for Arsenal was all that mattered to me. Having said that, no player likes to feel taken for granted. There is fair and then there is taking the piss.

Maybe I'd been regarded as a soft touch before, but players know what they are worth, know what they have contributed and, if their agent is on the ball, know what another club would pay. But it wasn't my agent pushing for more money. It was Arsene Wenger. Not that I realised that until much later on.

And something else that I wouldn't find out about straight away was the club's own calculation of the price tag it had placed on my head, my value to them as an asset. As an FA Premier League inquiry would later hear, my value was around £20 million.

Not bad for a lad they got for nothing from Puma FC. My worth was sort of irrelevant, though. It didn't mean anything because I was staying. All I could do was wait for the vice-chairman to start talking to me.

I was sitting with Sol Campbell and his then girlfriend, Kelly Hoppen, outside in the sunshine at Sopwell House, the hotel in Hertfordshire used by both Arsenal and England. It was June 2004 and, together with the rest of the national squad, we had an hour and a half of free time before the coach left for the airport and our plane to Sardinia and our training camp ahead of the Euro Championships in Portugal.

I was lazing around, eyes closed, feeling the sun on my face, when an eager voice called out, 'Ashley!' Mr Dein was stood there. 'Ashley, can I have a word?' He seemed flustered and there were beads of sweat on his forehead. We went into a little room just inside the hotel, like a little bar area. He caught his breath, then told me I wasn't earning enough, my salary was going to be increased, they intended to improve my contract and I should see this as recognition of my hard work during the past incredible season.

My face-cracking smile told him all he needed to know. I remember trying to be all serious, because it was the vice-chairman, but I couldn't stop beaming. I was buzzing, really buzzing. This was three years before my contract was due to expire. Normally, it's usual for new contract terms to be discussed with about 18 months left to run, because no club likes to leave a contract until the final year; it can't risk someone playing out his contract and being transferred on a 'Bosman', leaving the club with nothing. What Jonathan, my agent, and I had discussed previously was that Arsenal – say in June 2005 – were likely to offer a deal of around £65,000 a week. So this was exciting for me. It was a year early.

As I remember it, Mr Dein gave me some figures, saying this was the new offer and that I should have a think about it, but that it was take it or leave it. His tone soon wiped the smile from my face. I felt his attitude suggested he was doing me a favour, like I was a 17-year-old trainee.

The deal he offered was a £10,000-a-week increase to £35,000. A hell of a lot of money. But, when taken in the context of football wages and his own estimated value of £20 million, and when placed next to those other Arsenal wages of between £80,000 and £100,000 a week, his offer made me feel it was a piss-take. What I had hoped for was to be treated like my team-mates at Arsenal and England. I couldn't understand why, according to David Dein, I was worth only about half the wage of the players around me.

I don't expect anyone's sympathy or understanding over this. I can hear half my mates telling me that I don't know I'm born. But it goes back to my point about what is fair among team-mates.

Mr Dein carried on, telling me how I would be set for life and it was a huge wage for a lad my age. I wondered if I was going to get a pat on the head and a lollipop for being good if I accepted. It dawned on me then why he might have been rushing to this meeting and looked so flustered. I reckoned he wanted to bag my signature ahead of the Euro Championships, knowing full well that if I were to have a scintillating tournament, my value – and therefore my agent's position of strength – would grow. Mr Dein isn't daft. He's a shrewd operator and a clever businessman. He weren't going to get my signature, though. I told him I wanted to talk it through with my agent. 'This is a generous offer Ashley,' were his final words, as I headed for the coach.

I played our conversation over and over in my head on the way to the airport, when my mind should have been gearing up for Portugal and our first game against France on 13 June. I kept thinking, 'Would Arsenal treat Thierry and Patrick in this way?' – the team-mates who were to become opponents in that first Euro game in which our 1–0 lead at 90 minutes was turned on its head into a 2–1 defeat, with two French goals in stoppage time. Maybe Arsenal drew a distinction between a son of the club and one of the foreign imports – I don't know.

Clubs bang on about the importance of 'home-grown players' and how there needs to be more of them, but they need to cotton on to the fact that just because a talent has been harnessed and nurtured from an early age as opposed to being the subject of a big-money, headline-grabbing transfer coup, it doesn't mean that it's a talent that owes the club special discounts in negotiation. I was discovering that if you're on apprentice wages and come through the ranks, you don't get a bigger jump in wage than if you'd been scouted and transferred in.

If the dressing room was supposed to be a level playing field, and my input was to be recognised, the new offer was a slap in the face, not a pat on the back. That's what it felt like to me. And I couldn't stop thinking that the £360 million needed to fund the Emirates Stadium was the only budget the board was thinking about. As I've said, players get wind of it when one of their team-mates is not treated right. It sends out a message, whether they mean it or not, that your loyalty counts for little, and the club is focused on the new stadium, not in finding and recruiting talent for the pitch those new seats surround.

I rang my agent Jonathan from the coach and told him the score. He said he'd never heard me sound so deflated. 'What's up with you? You're on your way to play in the Euro Championships!' he said. He told me not to worry, that he'd take up negotiations. 'Now go show 'em what you are capable of!' he said.

Our Euro dream ended in the Estadio da Luz, in the quarter-finals against Portugal. I was pitched against that wizard Cristiano Ronaldo and we had a right old tussle that night, running each other ragged; one of those encounters I relish. But the game would be remembered for Wayne Rooney's broken foot, Sol Campbell's disallowed winner and Becks' spot-kick in the penalty shoot-out, when the turf gave way beneath his foot. We went out in sudden death, 6–5. I put away one of the penalties that night. I had never taken a penalty for Arsenal, let alone England, until Portugal. But it would stand me in good stead. For Sheffield United. And Manchester United. In the FA Cup.

By the time the 2004–05 season started, I was leaving the matter of a new contract to my agent. I had better things to think about, along with the rest of the Arsenal team, like how long could we keep the unbeaten run going?

It didn't matter to me that I was still on £25,000 a week. Every game we played was about winning and, as in the previous season, we went into each fixture thinking, 'We *are* unbeatable – we're going to batter this lot!' Invincibility had allowed us to forget what defeat felt like.

The football we'd played was out of this world. No-one was taking more than three touches on the ball: control, turn, pass; control, turn, pass. They couldn't get near us. It was the slickest, fastest, most fluid football, orchestrated by the boss. One other thing I remember from that immaculate season: every game we played, the sun was out. It was like we were blessed.

The new season got off to a flying start with a 3–1 hiding of Manchester United in the Community Shield at the Millennium Stadium; my cross on 79 minutes deflected off Silvestre's knee and went into the net for our third. Sadly, it went down as an o.g. But the best morale boost came just before the opener at Goodison Park against Everton, when we learned Patrick Vieira was staying at the club. It had been touch and go as to whether he was going to join Real Madrid in the same month as Michael Owen and Jonathan Woodgate. It had reached the stage where a transfer fee had been agreed between clubs, and everyone knows now how much Patrick agonised over that decision. In the end, though, the Spanish giants were not for him, and the boys were delighted.

I can't tell you how much of a boost that was. Such was his presence at Highbury that the inclusion of his name on the team sheet – even if he was not 100 per cent fit – was enough to give the team a lift and make any opposition think twice; they knew our commander-in-chief was up for the fight. Vieira in the team meant we were 1–0 up psychologically.

It was to be his final season before he actually did leave for Juventus for £13.75 million, but we still had one more year with the big man, and his input continued to be huge. He bossed games like I have never seen a player boss a game before. Everything went through him. He'd make us give him the ball and he'd take on all-comers, and, as a player, you knew anything could happen when he had the ball. He was the linchpin of that Arsenal team, and I'd have gone to war with that man. He was a great role model for me with his leadership, his ambition, his dedication to training, his hunger for victory. I doubt Arsenal can ever fill his boots because his spirit and dominance in midfield was that of a rare giant.

Before Vieira, fans used to rave about the famous back five of old: Seaman, Dixon, Keown, Adams and Winterburn and, after stepping into Nigel's boots at left-back, I had the privilege of lining up with those legends. I knew their brilliance and organisation from first-hand experience. But, I have to say, the 2003–04 back line – Lehmann, Lauren, Toure, Campbell and me – has to be up there, too, for numero uno contention as the best. We were rock solid, and conceded only 26 goals in that inspired season. No future Arsenal defence can ever better a season of 38 league matches unbeaten: it is only there to be matched. That was the scale of our achievement.

The achievement up front belonged solely to Thierry Henry – nicknamed Titi in the dressing room. I bet not many Arsenal fans thought they'd see a Gunner eclipse Ian Wright as the most prolific goal-scorer. It is hard to find words to describe this ultimate professional with his sublime skill and breathtaking acceleration with the ball. I think the boss said it best when he said, 'Sometimes you say that God has not given you everything, but with Thierry he has been given a lot.'

He scares people with his pace. I'll never forget how much I was in awe of him myself when we played Liverpool once at Anfield and Jamie Carragher thought he had him on the touchline. Just at that moment, Thierry knocked the ball on. Carragher tried to block him with a run down the same touchline, but Thierry outfoxed him, nipping and dashing off the pitch, onto the track, around Carragher and back onto the ball, as quick as you like. He is a monumental talent and, even in training, the goals he scores are show-stopping. It is a sign of what a perfectionist he is that he doesn't class converted penalties as 'proper goals'. He calls them 'fake goals' because they are too easy, no skill required. He always has to score wonder goals, what we call a 'worldie'.

But he's not selfish. He is a team player. It was Thierry who set me up for my first ever goal, scored at Valley Parade when Bradford City were in the Premiership under Paul Jewell. I remember scoring to make it 1–1, cancelling out a Stuart McCall goal, and I had done a short celebration and was turning to run back up the pitch when Thierry grabbed me, put an arm around me and turned me to face the travelling Arsenal fans. He brought his other hand above my head and started pointing down at me, as if to say 'He's the man . . . he's the man', and that was the picture that made the next day's papers. It's a mark of the man that he made sure I celebrated that first goal and got the recognition from the fans.

Arsene Wenger was the architect of Arsenal's amazing achievements. This man's love of football is contagious. He is everything a manager needs to be: intelligent, articulate, cool, calm but assertive, and a great tactician who brought continental flair to Highbury when he replaced Bruce Rioch in September 1996. He is a man who wants to win every game, and someone who wants to keep getting better and better.

He wants Arsenal to be the biggest club in the world. His vision is as simple as that. And he is a manager who cares deeply about the players: that they are treated right, have the best prep for a game, are paid fairly and are protected from media flak. The fitness of the mind is just as important to him as the fitness of the body, and his analysis of whether a player is mentally up for it is just as sharp and fast as his thumb on the stopwatch. He brought in a masseur and we started to have hot baths and massages. 'Helpful for the mind and the body,' he said. Mental strength is something he'll always drill into his players. His pearls of wisdom are viewed by the players as importantly as he rates our use of vitamin pills. The right diet is crucial to Arsene Wenger's football machine working well. It's that finely tuned that we'll have blood tests and sugar tests. I know exactly when to stop drinking Coca-Cola because the tests will tell me.

Pre-match meals are nearly always Dover sole and pasta, and we even have a resident chef at the training ground. The moment Arsene arrived at the club, Arsenal got healthy. Proper foods in, alcohol out. Before, there was lager in the players' lounge. Not any more. 'You can't survive at the top level in football if you don't have a healthy life,' he once said. In the early days, he used to go on about the English footballer not eating enough vegetables.

He's not a shouter or a bawler. Or as he said, 'I don't kick dressing-room doors, cats or even journalists!' The boss is as placid as you like, capable of inspiring a team with a quietly delivered insight that becomes his team talk. The man does give good team talks. When heads are down and we've gone into half-time being beat, he'll stress the positives, back the players, rouse us with some wise words and make us believe in ourselves.

He's always reminding us what we're capable of, what we can do, how we can turn a game around, how each individual has a massive game still to play. I can see him now, stood in the middle of the dressing room, looking each one of us in the eyes in turn, slowly revolving on his feet; this quiet passion and belief clenched into the fists of the hands that are always animated, urging us on. After a game, regardless of the result, he's not one for team talks. It's too late then. Whether we've lost or won, we'll come down the tunnel and the boss will be stood there, just outside the dressing room, his foot keeping the door open, to greet and encourage every single player. For his guidance and the opportunity he gave me to play, I owe him a lot.

The boss does have a sense of humour. He comes out with some dry one-liners and he's also able to laugh at himself. In Germany once, during pre-season, in the days of Tony Adams and Ray Parlour, the boss had got all the lads ready for a session in the steam room, and we were all stood in our dressing robes at the top of a staircase when he turned, slipped and fell arse-backwards down the few steps. It wasn't serious. But when you're used to seeing the boss in a tracksuit or looking dapper in a suit and tie, to see him flying like a clown in a dressing robe was something else. None of the players could help themselves: there was a chorus of snorts and Ray Parlour, who has the most contagious laugh, was the worst of the lot. The boss looked up, his resident frown deeper than usual. Then he smiled. He saw the funny side. In the sauna, all he could do was rub his leg and talk about being out of action for a number of weeks.

There was another time, in training, when Kolo Toure had come over on trial and was determined to impress. We were playing 'attack versus defence' and the boss had the whistle in his mouth, contributing with the odd pass here and there. When the ball goes to the boss, you let him pass it. No-one would dare tackle him. Not that anyone bothered to tell Kolo. So when the boss trapped the ball and was just about to bring his foot back to hit it, the new boy seized his moment to impress, steamed in and, bang, he put the boss straight in the air! Arsene Wenger was airborne, and we all stood there looking at Kolo like he was a man with a mission to rip up any chance of a contract. But the boss took it like a man, dusted himself down and congratulated Kolo on a good tackle. Seconds later, Kolo steamed in and did the same to Thierry.

'Aaaargh, that hurt!' screamed Thierry.

'Yes, and don't I know it!' laughed the boss.

Even Patrick was impressed. It's that kind of physical force that the skipper wanted from his team, and he continued to lead and inspire us as our unbeaten league record remained intact with wins 4–1 away at Everton, 5–3 home to Middlesbrough, 3–0 home to Blackburn, 4–1 away at Norwich, 3–0 away at Fulham, 1–0 away at Manchester City – where Reyes set me up for the 14th-minute clincher – 4–0 home to Charlton, 3–1 home to Aston Villa, plus a 2–2 draw at home to our bogey side Bolton. Forty-nine matches on the trot. Then came the match at Old Trafford on 24 October 2004; the day we were cheated out of our record. That's how I saw the game anyway. Others might not agree. Most of the 65,000 plus fans inside the stadium wouldn't, I know. But I can only say it as I saw it.

It sticks in my throat that we lost our 49-match unbeaten run to Manchester United that season. You don't mind losing if it's fair and square, but that October match was anything but, in my view: it was a joke. We had all wanted to knock up our half-century in football. Before the match, the press had been reporting that we had already had red and white T-shirts printed saying '50 Unbeaten', but that was bollocks. The headlines would have been enough. But, instead, our unbeaten record unravelled not because of a supreme Manchester United performance, but because of the decisions taken by referee Mike Riley. To nick a phrase from Alex Ferguson the previous season, '*they* were allowed to get away with murder'.

Reyes seemed a marked man from kick-off that afternoon. He had played a blinder when we'd beaten them in the Community Shield and if you can't out-skill your man, then go in with hard tackles. Alex Ferguson seemed to have resorted to tactics straight from the Hackney Marshes, and tackle after tackle went flying in. The worst of them was not reserved for Reyes; it had my name all over it, pretty much in the same way my knee had van Nistelrooy's stud marks all over it. Maybe it was his idea of revenge for a tackle I'd done on Ronaldo. It earned me a yellow card; the first of five that rainy afternoon. But if my tackle was rough, van Nistelrooy's on me seemed over-the-top dangerous in comparison.

I spoke to Rio Ferdinand about it later. He reckoned the reason for the challenge was that van Nistelrooy thought I was going to do him, so he done me first. And he sure did me good and proper. I went in for a tackle and was going to kick the ball with my right foot. Then – crash! Van Nistelrooy clobbered me; his studs going right into the knee of my left leg which was taking all my weight. The moment he whacked me, I thought it was broken. I literally felt my leg bow. This, according to our physio Gary Lewin, is because I've got 'hyper-mobile' legs, which is a good thing. Makes them flexible – and van Nistelrooy-proof. Luckily, it weren't broke, but I went down like a felled tree and was in absolute agony. What did the referee do? Nothing. Not even a free kick, let alone a yellow. The FA later reviewed the tackle on video and banned van Nistelrooy for three games: that's how violent it was. But Mike Riley just waved play on. Old Trafford is an amazing place to play when it is a full house, but it has never intimidated me. I'm not sure I could say the same for Mike Riley.

After the game, I nursed a gashed and swollen knee, and it was then that Gary Lewin told me that Sky Sports had not even replayed the tackle during its live coverage of the match. It was shown but not replayed over and over for pundit analysis. I was incensed. 'Right, I'm off down there,' I told Gary, and he joined me to go confront the Sky Sports reporter who was hanging around the tunnel, near the big red gates leading to the coaches.

'What's this about you not showing that tackle on me? How can you not show it?' I asked him.

He frowned at what he thought was me over-reacting. 'Well, we didn't think it was that bad.'

'Whaaaaat! Are you crazy!?' I yelled, and before I knew it Gary was leading me away before I went too far. Blindness was a contagious disease at Old Trafford that night.

From what I've seen and heard, van Nistelrooy seems to be hated among the Arsenal players. 'Despised' is probably more the truth. He hasn't been forgiven for acting up when Patrick got sent off in September 2003. You can respect him as a footballer and a striker but, in my opinion, sportsmanship does not come as part of his game.

He tries it on in every match and, somehow, gets away with his butter-wouldn't-melt-in-his-mouth act. I think he actually spends as much time on the floor, rolling around, as he does scoring goals. I find it hard to respect someone like him. I think he should have been red-carded for that tackle on me. And I reckon my England mate Rio should have been red-carded for a tackle, in the 18th minute, on Freddie. He was through one-on-one with the keeper, thanks to a superb ball from Dennis, when Rio just barged into him and sent him flying. The referee, again, waved play on.

Then, in the 72nd minute, Wayne Rooney 'did a van Nistelrooy' and dived. His pace is lightning fast and he was through in the box, taking a quick touch, when Sol went for a challenge, but then, realising Rooney was too fast, pulled his legs away. Rooney dived like an actor on the amateur stage. The referee blew his whistle and pointed to the spot. Even United players admitted afterwards that TV replays showed Sol never touched him. So Rio clobbers Freddie. Nothing. The Diving Dutchman clobbers me. Nothing.

Rooney's not even touched by Sol. And it's a penalty. And, of all people, it's van Nistelrooy who slots it away; the man I don't think should even have been on the pitch.

We then went gung-ho to get a goal back, but they scored again on the counter-attack. We lost 2–0. That penalty killed us, and every Arsenal player was justifiably livid at the end. We'd had the 'Battle of Old Trafford' in the 1990–91 season. This was about to turn into the sequel: the 'Battle of the Pizza'. Or 'Battle of the Buffet' as the media described it.

It started to kick off before we'd even left the pitch. Thierry was berating their keeper, Roy Carroll. He had been taking the piss out of his French accent throughout the match – rolling his tongue and speaking deliberate jibberish – and Thierry's patience, aggravated by the injustice we'd all suffered, snapped. By the time we were walking down that extendable plastic tunnel at Old Trafford, everyone was having a go at each other; there were shouts of 'you fucking cheats!', and players were running into a jostling huddle where the narrow tunnel opens into a wider mouth with the dressing rooms on the right.

I'm not the biggest so I was jammed in the middle; Arsenal in front of me, Arsenal behind. I heard the boss hammering Ferguson; incandescent French verbally sparring with bullish Scottish. The boss had made his feelings clear to Rooney's face and told him, 'He didn't even touch you!'

That's when Ferguson stepped in: 'Oh shut up!'

So they started arguing, and we started yelling in support of our manager, and their players started yelling in support of their manager. The more we shouted, the closer we got and the more threatening it became. The lads at the front were eyeball-to-eyeball when one of the United security lashed out and smacked our travel manager Paul Johnson on the nose. Then it kicked off, turning into a mass wrestling bout. Sandwiched into this melee, I looked up and saw Ferguson, swamped by his players, being pushed further and further away from the front, but still jostling and yelling, his face beetroot red.

Then it happened.

This slice of pizza came flying over my head and hit Fergie straight in the mush. The slap echoed down that tunnel and everything stopped – the fighting, the yelling, everything. It was as if all movement and sound stopped in that instant as all eyes turned and all mouths gawped to see this pizza slip off that famous, puce face and roll down his nice black suit.

Ferguson was steaming. I thought he was going to explode, but then he stormed off into the dressing room, cursing and grunting, brushing the crumbs and stains off his collar. That pizza definitely took the sting out of the situation, and both sides knew it had gone too far.

We all went back into the dressing room and fell about laughing. I was lying on the treatment bed, holding ice onto my swollen knee, but doubled up with laughter. We may have lost 2–0, and our unbeaten run was at an end, but the sound of hooting laughter filled our dressing room for a few minutes. Seriously, it was the funniest thing I have ever seen: to see this guy, a legend in the game, splatted like that. I almost wet myself, as did the rest of the Arsenal team. Arsene Wenger's serious frown even struggled to maintain its composure while the United boys did their best *not* to laugh. The missile had come from the food tray in our dressing room. I've got a fair idea who launched it, and his aim with a pizza is just as good as his skills with a ball, but I'm no grass and won't name names. All I'll say is that the culprit wasn't English or French, so that should narrow it down. What made me laugh was that my name was in the frame, even though I was stuck in the middle of the action. So, for the record, despite what the papers reported, it wasn't me. Not guilty to the pizza charge.

I told Rio after the game, 'You know it weren't me who threw that pizza?'

'Yeah, yeah, yeah . . . don't worry, the manager knows it wasn't you,' he said.

We all joked afterwards that the boss would back us up if ever asked about the incident and say, 'I didn't see it.'

Once the laughter had died away, it was time for reality to sink in, and the reality was a lot harsher than we had realised. That would become clear over the following weeks. We left Old Trafford with a sense of injustice, but felt we'd get over it, and put it down as a blip. As the boss drilled into us afterwards, 'We can start a new run next week.'

But we never did. We had tasted defeat for the first time in 49 games and it poisoned our system. We never got going again, and I'm convinced it was more psychological than anything to do with form or how we played. We drew at home to Southampton 2–2, but only thanks to a last-minute equaliser from van Persie. We drew 1–1 away at Crystal Palace, beat Spurs away 5–4 in an epic, but then drew 1–1 at home to West Brom. These were the sides we had been battering for fun the previous season, but that defeat at the hands of our old enemy became our tipping point, and we couldn't put our finger on why. Opponents began adopting the United approach: kicking us, bruising us, rushing us, not allowing us space to play our slick passing game. But, with every new game, we still believed we could get back on track. Even though we never did. We looked around the dressing room at each other and saw the same faces that had made history possible. There was not a shred of doubt in anyone's mind that we could still retain the title. But we had lost our grip, our confidence had taken a knock and, more importantly, that unique feeling of invincibility had deserted us, transferred across the capital to another team in west London. It was going to be the year of Chelsea.

By the time Jose Mourinho and Roman Abramovich came to Highbury in December 2004 and witnessed a 2–2 thriller – as well as Thierry handing out a lesson in concentration by firing home a quickly taken free kick as Cech arranged his wall – I'd already told my agents what I wanted in terms of a new deal. They thought I'd lost my marbles. I could tell by the looks on their faces. But I loved Arsenal, couldn't imagine playing for another club and wanted to stay.

'So get me £60,000 a week and I'll be happy with that,' I said.

'But, Ash, you're a £20 million-rated player – we can get you £80,000 a week, or more! We can have you up there with Sol, Thierry and Patrick!' argued my agent.

But it was never about the money for me – £60,000 a week is a lottery win. I didn't need more than that and didn't care what others were on. The way I saw it was this: a leap from £25,000 a week to £60,000 a week is a massive hike and I'd have been happy. For me, it was about striking a balance between the insulting £35,000 offer made before Portugal and the full whack I could have got.

'Fair's fair – £60k and a five-year contract is fine, Jonathan. That's what I want you to ask for,' I told my agent.

He thought I was bonkers. As did Patrick Vieira. At training he told me, 'Don't be stupid. Don't sign for anything less than between £80,000 and £100,000 a week.' Even Sol thought I deserved more.

To place my £60k in context, I'll re-use the *Evening Standard*'s figures about weekly wages in football: David Beckham – £100k, Frank Lampard – £80k, John Terry – £80k, Wayne Rooney – £80k, Rio Ferdinand – £65k. I believed I was being both fair and realistic. My mind was set on £60k. Nothing more, nothing less, and that was my position from day one.

The next thing I know, on 20 December, Jonathan is on the phone with good news: 'Ash, I've just met David Dein for breakfast at Claridges; we've shaken on £60,000 a week.'

That's what Jonathan told me. He said Mr Dein had said that he and the boss – Arsene Wenger – were going to recommend the deal to the board. Jonathan said that Mr Dein was confident that the board would approve the new terms. According to Jonathan, they shook hands and then wished each other a merry Christmas. As it turned out, Mr Dein didn't recall it happening like that at all. He says there was no agreement made. Even that he didn't have the authority to make the offer. I wasn't there so I can't know. What I do know is that Jonathan called me that day with the good news. I'd think he'd remember exactly what had just happened.

Negotiations had gone back and forth for weeks, but this was brilliant news. I phoned Mum straight away and she was over the moon. I remember it well because it was my 24th birthday. It was the perfect gift. It meant I would be at Arsenal until 2010. I was buzzing and went into Christmas with my future sorted.

But as it turned out the Arsenal board had other ideas about rubber-stamping Mr Dein's recommendation once the New Year arrived. Somebody, somewhere, clearly felt this home-grown player was getting too big for his boots. At a board meeting held two days before our 1–0 away defeat at Bolton in January, it was decided the maximum offer should be £55,000 a week.

I have since learned, from someone of authority at Arsenal who I trust implicitly, that the boss and Mr Dein came up against opposition from other directors when it was suggested I be paid the £60,000. It was apparently said that if the player weren't happy, then keep paying him £25,000 and then sell him for £15 million. Perhaps for the money men, the new stadium and making profits was all that mattered. I don't believe the board gave a damn about keeping me. It preferred to haggle over a difference of five thousand pounds. Five thousand pounds. In a football context, and when measured against the £20,000 a week I had decided NOT to haggle over, it was a strange way to behave.

I was still blissfully unaware of what was happening when I spoke to the *Evening Standard* after the Bolton game and the following quote appeared in the paper on 14 January 2005: 'I don't want to move, this is definitely the club for me. I love the place. As for the contract, what I want is to be paid on my ability and what I've achieved. I am not greedy – I want to make that clear.'

When I read my own quote in the newspaper, I thought it was fair enough and sent out the right message.

I had no idea minds had already been made up.

Only one voice – the same voice – stuck up for me: the voice of Arsene Wenger. As everyone sat around that boardroom table knows only too well, the boss stood up for me and questioned the wisdom of the offer. Bearing in mind it was a quibble between £60k and £55k, he was reported in the press as saying 'So you are prepared to lose Ashley Cole for £5,000 a week?'

It was at that moment, in that boardroom, that my Arsenal

dream began to unravel, because the board's answer to his question was 'Yes'.

And that's when all my shit began. It was the first act in what would become known as 'the Ashley Cole tapping-up scandal'.

2

Hotel Scandal

I don't know what I'd have done had I been there myself.

So it was a good job I was well away from it all, driving to Mum's house in Chigwell as agent and vice-chairman locked horns in an office in central London. It was 19 January 2005, four days before the 1–0 home win against Newcastle United, and I was sitting pretty, turning up the R&B tunes, thinking the deal was all but done at 60 grand a week and I'd be signing on the dotted line within 24 hours, securing my future. I didn't realise I was about to be kneed in the nuts. Not even van Nistelrooy could have winded me harder.

Somewhere along the A406 North Circular road, one telephone call changed everything about how I viewed and felt about Arsenal. Or, to be more accurate, about the people running Arsenal.

I knew Mr Dein was meeting my agents at their offices just

off Bayswater Road. It was supposed to be a formality. Then my mobile rang.

'Ash! Are you listening?' said a virtually hyperventilating Jonathan. 'I'm here in the office and David Dein is saying they aren't going to give you £60k a week. They've agreed £55k and this is their best and final offer. Are you happy with that? Because he's here and seems to think it's *me* making you not sign this contract!'

Best and final offer. That's what I remember the most: the words 'best and final offer'. That is important to know. Because Mr Dein claimed later that it was not a final offer at all, and he believed 'we would have come to an arrangement within a matter of weeks'. It was nothing but a game of tennis with the ball going back and forth over the net, he said. But, at the time, on that day, during that conversation, he'd called game, set and match.

When I heard Jonathan repeat the figure of £55k, I nearly swerved off the road. 'He is taking the piss Jonathan!' I yelled down the phone.

I heard Mr Dein in the background, scrambling to speak to me: 'Let me talk to him! Let me talk to him!'

He took the phone: 'Ashley, look, this is a good deal for you. What we need to do now is sit down, discuss this properly and run through some figures. Okay?'

'No, Mr Dein, it's not okay. I've told you from day one what I wanted. I'm not happy about this. You're not treating me right and you know you're not!'

'Ashley, if you don't sign, you'll lose out . . .'

I interrupted him. I was so incensed: 'I don't care, Mr Dein! It's not right and I'm not happy. I thought all this had been agreed, now you're telling me it's not, and I won't be signing,' I said.

He started to blame Jonathan, as if I were under the influence of my agent.

I said, 'Jonathan works for me. I tell him what to do, and I told him

60 grand a week. Not 100, not 90, not 80, not 70, but 60, and that had been agreed and you know it. Now put me on to him.'

I was trembling with anger. I couldn't believe what I'd heard. I suppose it all started to fall apart for me from then on. I'd trusted Mr Dein to push the deal through. Perhaps it was that he couldn't get board approval. I don't know, but to me and Jonathan, it was an agreement and it had gone tits up. I'd had six months of them trying to sort this out and it had been discussed at five board meetings. The conclusion seemed to be how cheaply could they get me.

I truly believe that the consensus of the board was that Ashley Cole would never have the balls to walk out on Arsenal.

I reckon Mr Dein's belief was that I owed a lot to Arsenal and particularly the boss. He didn't think I was just going to walk out on the club. That was his prediction. And maybe that belief gives the only confirmation that was needed: they were taking me for granted.

I don't disagree that I owe a lot to Arsenal and the boss, but that's no reason to believe I owe them a discount during salary negotiations. I'd like to think I've paid back what I owe the club in performances, assists and goals over the years. They gave me the break, but it was me who had to make the most of that break. When I had a loan spell with Crystal Palace – when I was 19 years old – I did think to myself, 'Am I ever going to make it at Arsenal?' Because they weren't doing me any favours back then. I had to prove myself at another club first. I worked my nuts off to get into the Palace team, play well, get Arsenal to sit up, take note and take me back, and then I had to fight my way into the Arsenal side. And when Palace wanted to buy me for £1 million, there was a lot of umming and ahhing going on at Highbury; a lot of 'should we, shouldn't we?' In the end, they didn't let me go and Arsene showed his faith in me, and I found myself playing Champions League football aged 20.

In fact, the one person I truly have to thank for turning me into the left-back I am today is a man called Tom Whalley, the youth team coach who took me under his wing as a wannabe striker and turned my playing position and game around. So, yes, I will always be eternally grateful, especially to the boss and Tom, for the opportunities I've been given. But Arsenal didn't make me. I made myself. What pissed me off about Mr Dein's attitude was that he seemed to think I owed him, owed the club, and he could therefore afford to 'squeeze' me.

The next day at training, I managed to have a private word with the boss. I told him that £60k was my position and the vice-chairman hadn't delivered.

'I don't want to sign for less than I think is reasonable,' I said.

He said the situation was very difficult and there was a wage structure the club could not break. He adopted the party line to my face, but he had already stuck up for me by asking that question about whether a £5,000 difference was worth the risk of losing me. Not that he could let on at the time.

The boss was behind me, even if the board weren't.

It will never matter how much money is in the game, the professionals out there will never stop playing out of their skins for their club and supporters. I'm not saying there aren't some lazy bums who don't give value for the wages but, for professionals like me, the desire to do the best for your club doesn't stop just because negotiations have broken down.

I might have sulked and bitched a few times away from the ground, but a dodgy patch weren't going to stop me giving 100 per cent to Arsenal FC. If I didn't have a fair deal in the bank, what I did have was a belief in and respect for the boss, my team-mates and the fans. I went into our next home match against Newcastle and gave it everything. The team created a hatful of chances that day and the 1–0 victory didn't tell the true story. It would have been six or seven, and I might have had one as well, had it not been for their keeper, Shay Given. He played a blinder. I was never going to let any of the off-the-field crap affect my game. If anything, it made me want to get out there and prove a point. Only when I was back home did I catch myself doubting my future at Arsenal and worrying about what options there were, because, all of a sudden, all the guarantees in my life had been ripped up.

I spoke to Mum endlessly about it, and I think she thought it would all get sorted in the end. It all went round in my mind: why was I being treated so differently to the likes of Thierry and Sol and Patrick? Nothing against them; they deserved all they got. But that was my point; players, myself included, deserving a fair deal. I had worked hard to prove myself. I was even voted by my peers into the PFA Team of the Year that season, along with Thierry, and that was a huge honour. Why weren't the club seeing me in the same light then? But when you've been given a final offer and you aren't happy with it, what then? What's the next move? For the first time in my life, I had started to entertain doubts about Arsenal. I'd think about all this, over and over.

I was well down on a particular day when I drove into town to see Jonathan at his offices. I'd hoped that maybe Mr Dein would have a change of heart, slacken off, reconsider and ring Jonathan, but there was nothing but silence. Inertia, Jonathan called it. And this is where I'll let him take up the story of that particular day. It sometimes helps to have it explained by an outsider looking in, especially because he observed a lot about me at the time, and he did prompt what happened next:

Ashley comes in to speak to me and says that he is absolutely devastated by what has happened at Arsenal. The boy looked gutted. He didn't really know where to turn. It's no good talking to him about what he's worth when he's in that kind of mood. Arsenal made him feel undervalued and unloved. He'd been disappointed right from the beginning, when David Dein gave him what he felt was the take it or leave it option at Sopwell

House. Take it or leave it sounds like disinterest to me. It's not something Thierry Henry will ever have been told, I can tell you. It's also the same reason Patrick Vieira left when the club told him they were 'neutral' as to whether he stayed or went. Players need to feel valued, wanted and respected. Ashley suddenly felt there was no future for him at Arsenal. It was hard to convince him otherwise when they had treated him like a muppet, and yet there I am, as the agent, knowing he's £20 million worth of talent; the best left-back in the world! I explained his options: a) go and thrash it out with the club, b) tell them how he feels and ask to be transfer-listed or c) wait two years, play out the remainder of his current contract and then he's a free agent who can leave on a Bosman for nothing. It's important to make clear here that Ashley had never once considered leaving Arsenal, so this was like asking a church-goer to suddenly start considering worshipping the devil. His head was all over the place. He was confused, angry, upset and hurt. He turned round to me and said he felt his heart wanted to stay with the club but his head told him to leave. Then he said to me, 'The problem is, I can't ever imagine playing against Arsenal!'

If you understand Ashley Cole, you understand that he is quiet, shy, reserved, and someone who is surprisingly insecure. He was worrying and fretting about the future because the future didn't seem so secure anymore. It's fair to say that relations with Arsenal had, by then, completely broken down. David Dein had shaken my hand, looked me in the eye and, I felt, agreed a deal and then the club had reneged on it. With Ashley, I toyed with various ideas and options. My only aim at that juncture was to reassure him, provide a morale boost. With that in mind, I told him I was in regular contact with the agent Pini Zahavi. He is a wonderful guy, and it's no wonder he's earned the nickname 'superagent', given some of the transfer deals he's been involved in.

Ashley wanted advice on where his future could be after his contract with Arsenal ended. I told Ashley that maybe his future isn't in England but abroad. Spain and Italy could not be ruled out. This was what Ashley had to think about at the start of 2005 – a possible future in Europe. At the time, I just wanted him to perk up and feel optimistic about the future again, but I don't think he had the ability to see further than Highbury or the Emirates Stadium. The whole Arsenal predicament affected him deeply. It's part of my job to make him realise his worth and to make him realise that if Arsenal don't treat him right, then one of the big clubs abroad would.

I knew that getting Ashley Cole to another club would be a breeze, even if he didn't. I told him there and then, 'Let's see how the land lies in Europe and what Pini thinks. He's the expert on everything international, and he'll be able to give you some pointers about your options for the future.'

Pini knows all about the big clubs. I rang him straight away. Anyone who has ever been in a room with me will tell you that if an idea comes into my head, or a suggestion is made to ring someone, I'll pick up the phone immediately. There's no room to stall or wait as an agent. The call to Pini was a spur of the moment thing; me thinking on my feet. I already knew Pini was in London because we were always in contact. So I get him on the phone: 'Have you got five minutes?'

'I'm just around the corner,' he said. 'I've got a meeting in a bit but if you pop round now, I'm free for about 20 minutes.' He never told me anything about his imminent meeting or who it was with, and nor was I interested. He was at a hotel conducting business as usual, cramming in meetings back-to-back, which is the norm for people with busy diaries. Ashley was up for meeting him and that's all that interested me.

So that's how it was. Jonathan grabs his coat and we're up and out of his office in no time. As a player, it's nice to know what options lie ahead, especially when your head is spinning. Everyone plans ahead: ask anyone on any kind of contract. You want to know what you've got to fall back on. Jonathan says I was insecure. I'm not sure it was that; more confused. My strong belief in Arsenal was shot.

I still had two years left on my existing contract but, within six months, if relations hadn't improved, the club would be looking to sell me anyway to maximise its asset. I was happy to stick to the current contract and slam in a transfer request right that minute. But, more than anything else, I wanted to feel in control again, settled in my own head, to know where I was going. It had been eight days since that phone conversation with Mr Dein, and everything seemed to be happening way too fast. My head had gone.

With an eye to the future, Europe seemed the only place where I had any hope of evolving as a player and moving onto the next stage of my career. Even before that meeting with Jonathan, I'd entertained European thoughts. Of course I had. Ask any player with ambition; they all do it from time to time. Nothing concrete, just tossing clubs around like a kid dreaming impossible dreams: Real Madrid, Barcelona, Juventus, Inter Milan. I imagined life in Spain and Italy and remember thinking, 'Not too sure about Italy.' I didn't know where the discussion with Pini Zahavi would lead, but, as I saw it, there was nothing to lose. What was the harm in going to discuss Europe and my options?

We jumped in Jonathan's Bentley and he told his driver our destination: the Royal Park Hotel.

It was Thursday 27 January 2005.

*

The day itself weren't nothing special. At training, that morning, it was the Bob Wilson Foundation Day, when young fans came to London Colney and we did photographs, autographs, that kind of thing. I also remember writing Patrick Vieira a cheque for £10,000 for his charity project, the Diambars Academy: a football and education academy in his native Senegal. I remember losing that cheque in the street (it must have fallen out of my pocket en route to Jonathan's office) and some kind soul returned it to the FA Premier League headquarters. It was also the day when all talk at training centred on my Arsenal team-mate Jermaine Pennant joining Birmingham City on loan. He's a Nottingham lad, a top bloke and a wicked right-winger, who joined the Gunners aged 15 from Notts County. After David Beckham, I rate him as the next best crosser of a ball in the game. He joined Birmingham when he was going through a tough time in his life, having just come out of jail for drink-driving, but he's bounced back like everyone knew he would. I'll never forget Penno for the trouble we used to get into with the boss.

One week, we were late three days running. The boss went crazy. Now, he doesn't go crazy often and he doesn't normally swear, so it was a fair mark of his anger when he yelled at us, 'For fuck's sake, you're late! Again!' He absolutely hammered us, and we still laugh about that week.

Penno left because he needed a fresh start and needed to be playing more. It was a sad day for me because I knew he wouldn't come back. On the short drive to the Royal Park Hotel, I remember having a conversation with Jonathan that Arsenal shouldn't be letting go of a talent like Penno – who has now signed for Liverpool.

It's worth mentioning at this point that, in its 'dossier of evidence' supplied to the FA Premier League about this day, the good old *Sun* newspaper cited a taxi driver who had spotted me climbing out of a silver BMW near the hotel at 10.30 a.m. I had been at the training ground at London Colney until about 2 p.m., seen by dozens of witnesses, and Jonathan's car is a dark-coloured Bentley. Not that those discrepancies would ever matter. It was actually around 3 p.m. when we pulled up outside the hotel at Lancaster Gate, near Hyde Park.

We walked by reception and into a meeting room called the Green Room where we found Pini sat alone. I had met him before, at the 2002 World Cup, at a dinner with Rio Ferdinand. Pini is a cool cat, loves his cigars and dresses dapper. A quiet, assured speaker, he'd win Coolest Agent of the Year if there ever was such an award. He must have just stubbed out a cigar because the smoke was still circling the room when we walked in. I couldn't have been more relaxed as the three of us sat in that tiny boardroom. Pini's mobile kept going off, Jonathan's mobile kept going off, and I laughed at the ridiculous number of interruptions. We eventually got to speaking about Europe. Pini focused on my situation, eager to know if I would stay at Arsenal until the end of my contract or whether the club would agree to release me earlier.

'I honestly don't know,' I said. Jonathan then chipped in to help me out.

'Ashley's not happy, but he's also not sure, Pini.'

Pini then told me not to worry about a thing. Whether it was now or later, there were plenty of clubs who would be interested, he said, before adding, 'Barcelona, Real Madrid, Valencia for sure,' and these magnificent clubs just rolled off his tongue. Just hearing their names, and a respected agent telling me they would at least be interested come 2007 or sooner, gave me a good feeling. I was impressed by this guy; the same man who had been the orchestrator of many of Chelsea's multi-million-pound foreign imports. Me meeting him in a hotel was entirely innocent, even though it would later smack of guilt.

'And Ashley would be happy with . . . wait for it . . . £60,000 a week!' said Jonathan, and both he and Pini burst out laughing at my expense. Mum and Mattie never laughed like that. They understood where I was coming from. That's agents for you!

I fired off a few questions of my own about the differences between Spanish and Italian football, the weather, the people, the lifestyles. I asked about the different clubs and how other English players had adapted and been made to feel welcome. It was while I was talking that there was a knock at the door. We must have been in there about 20 minutes at that point.

Pini suddenly flicked his wrist to look at his watch –'Time! Time! My next meeting . . .' – and he started to get up out his chair. The door opened and Jose Mourinho and Peter Kenyon walked in.

When it came to the FA Premier League tapping-up inquiry – a process this very incident led to – a lawyer called Mr Gay, the brief for the league, made a right meal of this moment, trying to make it sound all dramatic. He actually asked me whether I'd wanted to jump off my chair in surprise when the Chelsea management walked in.

Jump off my chair in surprise! Like I was some kind of wuss.

'I aint just seen a murder, you know!' I replied, and I remember there were a few sniggers at that one.

He asked me why I didn't panic because 'the enemy' had just walked in.

I remember thinking, 'Is this guy for real?' Perhaps he thought he was starring in an episode of 'Judge John Deed' or something.

What did he think I was like? I'm not a panic person. I'm quite relaxed and chilled.

But his view on how I *should* have reacted is an illustration of how this whole 'meeting' was interpreted, and how it all backfired and became an Arsenal player being tapped-up by Chelsea.

At the hotel, with Mr Mourinho and Mr Kenyon now in the room, I remember noticing Jonathan was gearing up to leave, reaching around his chair for his coat. As it was, the small talk, the pleasantries and the goodbyes lasted another 15 minutes. Had I known back then what I know now, I'd have been out of my chair and on the other side of those doors quicker than Titi can run from the centre circle to the penalty box.

Just like that lawyer bloke had imagined it should be.

But at the time, although I was a little wrong-footed about what to do or say next, I wasn't going to suddenly up and run. I'm a polite guy and I genuinely saw no harm in being there for a few extra minutes as these two meetings overlapped. Businessmen and women up and down the UK have meetings that run into one another, and I didn't get what was so strange about an international agent like Pini arranging to meet Chelsea people, like he has done umpteen times, after being good enough to squeeze me and Jonathan in beforehand.

It's like if you're a married man caught in a one-to-one with a decent-looking woman in a private room. You don't just up sticks and leave because of how something might look. It may be awkward. It may not look good if the missus walks in. But you respect the fact that you are married, as I respected the fact that I was under contract to Arsenal, and you know what not to talk about and how *not* to behave. Then, after a few minutes and polite chit-chat, you get up and leave.

When Mr Dein, in his role on the FA International Committee, travels with England, I have seen him in bars, having chats with the likes of Owen Hargreaves, Jermaine Jenas, and Jermain Defoe. No-one knows what he is saying, but he is trusted not to say the wrong thing. That's as it should be. I should also have been trusted to have handled an awkward situation like an adult. Because this accidental meeting could not have been more innocent.

We all stood up to shake hands when they walked in. Mr Mourinho was a nice guy, looked as sharp as ever and was as charming as you'd expect him to be. I liked him a lot. It was the first time that I had seen him away from the context of a football match, so that was the first thing that struck me as odd. Kenyon also seemed decent enough. Mr Mourinho pulled out a chair and sat at the head of the oval-shaped table and Jonathan was sat to my right. Mr Mourinho poured himself a glass of water from the jug on the table. He made a joke about it being his birthday the previous day and he raised his glass of water in mock celebration. It was normal chit-chat from then on. I mentioned how well Chelsea were doing in the league.

'Yes, and we are going to buy two more players – a midfielder and a left-back,' he said.

Everyone knew left-back Babayaro had recently left Stamford Bridge for Newcastle United, leaving Chelsea with only one player, Wayne Bridge, for that position.

And that's when Pini made a flip remark, 'Well, we *are* sat with the best left-back in the world!' and Mr Mourinho smiled and said, 'Yes, I agree.'

Agents never spare a player's blushes and they're incapable of not boasting about who they represent. Every agent believes they represent the best player. I suppose it's a bit like when fans at every club rush to boast and chant, 'We're the finest team in football the world has ever seen.' Even if they happen to support Portsmouth or Sunderland.

Two waiters arrived with sandwiches and more water. Pini had placed the order before we arrived. One bionic-eared waiter would later go to the *Sun* and say he overheard someone in the room use the words 'you have to sign this', suggesting a Chelsea contract was put before me. He'd probably overheard his own colleague, because the *only* piece of paper presented in that room for anyone to sign was a room-service bill. Another hotel employee claimed to have heard the words 'transfer' and 'Chelsea' in a room where the Chelsea chief executive and manager were seated discussing the form of Chelsea and how they were looking to sign new players! And as I've said, the 'transfer' of Babayaro had recently taken place.

Mr Mourinho was also reported to have looked me in the eyes and said, 'I never dreamt I could consider signing you. You are already the best left-back in the world but I want to see it in your face that you want to play for us.'

I'm tempted to say you couldn't make it up.

What he *did* say to me was general stuff about football, before asking how life was with me. Life's good, I told him. 'And are you happy at Arsenal?' he asked. This was not an unusual question in my book. Friends and family had been asking the same thing for weeks and Mr Mourinho had just walked in on a meeting with Pini Zahavi. It wouldn't take the most perceptive of people to get nosey on that one.

'No, I'm unhappy but it's a long story,' I told him.

He asked if it was because of Arsene Wenger. I told him it wasn't; the boss was brilliant, I had a very good relationship with him and my unhappiness was with other people. I could tell he was itching to ask more, but, at that point, Jonathan stood up and said, 'We better be going. Gentlemen, it's been a pleasure. We'll now leave you to your business.'

As I shook Mr Mourinho's hand to say goodbye, he made reference to the up-coming Manchester United game the following Tuesday night, 'Bad luck against Manchester!' he joked.

'We'll batter 'em, don't you worry!' I said. It was a match we went on to lose 4–2.

Not once was there anything mentioned about figures, transfers, further meetings or even leaving Arsenal.

I can only speak about what was said and not said while I was in the room, and in those 15–20 minutes, the chit-chat never strayed anywhere near what could be considered an approach by Chelsea. Firstly, I went there to discuss Europe, not London. Secondly, I had never dreamt of moving to Stamford Bridge. And thirdly, Jose Mourinho would later make it clear that he didn't want me.

And another thing. If it was supposed to have been a clandestine meeting, as it would ultimately be portrayed, why hold it in such a public place where we had to walk through a very public lobby to reach the Green Room? If pre-arranged tap-up meetings take place – and everyone in football knows that they do – they happen not in hotels, but in private houses. When Roy Keane was at Nottingham

Forest under Brian Clough and had 18 months of his contract still to run, he confessed to being tapped-up by Kenny Dalglish and Blackburn Rovers, and that was a secret meeting held at the Hertfordshire home of his then international team-mate David O'Leary. Tapping-up happens at every level of football. It can be a direct phone call, an approach from a friend at another club or a deliberate meeting set up at a private house. It goes on like head-hunting in other businesses. Tony Cascarino, in an article in *The Times*, said he got a phone call from Millwall once to join them on the sly, but he decided to stay with Gillingham. Keane also stayed on at Forest before ultimately switching to Manchester United. So every player knows it goes on, but when it does, it's done quietly and cleverly and not in a London hotel for all and sundry to witness and then go fill their boots with the press. William Hill wouldn't have even given odds on me or Mr Mourinho walking into that building and *not* being spotted. So no-one would be stupid enough to risk it.

Besides, if Jonathan *had* been interested in selling me to Chelsea, he would never have done it with me around. That would represent bad business on his part, because having me there would give off an eagerness that would devalue me and Jonathan is a sharper cookie than that. Not that any of this logic would matter later on.

After walking out of the Royal Park, I went with Jonathan to the FAPL offices in Connaught Road to pick up the cheque which I had earlier dropped in the street. Then I went home to Cheryl. As in the gorgeous Cheryl Tweedy from Girls Aloud.

We'd met in September of 2004 and we'd not long since moved in together. We laughed that night about a life in Europe and how it would make a change from north London, but the prospect seemed too far away to give it any serious contemplation. One thing I can say is that I never gave Chelsea a second thought after that day, not until that meeting blew up in my face three days later when the *News of the World* hit the streets.

3

Hung Out to Dry

I look back now and still can't get my head around half of it; how, in the space of 18 months, the dream was undone so fast.

It does my head in thinking about it all: the mess I found myself in, the storm that whipped up around me, the abuse of the fans, the charges laid against me. I'm not the first player, and won't be the last, to find himself knee-deep in 'scandal' but when you're in the middle of it all, it becomes all-consuming.

Life's a gig that works itself out in the end, and I'm cool with how things are now. But within months of that invincible ecstasy at Highbury, my football world was turned upside down.

Overnight, they stopped singing my name and the party ended as abruptly as someone pulling the plug out of the wall. I became the treacherous Ashley Cole, the Judas of Highbury; object of suspect loyalty in north London, subject of ridicule in every other stadium in England and villain of the piece in the newspapers.

I didn't know what to say or think at the time. Meanwhile the club was probably worrying about all-out war between Arsenal and Chelsea which I am pretty sure they didn't want.

War had not quite broken out, but the scandal had. Me, and that famous Gunners No. 3 shirt, had been caught out of position as piggy-in-the-middle between both clubs, an Arsenal player chatting with the Chelsea manager, and this is what was exposed in the *News of the World* as 'an illegal approach' by Chelsea. Tapping-up, in other words. Or, if you want to get technical, a breach of Premier League rule K3: the rule forbidding under-contract players from being approached by, or talking with, another interested club or manager. The tabloids called it 'Cole-gate', but that made it sound more like a scandal over toothpaste and I'm not sure that ever caught on.

Either way, my name was synonymous with the scandal of tapping-up in football. Punch the words 'tapping-up' into a computer search engine and I'm the first name on Google's lips. And, for the rest of the year, not a week would go by without 'the scandal' or speculation over my future being fodder for the press.

Mr Dein, like myself, hoped this so-called 'scandal in soccer' could be settled by the game's suits without the need for scapegoats. Even Chelsea FC tried to calm things down. 'Look,' said its chief executive, Peter Kenyon, 'we are *not* making a move for Ashley Cole. You have our assurances on that. There is no need for complaints or to take this matter any further.' And I reassured Arsenal over and over, 'I'm not going to Chelsea.'

But the FA Premier League was having none of it. The whole thing started as another one of the *News of the World*'s shock-horror productions, someone seemingly banged to rights until you get up close, check out the detail and see that its substance was nothing but a house of cards that can be knocked over in an instant.

I was forewarned of the storm brewing on the Saturday evening of 29 January 2005, the day Arsenal breezed into a 2–0 home win over Wolves in the fourth round of the FA Cup and, significantly, a landmark date in the preparation for the 2006 World Cup – the day the FA agreed to back England coach Sven-Goran Eriksson's bid to curtail the following Premiership season to ensure a four-week break before the summer's tournament in Germany. Not that my mind would be allowed any respite, or to wander anywhere near thoughts of Germany. The World Cup was still 17 months away.

The next day's papers were a matter of hours away. I was at home when my mobile lit up on the arm of the sofa. It was Jonathan. 'The *News of the World* reckon they've got you bang to rights having transfer talks with Chelsea,' he said.

We both knew the shit was going to hit the fan and we knew it was all caused by that hotel meeting two days earlier.

'What's going on Jonathan!? How the fu . . .'

'Calm down Ash! We're going to deal with it,' he said.

Minutes earlier, I had been lounging around at my gaff with Cheryl; chilling and making the most of some precious time together. Next minute, I'm bolt upright, shouting down the phone. Cheryl guessed it was serious. I could tell by the way she sat on the edge of the sofa, wide-eyed with curiosity.

'Look, it's probably a load of bollocks. We *will* deal with it,' said Jonathan. 'Let's see what tomorrow brings.'

I wanted tomorrow to be yesterday already. I wanted to know, to be in control and not blind. I didn't quite hear voices in my head, but there was a nagging sense of what I believed everyone would be thinking, whispering or saying out loud: 'Judas is going to bugger off to Chelsea.'

Shit. Shit. Shit. What have I done? I had so many emotions running through my head: frustration and anger mainly. Oh yes, and I told Cheryl, when she asked if I was okay, that I was shitting myself. The whole thing was killing me, hammering away inside. One minute I'd be reassuring myself that I'd done nothing wrong, the next I was scared shitless about where all this was going to lead.

What would everyone think of me? My family and friends? The players? My mum? What would she, my biggest and most ardent fan, make of all this? Arsenal was in my blood. She knew that. But she'd be hurt for me. I knew I couldn't ring her until I saw the actual headlines. She'd only have worried. The boss? I bet he's already on the phone with Mr Dein, I thought. But if he knew me for real, he'd know it was never about the money. I kept reassuring myself like that, concerned about Mum, the fans and the boss more than anything. The very people I'd busted my guts to impress since joining Arsenal were going to be so let down when they read all this rubbish and, let's face it, people tend to believe what's printed. Whether you're in football like me or showbiz like Cheryl, perception can be as damaging as reality, especially when aided and abetted by a tabloid.

'I've too much pride for this shit, babes,' I said to Cheryl. 'People are going to believe that I want to join Chelsea!'

Cheryl's support, arms and words of advice that night, and since, are the reason why she is so amazing. My special Geordie lass is a brick. She'll never let me brood or withdraw into myself. She'll keep me talking. It's like I said to her that night: I was hurt and angry; money has never driven me and, at that time, I wasn't thinking about Chelsea. And I know that in 2005 Chelsea were not interested in making a move for me. I know all that information because it is there, in black and white, in the 'Ashley Cole Investigation' bundle, an arch-lever file containing so many taped interviews, witness statements, affidavits and dossiers that, at first glance, you'd be forgiven for thinking I wasn't a footballer but a criminal. This bundle came about after my 'crime' was reported by the *News of the World* on Sunday 30 January 2005. '**CAUGHT! CHELSEA TAP-UP COLE**' screamed the headline above an article that began: 'Chelsea have made a scandalous

WINNING

25th April 2004. We clinched the Premiership title in Spurs backyard. Sweet.

Invincible! Played 38, Won 26, Drawn 12, Lost 0. My future was set. Nothing could possibly go wrong…

Celebrating my first Arsenal goal. Thierry made sure everyone knew I was the man that day.

EMPICS

GETTY IMAGES

My diving header in the 88th minute against Dynamo Kiev in November 2003 is a moment I'll remember forever.

Followed by one of the greatest nights of my career. Inter Milan 1 Arsenal 5. 'I bet you can't jump this high Thierry. Oh, I guess you can!'

EMPICS

That'll shut them up.
Five days after the
tapping-up scandal, I
scored in our 3-1
victory over Villa. But
there were decisions
taken that day that
would affect the rest of
my life.

1st March 2005. Pure relief and joy. Totally knackered, I changed from villain to
hero in one kick. The penalty that beat Sheffield United in the FA Cup Fifth
Round. The fans could see how much the club meant to me.

A troubled week.
FA Cup final 2005.
Penalties. The fans
were at last singing
my name. I step up,
side foot, hit it
high. Goal! Four
months of grief
roared out of me.

If the FA Cup final was to be my last match as a Gunner – I wanted to capture every sweet moment forever.

ACTION IMAGES

GETTY IMAGES

Fast forward a year. A new deal and I'm still at Arsenal. It's May 7th 2006. Arsenal 4 Wigan 2. The last ever game at Highbury. Thierry and I alone at the end. 'They'll sing your name next Ash.' But nothing.

'I love this place. But I can't do this no more.'

GETTY IMAGES

LOSING

GETTY IMAGES

No longer invincible. Our run of 49 games unbeaten comes to an end at Old Trafford, October 24 2004. But we felt cheated.

The boss and Sir Alex – before the Battle of the Pizza. I bet Fergie wishes he'd been wearing that wipe-clean jacket when he got into the tunnel…

EMPICS

February 2005 Fortress Highbury. 32 games unbeaten. I was ready to keep that run going no matter what was happening off the pitch. Only it didn't quite work out that way…

EMPICS

Intelligent, articulate, cool, calm, assertive, a great tactician, with flair. And the man who stood up for me when I needed him. I so wanted to win the Champions League for Arsene Wenger.

EMPICS

EMPICS

Fourteen minutes to go in the final, and the game turns on its head as Barca equalize.

Walking past the trophy when it wasn't ours to hold. That was the worst.

illegal move for Arsenal star Ashley Cole that has stunned Highbury and will trigger an urgent FA probe.'

The *Sun* followed up a few days later with '**CHELSEA GUILTY – Summit Stinks**'. It was as bad as I had thought it would be. An accidental meeting was being played out in the media as a conspiracy going on behind Arsenal's back.

The 'case' as it later came out seemed to rely to a large extent on witnesses who were probably paid (as often seems to be the case when things like this hit the papers) thousands of pounds in newspaper deals. If payments were made – isn't there an issue of reliability there?

The daft thing is that in criminal law, when prosecution witnesses have been paid by the media, cases collapse because it is recognised there is a danger of the truth being stretched to secure a conviction in order to get hold of the cash. It's a carrot that don't belong in fair justice. The FAPL, in my experience anyway, seems to be much more bothered about pressure from the press and appearances. Regardless of the dodgy story, the small matter of 'Ashley Cole & Chelsea FC' was going to be taken on face value and blown out of all proportion.

As I watched events unfold the only conclusion I could reach was that the FAPL chief exec, Richard Scudamore, couldn't wait to come after me. Maybe so the league could appear tough in the eyes of the media and football world? I don't know. The only problem was that he was in a bit of a fix about how to proceed because no complaint had been lodged by Arsenal, and he needed one to be formally made.

The media was under the impression, like I was, that Arsenal and Chelsea were sorting it out between them. As a report in *The Times* said, 'Kenyon and David Dein . . . are believed to have been in contact to try to resolve the issue. If Dein and Kenyon manage to reach a private agreement, the Premier League could not become involved. It can only act if a complaint is made by Arsenal.'

But Scudamore seemed to have other ideas, probably feeling the pressure from people like Steven Howard in the *Sun* who demanded to know in one column, 'So what will the Premiership and their chief executive Richard Scudamore do about it?'

Scudamore was already turning on the blue flashing lights and sounding the sirens, and seemed determined to get a complaint, applying pressure on Arsenal from behind the scenes. Over a period of three days, the calls between Highbury and Connaught Road must have been relentless.

It's that sort of thing that's out of order. It seems to me that the FA Premier League stoked the fire so that it could come out and act like the tough guy, putting its house in order. That is what goes on behind the scenes that the fan needs to know about.

That's probably why Scudamore couldn't wait to get on the phone to the Arsenal vice-chairman, turn the screw and get the complaint.

It seems Mr Dein stuck up for me at first, telling the league that it had to police the rules itself. In other words, 'If you think there is a case against Chelsea, get off your arse and do it yourself.'

But the Premiership 'police' struggled to find the balls to launch an investigation off their own backs. They needed Arsenal to pipe up. Then they could hide behind one of the biggest clubs in the country and, with justifications for an inquiry in place, speak boldly about acting in the interests of football. Scudamore needed courage in numbers. When a complaint was not forthcoming, it was as though he bartered for one.

I imagine it went something like this.

Write a full letter of complaint to the Premier League, Scudamore suggested to Mr Dein. But this was refused.

Okay, we would settle for just a two-line letter instead. Again, Mr Dein didn't back down.

The next option they'd settle for was a verbal green light.

But Mr Dein refused to put forward a formal complaint.

The vice-chairman also wanted to make something else crystal clear behind the scenes: that there was no allegation of me approaching Chelsea; and that there was no complaint by the club against me. Mr Dein told me I was under enough pressure and he didn't want to add to it.

So who had given the league the go-ahead to launch an investigation? If Mr Dein had resisted a formal complaint, then how did the ball get rolling? Because Mr Dein was supposed to be the man in control of all this from Arsenal's side. At least to me, he was the face of the board, with the authority. So who was it that issued the verbal green light? If Arsenal as a club was behind me and determined not to start a process that would drag me through the mud, then what happened?

The answer is that I have the Arsenal chairman, Mr Peter Hill-Wood, to thank for pressing the button: 'With all the speculation we felt we probably should ask the Premier League to investigate to see what was true and what was not true. It was a board decision.'

He wasn't letting Chelsea off the hook. Even more surprisingly, and this rankles deep this does, it would also later come out that Mr Dein, despite everything he had said, had actually told Scudamore that an inquiry was justified, but backed away from giving the green light officially and that's probably why he didn't put anything in writing.

One minute the vice-chairman is making it clear he didn't want a war and reassuring me that everything was going to be alright. The next, the FAPL seem to be acting on complaints they'd received.

No-one seemed to realise that if they went after Chelsea, they'd take me down with them. 'We would not want Ashley Cole to be put under more pressure . . .' What crap.

The chairman wasn't even thinking about me. As I understand it, and this is borne out in the league's own statements, he telephoned

David Richards, the non-executive chairman of the FA Premier League, on the morning of Sunday 6 February.

It was the day after we had beaten Aston Villa 3–1 away; a match in which I had provided the perfect answer to the critics by scoring in the 28th minute. That should shut them up. That should restore some faith in me, I thought. I just wanted to get back to concentrating on playing. We were still the reigning champions. Chelsea may have been dominant and topping the table, but they were not out of reach – they had something like an 11-point lead – and the boss kept instilling into us that we had the spirit to fight back, so it made no sense to fight a distracting off-the-field side-show. I wasn't going anywhere, let alone to Chelsea. There was no 'transfer approach' or move for anyone to sabotage. The only person in danger of being destabilised was me and, ironically, one of the very purposes of rule K3 is to protect players from being destabilised. Arsene Wenger believes an approach has the potential to distract an under-contract player with dreams of more money, more glory, a new life. But my mind's eye was focused on nowhere but Highbury, on pursuing more glory with Arsenal, in the interests of Arsenal. My goal at Villa Park illustrated that much.

How ironic, then, that Mr Wenger's own executives were, at the same time, contemplating how to turn a molehill into a mountain.

If Chelsea were to be found guilty of breaching rule K3, the FAPL had the power to sanction them. The media hyped all this up. 'DOCK 'EM' screamed the *Sun*. It was as if someone had flicked on the floodlights at a darkened Highbury and enlightened the board. Perhaps they thought here was a way of possibly reining back the runaway leaders.

That's what I genuinely believe. That Arsenal's thinking was 'We can get one over on them here,' even though the club later denied this was a motive. I do know the boss wasn't interested in any of that. He made it quite clear publicly that he was only interested in winning the

Premiership on the pitch – not by deducted points. Who knows if that was the widely held view of the board.

Had I been caught in a hotel crossing the path of David O'Leary or Graeme Souness, I reckon there is no way Aston Villa or Newcastle would have been pursued so vigorously. This was all because of the Chelsea factor. Was I deemed expendable if it meant getting back at the club whose supremacy was bringing Arsenal and Manchester United to heel in the 2004–05 season? I know what I think – that I was naive to believe my years of loyalty counted for anything.

So the decision was made the morning after that Villa game. It was at the game that the board discussed it all.

Five days earlier, on 1 February 2005, *The Times* had reported: 'With Cole having reaffirmed his desire to stay at Highbury . . . the likelihood of an inquiry into this matter is already receding.'

But Scudamore had got what he wanted: Arsenal had given the verbal green light that allowed the league to hang Chelsea – and me – out to dry.

Within two weeks, formal interviews of all witnesses, including myself, would begin.

4

'Real Arsenal Boy'

'You off to Chelsea then Ash? Good luck mate!'
shouted a man in the street as I stopped for petrol.

It was a crisp, chilly Monday morning after the previous day's 'revelations', and I might as well have had the worst of hangovers; all I wanted to do was stay in bed and pull the duvet over my head. I'd gone to bed early on the Sunday night – sleep had seemed the only way to escape the ringing of the telephone, the news on the TV, the debate on the radio, the reports on Teletext and the sense that the media was man-marking me. It's sweet when you're making headlines for a football triumph or a nice goal. It's a different thing when you're made out to be a deceitful villain and you've become *the* sporting headline of the weekend.

Funnily enough, I'd slept soundly. The worst bit was waking up, knowing I had to face the music. So hearing some random bloke in the street wishing me luck was like the initial grating bar of the first symphony, and it confirmed that everyone believed a move to Chelsea was guaranteed. Unless he was a Spurs fan trying to wind me up.

It's about a 20-minute drive from my place to London Colney training ground. I must have driven there on autopilot. I had deliberately not got any of the morning newspapers or watched breakfast television. Normally, I'd have an R&B CD blaring throughout the journey, thumping the roof of my black Range Rover, but not that day. It was playing but the volume was down, as subdued as the driver. People often say that nothing seems to bother me, but, while I'm not the deepest of thinkers, I do store quite a lot up inside and the situation must have been seriously weighing on my mind if it made me turn the R&B down.

The tinted windows and a quick acceleration through the black iron gates at the training ground entrance meant the loitering photographers got no sight of me. There was only the odd one anyway so, as I grabbed my wash-bag from the back seat, I started to wonder if this weren't going to be so major after all.

A few paces into reception and that over-optimistic thought was soon sent flying. There, on the table in front of me, were some of the daily national newspapers, fanned out for everyone to see.

'**Chelsea in Cole tap-up storm**' screamed the *Sun*. '**Mourinho: I didn't tap-up Cole**' in the *Daily Mirror*. '**No comment won't do**' said the *Daily Mail* and, more soberly, in the *Independent*: '**Chelsea face points cut over tap-up of Cole**'.

I wanted to turn around and walk back out of the door. As I walked towards the dressing room, I could hear the usual loud murmur of banter coming from behind the frosted glass of the double doors. I walked in. It was as if a piano had stopped playing. There was such an awkward hush, broken only by the odd sound of someone clearing their throat, the shuffling of flip-flops on the white floor tiles, a tap gushing at a sink, the 'zzzzpp' of bags being opened.

The Arsenal dressing room weren't generally a boisterous din of activity; it was a surprisingly quiet place these days. But today it was noticeably quieter – an uncomfortable lack of noise, with all eyes on me. I didn't say a word to anyone because I weren't much in the mood for talking. I'm sure some players doubted me and criticised me, but no-one said anything to my face. It's at times like this when I wish I was a different character, could cut the crap, command the attention of the dressing room and put into words what a load of rubbish it all was. Like I imagine Roy Keane would have done. Like Tony Adams did. Instead, I withdrew and shirked from confronting it, allowing a big, fat issue to sit there. Once changed, I sat there in my yellow T-shirt and grey shorts, staring into space, hiding behind the usual chit-chat which had started again.

Our next league game was the following day, at home to Manchester United, and I needed to focus, focus, focus. I kept telling myself that, silently psyching myself up, visualising the marking of that skilled live-wire Cristiano Ronaldo. He is the worst guy by far to mark in football. His skills are slicker than his hair, and any defender has to be on top of his game to stand a chance of keeping tabs on him. Even the way he wears his socks above his knee tells you he means business. I knew I'd have to be 100 per cent razor-sharp because the man is unbelievable.

In the chill period before training, I was sitting next to my good friend and team captain Patrick Vieira. He asked if everything was alright.

'Have you not seen the papers, man?' I said quietly. 'I've been kippered in the *News of the World* and now the world and his brother think I'm off to Chelsea.' I didn't want to explain the intricate details. Not to the skipper. He doesn't want his players talking to another team and he may have doubted me. I couldn't have stomached Patrick doubting me.

'Well, are you?' he demanded.

'I'm not. Honest I'm not!'

'Then that's it then.' Enough said. Patrick knows me and he knew what Arsenal meant to me. 'A Gunner's heart' is how he described it. I trust Patrick and respect him as a friend and player. He is an intelligent footballer who can be funny, serious, chilled, fiery – all in the same hour. Nobody in the Arsenal dressing room had the same presence as him, not even the boss. Patrick was a colossus, both on and off the pitch, and knew more than anyone how to develop broad enough shoulders to deal with the press. Even when this man regularly threw my flip-flops across the dressing room as a joke or mobbed me for sitting on his part of the bench, I couldn't help but like him.

To me, he was a consummate pro and a true leader. I've played under him and his predecessor Tony Adams and I couldn't have had two better, more inspirational captains. Our Cameroon team-mate Lauren used to call Patrick the 'lungs of the team'. I would add that he was also the heart and soul of the dressing room and, regardless of his status as a foreigner, he was every inch a true Gunner as someone like me from Stepney.

As I dismissed the newspaper story, the dressing room door opened halfway and Arsene Wenger, wearing a dark blue tracksuit and a frown, stood in the frame, his foot keeping the door ajar. He looked over to me. 'Can I please have a word?' he said, and no-one could have looked more serious than him if they'd tried. Not even Patrick Vieira. Even when the boss tells a joke (normally a very bad one) he looks beyond serious, so there was no accurate reading of his mood. Except to say a farmer could have planted bulbs in the furrows on his brow.

He turned, walked away and the door fell shut behind him. Oh shit, I thought, he's not wasting any time.

There was a mocking chorus of 'oooos' from the dressing room, followed by fits of laughter. Well, I suppose something was needed to break the ice. Patrick patted me on the back en route to the managerial summons. I've loads of respect for Arsene Wenger; he's such a nice guy, extremely fair and a gentleman of the game. His passion and fire bubbles beneath a very tight lid, but he's not a volatile character who has out-of-control hissy-fits like some managers out there. The boss is controlled, measured and placid, so I knew he was not going to blow up at me. But I was concerned about his opinion of me. When you respect someone as much as I respect the boss, the thought of letting him down is potentially more wounding than any screaming rant could ever be. If I knew one thing, though, as I stepped inside the already open door to his office, it was that he would give me a fair hearing. When you have the boss's attention, he listens intently.

Walking into his tiny office at London Colney, the first thing to draw the eye is the photo gallery on the walls of Arsenal teams dating back to 1996, his first year in charge: a picture story board, squad by squad, of the evolving process from 'Boring, Boring Arsenal' to 'The Invincibles', the teams which each played their part in that historic journey. His desk is to the left and there are two sofas, at right angles to each other, to the right and that's where we sat.

'You don't have to tell me about it,' he said, his French accent thick with both reassurance and assertiveness, 'but, let me tell you, I know something happened.'

He was sat on the edge of the sofa, his forearms resting on his knee, his hands clasped together, and I was fixed by that deadly serious stare. The cat seemed to have got my tongue for a few seconds.

'I *know* you were there, Ashley,' he said, filling the pause for me.

'Fair enough,' I said, 'but I'm telling you boss, I wasn't there *with* Chelsea.'

I was choosing my words carefully because I knew I'd been in a room with Chelsea but didn't want an innocent situation to be misinterpreted as a guilty one. I was ducking the issue, I know I was. But when you walk into a place and accidentally come across someone you know, an associate or a friend or whoever, you *see* them there but are not exactly *with* them there, and that is an important distinction. It's why I made a point of saying I was not *with* Chelsea.

I have always been honest with the boss and I was just hoping he would believe me, but the look of disappointment in his eyes suggested otherwise. In turn, the weight of his unspoken accusation that I was not being truthful made me feel guilty, and there's nothing worse than being thought of as guilty when you know damn well that you are innocent yet you're also aware how a particular situation may appear.

The boss didn't believe me, I could tell. He would later tell the Premier League that he had a gut instinct that the meeting had happened, even though he conceded, 'I have no proof of that.'

'Okay, Ashley,' he told me in his office, 'don't tell me what happened. I just want you to tell the truth to the Premier League if they ask you. It's down to you to tell them the truth. No need to tell me, tell them.'

I will give the boss credit for not labouring the point or making a big song and dance about it. There was no dressing-down, and he was genuinely concerned about the impact the story was having on me. He knew the pressures of being in such an intense media spotlight and he knew the whole sorry saga was affecting me, this player he referred to as 'a real Arsenal boy'.

He kept asking if I would be okay for the Manchester United match. He asked if I wanted some time. No way, I told him. 'That is good,' he said, and he reminded me, just before I left, that his door was always open. That man is, as they say in east London, a real diamond geezer.

He only needed to look into my eyes to see the hunger and determination. I didn't need to be fired-up for the next fixture. Manchester United were coming to Highbury, the fortress where we had gone unbeaten in 32 games. Nothing was going to stop me from playing in this one.

This was my chance to play out of my skin.

*

It was guaranteed to happen. 'Fortress Highbury' was always going to be breached one day. It was only a matter of time before a team came and turned us over on home turf. We all knew that. We just didn't want it to be Manchester United. Anybody but the 'enemy', the same team that had so cruelly ended our 'invincible' 49-match unbeaten league run on 24 October at Old Trafford that same season.

Not them again. Not at such a crucial stage of the season, now that we were into February. Not when we were lying second, ten points behind Chelsea on 51 points, and United were on 50, and when we were looking to avenge a 1–0 defeat that had knocked us out of the Carling Cup in the quarter-finals in December. Not within 48 hours of being accused of wanting to join Chelsea. Not when every mind in the stadium would be wondering if I was going to mentally buckle, when every eye would be checking out my performance. Any game but this one. Way too much was at stake on a professional and personal level.

I remember being stood in the tunnel before the game, both teams boxed in by plain white walls, ready to run out on to the pitch. I was at the back of the line, up on the steps leading down from the dressing room corridor, staring straight ahead, determined to focus, wondering who would be my biggest opponent on the pitch: Cristiano Ronaldo or the Arsenal fan.

As if there wasn't enough to contend with in Manchester United fixtures. I've seen less bad blood between Freddie Mays and Lennie Taylor in one of my favourite films, *Gangster No. 1*. The intense rivalry between both clubs borders on spitting hatred and stems back to the 'Battle of Old Trafford' and a 21-man brawl in 1990–91, so they say. It was always going to be a grudge match for us.

The agitation of adrenalin and that simmering feeling that it could all kick off at any time kept me on my toes in the tunnel. Roy Keane and Patrick Vieira eyed each other up at the front like boxers before a bout, two of the most fierce midfielders in the game locking horns before they were on the pitch. If anyone had lit a match there and then, the whole place would have gone up.

I looked to the side of me and saw my old mate Rio Ferdinand psyching himself up, pouring a bottle of water over his head; it's what he does before every game. He shook his head as if it was a cold shower.

Freddie Ljungberg went down the Arsenal line, as he always does, slapping each hand all the way down to the front: 'Good luck . . . Come on . . . Good luck . . . Come on boys!' and then returned to stand in front of me. 'Good luck, Ash,' he said.

We could hear the constant roar contained within the tight, steep stadium that is Highbury; the fans bursting their lungs, stirring the night air, singing, 'Ar-ser-null . . . Ar-ser-null . . . Ar-ser-null . . .'

In the build-up to the big game, all the press seemed to ask the boss was, 'Is Ashley Cole ready for this game? Is he going to be focused?'

Take this match preview from *The Times*: 'When the players walk out at Highbury this evening . . . the focus of attention will be Ashley Cole, the Arsenal and England left-back . . . As Arsenal take on United at high-stakes poker tonight, when a defeat or draw could end the realistic championship hopes of either side, Wenger offered a conspiracy theory to add extra spice to the occasion. Instead of the usual verbal crossing of swords with Sir Alex Ferguson . . . he found himself distracted by Chelsea and Mourinho. "The timing is not welcome before such a big game, and I find that coincidence just a little bit troublesome," he said.'

I'd read that before the game. It pissed me off that the spotlight was on me. It pissed me off that it had ever become a 'distraction' in the boss's eyes. As I stood there in the tunnel, I was determined to prove to the boss, the fans and the press I was focused.

Robbie Williams's song 'Let Me Entertain You', a song often played in the run-up to kick-off, was lost in the din of the stadium as the crowd anticipated the match.

Then came the Highbury cue to walk out: Fat Boy Slim's 'Right Here, Right Now' kicked in. Love that song – it has a real energy about it. We always run out to that, as the chants break out into stadium-filling applause, and it never fails to make the hairs on the back of my neck stand on end. As soon as those boots touch grass, I quickly tap the ground with both toes – right then left – as I run. No idea why. It's just something I do. Rio and Freddie have their habits. I have mine.

So there I was, out on the pitch, going down the line of Manchester United players with the rest of the team, shaking hands in front of the East Stand. And that's when I first noticed it: the reaction of the fans.

The club's public announcer read out the team and got to my name: 'ASHLEY COLE!' At first, I didn't know if it was my mind playing tricks on me. I heard boos among the half-hearted cheers. Must have been Manchester United fans. But it can't have been. It came from the East Stand. Or was it the Clock End behind the goal? All this was going through my mind when I should have been concentrating on Ronaldo.

The Arsenal fans had always been brilliant and never failed to get behind me. As someone who grew up at the club, that recognition was always important to me. Nicking one of the boss's pearls of wisdoms, 'The imprint you make in the spirit of the people is more important than the result.' And he's dead right.

I never wanted anyone to think badly of me, let alone the people whose spirit and support I thrived on. My favourite chant had always been this one (sung to the tune of Spandau Ballet's 'Gold'): 'Ashley Cole . . . COLE!/Always believe in your soul/You've got the power to know/You're indestructible/Always bel-ieeeve-it. COLE!'

But they weren't singing that any more. They weren't even cheering my name. I had been left with the killer of indifference and the odd chorus of boos. I wanted to shake them out of my head. But they were there, rattling around in my thoughts all through the match.

There is not a player in the world who can honestly tell you that he's not lifted when the fans sing his name. Nor is there a player in the world who can tell you that he's not bothered if the home support turns.

Maybe some players have crocodile skin, but I don't. This was like hearing jeers from relatives in your own home. And it hurt. It hurt just as referee Graham Poll blew the whistle for kick-off.

Eight minutes later, the place was lit when Vieira nodded one into the net. We seemed in control in the first half. It only started to go wrong in an ill-tempered game (Sylvestre was sent off for head butting Freddie) in the second half, which we started 2–1 up after Bergkamp had re-established our lead after Ryan Giggs, who was a real menace that day, had equalised, assisted by a wicked deflection off my boot. His 20-yarder was never going in until it got my assistance.

I remember cursing my luck as the Manchester United fans celebrated. Just my luck. Wants to join Chelsea. Helps Manchester United score.

I'd be lying if I said I was mentally strong that day, and what happened when I came to take a throw-in early on in the game from in front of the East Stand didn't help matters. As I spun the ball in my hands, I heard the shouts from behind me. Boos. Jeers. Then someone shouted, 'Fuck off to Chelsea then you Judas!'

I'd also be lying if I said I didn't want to turn round and punch him in the mouth. What did he know, this fickle fan who believed everything he read in the papers? I think I got some of the fans back on side when I went in hard on Ronaldo to show him, and the fans, that I meant business. But from that moment on, from that match until the end of the season, they didn't sing my name anymore and I've struggled ever since to understand why so many fans were so quick to judge and then condemn me. Freddie Ljungberg can do bugger all for around 75 minutes, have one magic touch and the fans are falling over themselves to hail him. Or he only has to fart during a warm-up and they're singing his name from the rafters. The Arsenal fans don't half know how to make you feel special, but they also know how to make you feel lousy. I was going to have to get used to being regarded as the traitor in the same way the team was going to have to get used to the taste of defeat at home. Both were bitter pills to swallow.

Like I said, we lost our grip on the game after the break, Ronaldo scoring two in four minutes before O'Shea tucked away a late clincher. We'd been turned over 4–2 at home. None of us could believe it. It was a pig of a game, and allowed Manchester United to leap-frog us into second place. We sat, despondent, in the dressing room afterwards. Heads were down and not much was said. What filled the silence was the sickening sound that drifted down the corridor: the gloating cheers of Manchester United.

Somebody, and I can't remember who it was, said to me afterwards that it looked like I played 'with all your troubles on your shoulders'. Maybe I didn't run up and down as much as usual and, okay, two goals came from my side, but it weren't all my fault. Every time I attacked, as I was expected to, Ronaldo stayed up front, so if I was on an attacking run and we lost the ball, one ball over me killed me. Ronaldo, with his step-overs and pace, had been determined to give me a torrid time that day. I had a poor game. Perhaps the fans' reaction affected me more than I thought it had. But I didn't think I'd had a stinker.

Unlike the boss. It got back to me that he'd said I was not the normal Ashley Cole on the pitch. I think he thought the whole controversy was weighing me down and that I was a little lost.

All players' performances are marked of course. But what I didn't realise was that I was under even more intense scrutiny than normal, with certain people looking for problems with my game. That's what it ended up looking like to me. And it wasn't just management. The board was taking a keen interest, I guess looking for clues of destabilisation caused by Chelsea. They were checking a system called the 'Opta Index'. This provides a computerised calculation of each player's contri-bution to each game for the manager and issues points on passing accuracy, ball possession, fouls won, fouls conceded, offsides, clearances, headers, chances made, chances given away. All this information is calculated to a total score, either a negative or a positive, and the highest scorer is the best performer on the day. It shows how much of a science football has become. I was one of the club's robots under inspection for any signs of malfunction. I didn't find out about any of this until the end of the season.

When I did, the club's very own Opta Index findings were used as damning evidence against me at the Premier League two-day inquiry three months later. It didn't make for pretty reading. I scored something like 160. Which means nothing in isolation. Until you realise that normal scores for top performers – like Vieira and Henry – would be above 1000. I've been told I was normally in the top three or four performers at any match so apparently this reading *proved* that the Chelsea saga had made an impact.

What he failed to mention was that others had also scored low like me in that same match and none of them had been linked to Chelsea.

Sometimes, footballers have off days. We like to speak about our best goals, brilliant passes and career highs, but we're human: we make mistakes, we sometimes have complete howlers and, mentally, we may not be 100 per cent all of the time. I did have a lot on my mind going into that match, but didn't anyone think that maybe what was weighing on my mind was the false accusation made in the *News of the World*? I'd met Pini to discuss Europe, not Chelsea, to discuss a hypothetical deal, not a real one. Feeling media pressure is a world away from feeling guilty, and it's bang out of order for anyone to jump to conclusions based on the bare facts of those Opta Index figures and use them against me.

Even without considering those figures, I knew in myself that my game had to improve for the following Saturday and our away fixture at Villa Park.

I remember walking out of the tunnel in a completely different frame of mind to the one I'd had before the Manchester United game. I couldn't wait to get started. We were wearing our blue away strip that afternoon, so that gave the Villa fans all the ammunition they needed to taunt me about looking good in blue. But I was not bothered that day.

Early on, I pressed forward and shot just wide. It was a good sniff of goal and that set me right up for the rest of the match. I was buzzing then. I wanted to see that net billowing more than ever. I wanted to prove so many people wrong. For every questioning look, for every boo at Highbury, for every Villa fan that had taunted me, for anyone within Arsenal who might have doubted me, I wanted to stick the ball in the back of the net and shove all their crap down the back of their throats.

My moment came on 28 minutes when we were already 2–0 up, thanks to Freddie and Thierry. Our mercurial Frenchman turned provider for me when he did some great skill on the right, nutmegged someone and hit a great diagonal ball to pick out Dennis on the left. Their guy went to close him down and that's when I made a dash down the inside left, running into the space. One touch from Dennis and the ball came right into my path, and I struck it on the run, on the half-volley before Liam Ridgewell could get in a blocking tackle, and it sailed into the corner of the net.

The elation I felt was something else. Maybe it was the release of a week's worth of shit coming off my shoulders, but I screamed like mad, clenching both fists. I slid on my knees and ran up to where the Villa fans were – those fans calling me Judas, mocking the colour blue – and put my index finger to my lips and 'Ssshhhed' the lot of them. It sounded like a major decompression in my head even though they probably never heard a thing. It was such a great feeling. All the boys came rushing over and mobbed me. They knew the significance of the moment and shared the relief with me. I remember Thierry behind me, yelling my ear, 'What a gol! What a gol!'

Even referee Steve Bennett, eager to usher me away from the Villa end, knew what it meant, I think. 'That was a good goal. Well done,' he said, before adding, 'Now let's get back.'

On the run back up the pitch, Patrick grabbed me so hard that he squeezed my head into the 'V' of his neck, where he rubbed in dollops of Vicks before every game.

Now, it's true that I had been feeling emotional at that moment, but my eyes were watering for a different reason before the re-start. The Vicks from his neck had gone into my eye and it was stinging like hell. So, as I'm running back up the pitch, I'm pinching a section of my shirt and lifting it up to wipe the stuff away. Everyone thought I was lifting up my shirt to kiss the Arsenal badge or wiping away a tear. But it was Patrick and his bloody Vicks.

It turned out to be a great day, the day when both Arsenal and myself bounced back to form. We dominated that match like reigning champions. And my Opta Index score for this game? 1510 – the fourth highest score on the pitch.

So much for my game being affected.

I've got to be honest, I've lost some respect for the vice-chairman. He may well have overseen my years at Arsenal and provided some much needed and appreciated advice in the years when I grew up at the club, but he seems to have forgotten that the Arsenal boy has become a man, that the boy he regards as a son of the club cannot be taken for granted just because there is an affectionate history. You don't stick around because of history. You stick around for the future. And I thought I had one at Arsenal.

The fans were led to believe I had one, too. Mr Dein issued a reassuring statement to the press: 'I can assure our fans we are not going to allow this situation to develop into one where Ashley Cole says he wants to go.'

I'm not sure all of them would have been bothered. Not the ones who booed me. Or the ones who had made up their minds having read the newspapers. 'Whenever I see Ashley Cole's face on a website or newspaper, I think money-grabbing mercenary,' said one fan, posting his thoughts on the Arsenal Mania website. 'This is a major betrayal by Cole,' said another.

'Cole must have chapped lips from kissing the badges of other clubs,' was another comment in another chatroom. And my actions were 'disgusting and insulting', even more so because I was an Arsenal fan as well as a player. I tried to understand what they were thinking and why they were thinking it, but became angry that their reaction was so swift and so damning. But that's the football fan: quick to judge. I soon learned to stop wanting to know what the fans were thinking. I had to develop a thick skin and start letting my feet do the talking.

5

Nicked and Dropped

It's funny how you only remember certain details when life moves you on. When you're there, in the middle of it all, focused on playing and hungry to win, the environment around you passes by without much thought. Maybe I was guilty of taking something for granted, too.

I'm not really one for nostalgia, but, looking back over my time at Arsenal and despite my runs-in with the board, nothing can embitter the memories on the pitch and from the dressing room. Times were too good for that. Even at training.

I loved training. We used to have so much fun and, unlike some clubs, it never turned into a gruelling obligation. With the lads at Arsenal, and the way Arsene structured it all, training was almost a joy. Unlike some clubs that seemed obsessed with running players up hills or doing endless, mind-numbing laps of the pitch, Arsene always made sure we worked with the ball. Even if it was the second day of pre-season. He is the master of touch and technique and he never has seen the point of running the legs off players, unless they're using the ball at the same time. 'Attack versus defence', 'Five versus two', 'First XI versus reserves'.

Training was all about football. As it should be. The best fun was in the dressing room when the lads' varying tastes in fashion would be the source of much piss-taking. The smartest dresser was, without doubt, Thierry. I think the man is a perfectionist in every sense. I can see him now, standing in front of the mirror, putting the creams on his face, patting both sides of his cheeks and neck with aftershave. And no-one is more colour co-ordinated than him, from the top of his head to the tip of his toes, baseball cap to trainers – it all just *had* to match. His collection of trainers and caps beats even mine! If Thierry was the smartest, Freddie was the most stylish, most outlandish. He was the man that gave me the courage to wear ripped jeans.

The Arsenal training ground was the platform for a regular humiliation ceremony. The changing room is all modern, with metal bars and exposed air-conditioning pipes running above the benches where we sit. The worst fashion culprit will return from training to find his clobber hung from the roof, on show for everyone to see. I remember it happening to Thierry once when he came in wearing an army camouflage jacket and Martin Keown dived across the dressing room, pretending to be a soldier firing a machine gun.

Thierry got so wound up, but Martin is such a joker, with a sense of humour and personality essential to a lively dressing room. He also happens to be the only player I know who has ever pulled a hamstring while vigorously brushing his teeth at the sink! It was always a treat, though, to come in from training to see whose clobber was hanging up in shame for everyone to see.

That was life at London Colney. But nothing beat the atmosphere of 'home': Highbury. I can still smell that place. Like the smells of childhood that never leave you, the smell of match-day in that cavernous red-and-white-tiled 'home' dressing room will always stay with me: the warm, musty air; the scent of massage oil, fused with the Vicks that Patrick dolloped onto his chest and the Deep Heat Lauren smothered into his legs. I can still hear the flip-flops shuffling across the tiled floor, still feel the warmth coming through the soles from the under-floor heating.

And I can still visualise it all: from the banter at the Four Seasons Hotel at Canary Wharf on the eve of a Saturday home game, to the coach journey to north London and up the famous marble steps into the pre-match verve of the dressing room. Through the double-doors. Treatment room on the right. Vaseline, scissors, tape and bandages scattered around two shelves. A chalkboard to the left with bottles of water beneath. And then, facing me, the pristine shirts hung with their backs facing out: LEHMANN, LAUREN, COLE, VIEIRA, GILBERTO, LJUNGBERG . . .

I can still see the usual gang, me, Hleb, Reyes, Lauren and Cygan, playing ball in the wide corridor of the dressing room, just outside the toilets. It became a sort of pre-match ritual, each player getting four lives and one touch to keep passing the ball in rapid fire, and the one who messed up got flicked on the ear. In a tight area, in bare feet: nothing sharpens up the passing game more than that. And, no, it wasn't the boss's idea. For once.

I can still see Pat Rice, the assistant manager, coming over to each player, revving us up one by one, with the team sheet in his hand, reminding us what our duties were that day, who we had to keep our eye on, the men we should be marking, drilling into us his own enthusiasm and determination. He's full of brilliant advice on opposition detail is Pat. Although not every time. Martin Keown tells the story of how Pat drilled it into Steve Bould that Emile Heskey, in his days at Leicester, was weak on his left foot. 'So show him on his left foot . . . show him on his left foot!' Pat kept saying over and over. So

Bouldy did just that. He never allowed Heskey on his right foot and got him on his left instead. And Heskey shot with his left foot and it sailed into the net. So now, Pat will always be a little bit more careful. These days, when he's spotted someone's weakness is their left foot, he'll say, 'Show him on his left foot . . . show him on his left foot – but remember he can shoot as well!' I can hear him saying it now.

I can also see Thierry sat there, focused, in his own world, with his iPod playing on his speakers. Something crap like Michael Jackson would be playing. Then, just before the game, he'd belt out a song dedicated to me and to lift the team. '21 Seconds' – nothing pumped me up better for a match. It was like our own countdown. '21 seconds to go . . . 21 seconds to go . . .'

And then we'd be out on that pitch, hearing the roar of Highbury. Just thinking about it now brings back the tingle. It's something I will never forget.

To me, the Villa game and my goal spoke volumes about my commitment to Arsenal. I'd hoped it had made a point with the manager, the players, the fans and the board. But it seemed that Mr Dein was hooked on believing the newspapers, not his player.

Which is why he wanted to talk to me away from Highbury.

I think he saw himself as some sort of father figure and looked on me as a son of Arsenal. He recounted many times how he had stood on the touchline, like a proud dad, cheering me on when I was playing for the club's under-17 side. To be fair, I regarded myself as a son of the club, too. Highbury was not just a club or a stadium, it was a second home.

So Mr Dein wanted a 'father and son' chat. I suspect it also had a lot to do with prising me away from Jonathan. Of course, I told my agent all about it. Just tell him the truth, he advised me.

I met Mr Dein at his house, set back off a dark, leafy road on the outskirts of north London, about 15 minutes' drive from me. It was about six weeks since the *News of the World* story. It's not every day a player gets an invite to the vice-chairman's gaff, and I was as nervous as anything. It's funny. I can run out before more than 65,000 people at intimidating stadiums such as Old Trafford, when the pressures are huge and the expectations massive, and yet not feel the slightest tremble. When my studs touch those blades of grass and my feet do the talking, my confidence rides high and I'll take on all-comers. Yet, the moment I heard those same feet crunch on the gravel of Mr Dein's driveway and his front security lights flicked on with a dazzling beam, this sweaty heat crept up my back and the palms of my hands became all clammy. Away from a stadium or training ground, where I feel most at ease, I'm a shy person. I never have been a big noise, not at school, not in the dressing room, and I get nervous in serious meetings with heavy conversation. And this was going to be a seriously heavy one-to-one. A lot had already been said, and it was going to be very awkward.

Even as I rang the doorbell, I felt like doing a runner, like I had as a kid when I knocked on the doors of rows of houses in Stepney before running away in a pointless game we called 'Knock Down Ginger'.

Knock, knock, knock. Run, run, run. It was funny at the age of ten and, who knows, maybe it's where I get my pace from. I felt as uncomfortable as a naughty child when that particular door opened, in a street a world away from Stepney, and Mr Dein was stood there, looking as suave and debonair as ever in a suit, while there I was in jeans and jacket, feeling more than a little intimidated.

'Hello, Ashley. Come on in.'

In the sumptuous lounge, I took a glass of water and sat down, bolt upright, on one of two sofas. Mr Dein sat on the other one to my left, relaxing and reclining backwards. There was the usual amount of small talk to break the ice and then the vice-chairman cut to the chase.

'So, c'mon, Ashley, what really went on that day?'

'Listen, nothing went on. I'm telling you, nothing went on.'

He raised his eyebrows with a questioning look.

'Mr Dein. I don't *want* to play for Chelsea. I'm not going to Chelsea. Nothing went on.'

I didn't say much and Mr Dein didn't seem to listen to the little I did say.

'Look, Ashley, we are not after you. We know it's all Chelsea's fault and . . .'

I interrupted him. 'They've not done nothing wrong,' and I could hear my voice straining, 'I don't know what more I can tell you.'

Mr Dein carried on regardless. He just kept going on and on about Chelsea, why I should trust him, tell him the truth, tell him what happened. He tried turning the screw on the salary. I told him that I thought someone on the board had it in for me, didn't like me or wanted to see me go. How else could he explain the squabble over £5k? Maybe it wasn't Mr Dein. Maybe it was Peter Hill-Wood who, despite my five years in the first team, I'd never met one-to-one in my life.

I just laid it on the line. 'I feel betrayed and let down by a club I've given my heart and soul to.' I told him I had wanted to re-sign for Arsenal, but the whole thing had left me feeling upset and confused.

In return, he turned on the charm. 'Ashley, you have been here since you were a boy. I almost think of you as a son. You're talking rubbish: this club loves you. What you need is better representation.'

Mr Dein and the board must take me for a right mug, I thought, as the words dribbled off his tongue. What a load of patronising crap. After 45 minutes of going round in circles, the meeting came to an end.

'Look, Mr Dein, I'm happy for now at Arsenal. Let's just leave it at that,' I said, referring to my existing contract. I needed head space to work things out.

We stood at his front door and shook hands. Not that a handshake seemed to carry much weight before. 'Remember,' he said, 'this little chat is between me and you.'

The most effective contract I can ever enter into is the unwritten one where I look someone in the eye and give my word, which is why it bugged me so much when I gave my word about the events of 27 January and my word was dismissed for that of a tabloid.

'Mr Dein, I won't be telling anyone,' I reassured him, and then we said farewell.

And I wouldn't have told anyone, except one week later, I got a call on the mobile from Jonathan. 'Did you tell David Dein that you wanted to re-sign for Arsenal? Through a mutual friend, he's making it clear that's exactly what you said.'

I'd said I had wanted to re-sign for Arsenal, 'had' being the operative word. Circumstances had changed and made me re-think my future, but if what Jonathan had told me was true – and I have no reason to think it wasn't – then the vice-chairman had somehow twisted my words. So much for the chat being between me and him. It seemed to me he was letting me down at every turn. And if he thought relations had soured because of the Chelsea incident in January, he was mistaken. Relations had soured the moment he went back on a verbal agreement in December. But to be fair, maybe it wasn't his doing. Perhaps he had no choice in having to go back on the £60,000-a-week agreement after he had recommended it to the board and it was knocked back.

When a Premiership team scores at home in the 78th minute in an FA Cup tie against a Championship side, fans expect that goal to be enough, or the first of a late flurry. It says much, then, about the spirit of Neil Warnock's Sheffield United that, with a 90th-minute penalty, they forced us back for a fifth-round replay in the first week of March at Bramall Lane. We were badly weakened for the trip to South Yorkshire, missing Thierry and Robert Pires through injury, and Dennis, Jose Antonio Reyes and Robin van Persie through suspension, and so were forced into fielding a young side. It turned out to be one of the most gruelling matches I ever contested. I remember taking a breather on the touchline while there was an injury up field and Neil Warnock was in the technical area.

'You're never gonna be in a game like this again for a long time!' he said, when he saw me looking knackered.

If he said it to get a reaction he probably didn't expect the reaction that I came out with: 'You're not wrong!'

His right wing-back, Derek Geary, couldn't half run. He was even smaller than me and was a little dynamo. I told him at one point to stop bloody running so much. He thought it was a joke but I was dead on my feet and cramping up all over. The Blades were at us at every turn, niggling, kicking, harassing us, and it was a hard, hard game that was. Having said that, we should have finished them off with the chances we created, but we just couldn't find the back of the net, so it went down to penalties. And when people say it is 'the longest walk' from centre circle to penalty-spot, they aren't kidding. Whether you're in a Euro Championship quarter-final in Portugal or an FA Cup fifth round in Sheffield, the climate of fear is the same when you're walking with that rucksack of expectation strapped on your back. You're looking at your team-mates, not wanting to let them down, looking at the opposition, knowing they're praying for a balls-up.

And there is an entire stadium around you, apart from a little pocket of Arsenal in a corner, willing you to miss, jeering, whistling, cackling, booing. It's hard to relax in a penalty shoot-out, the tension seems to stiffen the muscles, and when it gets decisive, you know as a player that the difference between hero and villain is a knife-edge. Okay, this was no England shoot-out where an entire nation expected. That would come later in June 2006. It was much more important than that: it was for the Arsenal faithful, and God knows I'd had enough of being a villain in their eyes for the previous month. Here was a chance to be a hero. For a few seconds at least. We'd practised penalties the previous day, but the tension is missing, so there's no comparison. We'd do smart dinks and slow kicks and try to be clever, but there's few I know who'd have the nerve to do that in a real match shoot-out. All I knew was that I could not afford to miss, and it was only my second penalty in front of a crowd. As I walked to the spot, I was heaping more and more pressure on to myself. Lauren, Patrick and Freddie all put theirs away but the true hero of the hour was our keeper Manu Almunia who pulled off two superb saves to deny Alan Quinn and Jon Harley. So it was down to me to perform on the platform our keeper had built. Score, and we were through 4–2.

With the side of my left foot, I slotted home and the relief roared out of me once more as I reeled away from goal and dropped into my customary knee-slide across the greasy pitch. All the players pounced, but I fought them off. 'No, no, no . . . to Manu! Let's go to Manu! He won it for us!' I yelled. We found Manu, both gloves aloft in the air, and jumped on him instead. That young team groaned like old men back in the dressing room – cramp had taken over from jubilation. Sheffield United had given us the toughest battle in an FA Cup journey that would take us all the way to the final at the Millennium Stadium – against Manchester United.

Away from the football pitch, the FA Premier League were still carrying out their interviews like detectives, but the one thing that always gnawed away at me was how this story had ever got the legs in the first place. I'd been shopped by a waiter and a sandwich server, that much was clear. But both the league and *News of the World* made it sound like they'd cracked the biggest conspiracy of the century, the way they were going on, acting like moral heroes.

From what I can see, the FA Premier League can't help but fall over itself to launch an inquiry. I'm surprised they've not yet launched an inquiry into the terrace chant 'Who's the bastard in the black?' It started 2006 in the same way it started 2005: with an inquiry. Not into tapping-up this time, which everyone in the game *knows* goes on, but into 'bungs and corruption', which everyone in the game *suspects* goes on. So when the England boss Sven-Goran Eriksson was caught on tape by, you've guessed it, the *News of the World*, talking generally about deals, the FAPL was off like a shot again, it seems to me, just to try and look tough in the eyes of the football public.

Des Kelly, sports columnist in the *Daily Mail*, summed it up best with a phrase that could apply to both the allegations surrounding Sven and the tapping-up allegations against me. He wrote, 'Nobody had seen a rat, you understand. Heaven forbid. They just wanted someone to stop people saying they could smell one.'

I smelled a rats' nest at the *News of the World*. It had always said that it had had a tip-off that 'Chelsea were going to meet Ashley Cole' at 2 p.m. that Thursday 27 January. I reckon its source must have been its own astrologer Mystic Meg, because not even I knew I was going to the Royal Park Hotel until shortly after 3 p.m. that day. And if it was so sure this was happening, why didn't it have photographers ready and waiting at the hotel? Or why wasn't one of these crack investigators on to me from the moment I left the training ground at London Colney? Not one piece of photographic evidence was produced. Instead, its sister paper, the *Sun*, created a cartoon to illustrate its story, then quoted one of the waiters saying, 'They were definitely talking about a transfer. I clearly remember the words, "This is what we're prepared to do if you come to Chelsea." '

So, not only were we apparently reckless enough to hold such a hush-hush meeting in a public hotel, we were also daft enough to hold transfer negotiations while the waiters laid out prawn and chicken sandwiches!

One of the so-called informants was a waiter called Ray Mason. He came from Stepney, of all places. I was being killed by someone from my home territory. I would soon learn that he couldn't count, let alone tell the truth. When interviewed by the FAPL, he said he walked into the room and there were four people. There were five. The dossiers of evidence the *Sun* and *News of the World* sent over to the league made for fascinating reading. An 'investigator' from News International had rung the hotel, posing as 'Martin from Chelsea', conning details out of hotel reservations to confirm that Pini Zahavi had booked the room. Then a reporter was sent to the front desk, posing as a guest who remembered seeing Jose Mourinho walking through the lobby and one of the receptionists confirmed it but added, 'That's a secret!'

So, between them, the league and the newspapers were putting both Miss Marple and Poirot to shame, establishing that Ashley Cole and Jose Mourinho had been spotted in a hotel room, talking together, daring to mention Chelsea around a table where tea and sandwiches were available. It was an open and shut case if ever they had seen one. The 'police' could place us at the scene and weren't too fussed about getting any hard evidence.

Two days before I was officially interviewed, on tape, by the FAPL investigators, Arsenal played Bolton at the Reebok on Saturday 12 March in the sixth round of the FA Cup.

Steve 'Winky' Jacobs, a good friend and the club counsellor, who had proved a rock to both Tony Adams with his alcoholism and Paul Merson with his gambling and cocaine addiction, knocked frantically on my door at the Lowry Hotel, Manchester, on match day.

Steve stood there looking like a man with grim news, and the clue was clutched in his hand: a copy of that morning's *Sun* newspaper.

'You ain't gonna believe what's happening now!' he said.

'EXCLUSIVE: COME 'N GET ME', and that headline and my mug was staring out from the back page. My 'scandal' had taken a new twist. The story started, 'Ashley Cole's agent Jonathan Barnett made a phone call to Pini Zahavi asking him to set up a meeting about a move to Chelsea, the Premier League inquiry was told yesterday.'

It went on, 'The *Sun* understands that, according to Chelsea's evidence, Barnett called Zahavi . . . and the bombshell revelations turn soccer's biggest tap-up row on its head . . . indicating Cole tapped-up Chelsea rather than the other way round.'

Now it was no longer just about Chelsea being accused of breaching Premier League rule K3. I was being accused of breaching rule K5 which states that 'a contract player, either by himself or any person on his behalf, shall not, either directly or indirectly, make an approach to another club without having obtained the prior written consent of his club'.

I scanned the paper, sitting on the edge of the bed. I couldn't believe what I was reading.

What Peter Kenyon said on tape – just 24 hours before the Bolton game – in his official interview was that it was a meeting arranged by Jonathan Barnett and me with a view to understanding my position at the club.

The next day, the *Sun* conveniently learns of this 'admission', from what was supposed to be a confidential interview, from a 'source close to the inquiry'.

What eats me is that I'd been with Jonathan when he made the phone call from his office to Pini Zahavi, not Peter Kenyon, and I heard every word of that conversation. I was livid, throwing the paper on to the bed like I was John McEnroe slamming down a racquet.

'It gets worse,' said Steve. 'The gaffer is reading every single word over breakfast and he's got a face like thunder!'

It was not the match preparation I needed.

I went downstairs for breakfast and, in the lift going down to the restaurant, kept telling myself the boss knew I was committed 100 per cent. I'd been telling him since January that the newspapers couldn't get to me and he was the first person to advise players to take what the press said with a pinch of salt. Sure enough, it was a read-all-about-it scene downstairs, all eyes on the folded papers beside their breakfast bowls. I sat down with Steve Jacobs on a table with Graham Stack,

Stuart Taylor, Justin Hoyte and Paul Johnson. Half of that lot couldn't help but snigger. I looked left and there was the boss, two round tables away, staring at me with a face darker than thunder. 'Told ya,' said Steve.

I could not look in the boss's direction again. I had some fruit, slurped down some tea and we all went for a walk outside after breakfast. I needed the fresh air and the rest of the lads needed to wonder out loud what the boss would say. On our return, he was stood at the rear of the hotel lobby and he pulled me to one side. We sat down on two chairs.

Then he came right out with it: 'Ashley, I think you need a rest. I'm not going to play you today.'

He might as well have slapped me in the face, it stung that bad. Then I felt my blood boiling. I was so taken aback that I didn't know what to say. I wanted to lash and kick out, and scream at him, 'Why the fuck not?' Instead, I just felt this need to rush off.

'Right then!' I said, jumped up and started to walk away. The boss grabbed my arm.

'No stay and we will talk. I know you are disappointed but stay . . . please,' he said.

I wish I hadn't stayed, because he went on to talk about my welfare and the more he spoke, the more my sense of injustice multiplied. 'I think you are looking tired, and that is why you need the rest,' he said.

This was bullshit as far as I was concerned. 'But I'm not tired. I'm NOT tired!' I told him. It was no good, his mind was made up. The previous day, I had been picked for the team and we had done the team shape and put our tactics into practice on the training pitch; the team that would line up versus the rest of the squad. I was sharp in that training match, and he knew it. Yet, 24 hours later, he's telling me I'm too tired. I knew the *real* reason. If he had come up to me and said, 'Look, I'm not playing you because of all this stuff in the papers' then, as hard as that would have been to hear, at least he would have been giving it to me straight.

I was relegated to the bench and Gael Clichy stepped into my shoes. Gael is an exceptional player and this was not about him – we're both there to make each other fight for that left-back spot. This felt like a punishment dressed up as fatigue, and that's what pissed me off. The press had been handed a story on a plate. Sure enough, they pounced on this as a sign of friction, unrest in the dressing room, more fall-out from an endless saga.

'COLE DUMPED!' yelled the *Mail on Sunday*. '**Cole dropped as agent comes out fighting**' said the *Sunday Times*, quoting Jonathan as saying the latest claims were 'appalling and offensive'. The tone of all the sporting reports was that the boss had 'left Cole out in the cold' and this 'heralded Ashley Cole's departure from Highbury'.

It had been the moment the press had been gagging for since the story broke in January. The boss's official line that I'd been left out because of a hamstring strain weren't being swallowed by the reporters. I think he'd have been wiser to play me, as intended, and we could have risen above it as a team, at least on the surface. Instead, he played straight into their hands and wrote the headlines for them. It was probably the most winding blow he had ever dealt me in my time at Arsenal.

I'd like to say here that I took it on the chin and acted like a true pro. Only I didn't. I was an embarrassment to myself. I remember being stood in the tunnel, with a big chunky coat and a woolly hat on, while the rest of the lads warmed up on the pitch before kick-off. I found it impossible to put on a brave face and hide my darkening mood, and the more I dwelled on the situation, the more I felt robbed and the angrier I became. It only got worse as I sat huddled on the bench in the Arsenal dug-out alongside Robin van Persie, Cesc Fabregas, Emmanuel Eboue and Stuart Taylor. A bank of orange-bibbed photographers trained their lenses in my direction and clicked away, capturing and completing my humiliation, frame by frame. I ground my teeth.

There was no way I was even going to attempt to look happy. 'This is what the boss wants, so this is what the boss will get,' I thought. That was until I saw the photographs the next day and winced with every turn of the page. I looked like a sulking child. All my friends rang to say, 'Jesus Christ, Ash, what do you look like?!'

Towards the final quarter of the match, the boss turned to me and said, 'Go warm up.'

All I could think was, 'Hang on a minute, you thought I was too tired before the match and now you want me to warm up?' I'm not proud of my reaction or the emotional rationale behind it, but that's how it was. I refused to warm up properly and only jogged down the touchline and went through the motions. The Bolton fans had a field day: 'Chelsea rent boy!' they yelled.

'Off for the money – you're only off for the money!' they chanted.

I got to the corner flag and looked to my right where the Arsenal contingent was seated, perhaps hoping for some support. There was nothing. Not one clap or cheer. This was the rock-bottom moment. I've never seen so many pissed-off faces staring back at me. The drip, drip, drip of the day's events was trying my patience and I couldn't wait for the match to end so I could get the hell out of there. I stretched, but didn't warm up. Pat Rice, the assistant manager, stood out of the dug-out and rolled his forearms, ordering me to warm up. I looked away, pretending I hadn't seen him. I know all this was really bad and unprofessional, and it weren't like me at all, but, then again, I don't think I've ever felt so low in my whole career. At the next England match, Sammy Lee had a word with me. He had been at the Bolton game (this was in the days before he became Sam Allardyce's number two) and said to me, 'Listen, I know you're going through a bad time, but everyone was looking at you and saying how you weren't bothered.'

The last person I wanted to see after the match was Mr Dein, who was going to the dressing room as he always did after every game. 'You okay, Ashley?' he said.

'No, I'm fucking not okay, Mr Dein! Does it look like I'm okay!?'

The look on Stu Taylor's face when he saw me let rip at the vice-chairman like that! I'll shake Mr Dein's hand if he reaches out to shake mine, but our days of friendly conversation are over. Given the choice between saying ten words or one to him, I'll go for the one.

We won the match 1–0, thanks to a Freddie goal in the third minute. On the team coach to the airport for the flight back to London, I sat at the back with Steve Jacobs – there's no-one who can sort heads out like that guy. I spent the next four hours chewing his ear off and he listened. Steve looks like a younger version of that batty professor in *Back to the Future*, as wild-eyed and as manic, and the man has a heart of gold. When the shit's hitting the fan, this man's wisdom and advice helps make sense of a lot of things. We were bitching like girls over what the boss had done and how he'd made it worse. I bitched to Patrick. I bitched to Sol. I went out with my mates to a restaurant that night and bitched to them all night long as well. The next morning, I was lying in bed flicking through the papers, looking at all the headlines – *Sunday Mirror, News of the World, Sunday Express, Mail on Sunday* – bitching to Cheryl, stabbing and jabbing at each headline about me, telling her I'd told her so. She nipped out to McDonald's to cheer me up with a burger for breakfast.

'Now put that in your gob and stop moaning!' she said.

'My name is Ashley Cole and I am employed by Arsenal Football Club.' The tape was running and I was being interviewed by a lawyer called Nick Fitzpatrick, the man assigned the role of 'fact-finder' for the league. I was just going to tell it like it was and hope I was believed. On the same day, somewhere else in London, Jose Mourinho would be interviewed too.

There were times during my interview when I thought it was the police who were sat opposite me and that perhaps I was being investigated for a larger crime. I had to keep telling myself it was a football tapping-up inquiry because the questions got a bit intense.

I remember dead clearly one bit which seemed way over the top. It went something like this: 'I want to know your movements,' said Mr Fitzpatrick, recalling my journey into London on the day of 27 January. 'What were you driving?' he asked.

'A Porsche jeep,' I replied.

'Is that a dark one, by any chance?'

'No, light grey. Light metal.'

'Does it have dark windows?'

'Yes.'

And the questions kept coming: 'Do you know whereabouts you parked?', 'Did you just leave your car and walk to the office [of Jonathan Barnett]?', 'What sort of time did you arrive at the office?', and on and on he went. Thankfully, he didn't swab the inside of my mouth or ask for any DNA. But they did seize the phone records of myself, my agent, Jose Mourinho and Peter Kenyon. And, of course, when they found out that Jonathan Barnett had rung his old friend and business associate Pini Zahavi, two and two seemed to equal six. It was all becoming that tedious, as the FAPL treated the Great Case of the Ashley Cole Tapping-up Scandal like some kind of unsolved mystery. Around 20 people were interviewed, from football managers to sandwich servers, between January and March 2005.

There was a lot of speculation about charges against Chelsea and the sanctions open to the league, but not once did I think about being charged myself. It never entered my head. Even the boss had reassured me that I wouldn't get into trouble and there was nothing to worry about. And nearly every commentator or football writer, except one in the *Daily Express*, had predicted I would be 'in the clear' and 'escape punishment'.

But on 23 March 2005, the FA Premier League issued a statement. It was charging me for a breach of rule K5 and Jose Mourinho and Chelsea Football Club for a breach of rule K3. It couldn't make up its mind who had approached whom, so it covered both bases. Whatever Arsenal may or may not have said about me not being to blame, the very investigation it had kick-started was now coming after me. Arsenal's pursuit of Chelsea had backfired against their own player, and I couldn't believe what was happening. I had to issue a formal statement through my lawyer, saying how we 'accepted receipt of the Premier League charges', but I didn't accept it. I couldn't accept it. None of it made any sense. 'YOU'RE NICKED' crowed the *Sun* the next day, and the media got all revved up again over me being 'sensationally charged'. I felt like a scapegoat, the player sold short by Arsenal, the player the FA Premier League was piggy-backing in a show of strength to protect itself. I felt completely deflated and disillusioned with the whole business.

The one person who was happy was the vice-chairman David Dein who couldn't wait to heap praise on the *News of the World*. 'It is congratulations to you and your team,' he wrote to the editor, 'for all the work that you have done in exposing this.'

Nine months later and, curiously, Mr Dein was in no mood to rush to the editor of the *Daily Express* to congratulate them for their investigative work.

I don't know what happened. I've just read the press reports like anyone else. So I'll let you decide whether this smells of hypocrisy and double standards. It all had to do with the £4.5 million transfer of Gilberto Silva from Atletico Mineiro to Arsenal which attracted the close scrutiny of a High Court judge. Mr Justice Jack presided over a civil matter concerning agents' commissions involved with the transfer. As a result of that case, it emerged that Arsenal had used an international sports consultant to make enquiries and 'sound out' the appropriate people in Brazil about Gilberto moving to a 'European club', without ever mentioning Arsenal.

From reading the reports, it seems Mr Dein protested that there was nothing 'covert' about that approach. Now I would say, nor was there anything 'covert' about me meeting Pini Zahavi in a busy London hotel, but I still got hauled over the coals for it. The FA brought the Gilberto case to FIFA's attention but, surprise, surprise, nothing came of it.

Look, tapping-up takes place in football. And if it's not blatant tapping-up, it's a diluted, more subtle form of the same thing. Whether it's a FIFA-licensed agent, a third party, a conduit or a friend of a friend, players or their agents are sounded out all the time. I'd be amazed if every club doesn't do it. So how Arsenal could take the moral high ground in my case was a joke.

As the Aston Villa chairman, Doug Ellis, wrote in the *Daily Express* in November 2005, 'It makes me laugh when I see how Arsenal made such a big fuss over the way Chelsea supposedly tapped-up their defender Ashley Cole. Let me state the blindingly obvious – it happens all the time. By definition, that means Arsenal must surely be up to the same tricks as everyone else.'

What was blindingly obvious to me was that there was only one reason why Arsenal were making such a meal out of my case – because it was Chelsea. I wish the Gilberto case had come to light a few months earlier. It would have made for interesting ammunition for my legal team. But in the spring of 2005, all we could do was await a trial date.

6

Rough Justice

No-one could accuse them of not being in fine voice or not getting behind me.

'One Ashley Cole . . . There's only one Ashley Cole . . . Onnne Ashleeee Cooole . . .'

But for once, I wished to God they weren't singing my name. For once, the hairs on the back of my neck weren't standing on end. Because it was the Chelsea fans.

They were determined to rub it in and adopt me for the afternoon, clapping when I came out for the warm-up, cheering my every touch of the ball. Chelsea versus Arsenal, a mid-week fixture on 20 April 2005, was a weird experience when the fans in blue cheered the bloke in red and white. What made it more perverse was that it was probably the best reaction I'd had from a crowd that year. England team-mates John Terry and Frank Lampard had a laugh about it afterwards, saying I'd shown balls that night.

I'd been buzzing for the match ever since our defeats of Blackburn, Norwich, Middlesbrough and then Blackburn again in the FA Cup semi-final. Friends had been asking if I was dreading the London derby, but there's nothing better for my motivation than what the press would call a 'grudge match', and this one was extra-loaded with spice for obvious reasons. I'd never been more focused for a match and was ready for anything – except the fans' reaction.

I first noticed something was up on the team coach, where I was sat at the back, listening to R&B on the iPod, gazing out of the window as a police escort cut through the crowds on Fulham Road. We all get used to the moronic stick over the seasons; brainless idiots giving us two fingers or making tosser signs, somehow thinking we'll be offended.

From the outside looking in, I must have looked as expressionless as the rest of the lads until I caught sight of a big woman with a blue scarf who was excitedly pointing me out to her husband. Then a bunch of Chelsea kids clocked me and cheered as their dads smiled and two lads gave me the fisted salute. I sat up, a tad self-conscious, and looked around to see if anyone else had spotted this, but they hadn't. Not until we stepped off the coach at the ground. I was last off. Every Arsenal player ahead of me got booed. As I appeared at the door, this crowd of blue cheered. There was a placard held up which read, 'Welcome Home Ashley!' A steward stuck out his hand to shake mine and one bright spark shouted, 'When you gonna come and join the *real* champions Coley!' I've never been sure whether it was collective sarcasm or a genuine belief that I was about to join them.

The reaction of the Chelsea fans was in sharp contrast to the hostile reaction that faced me at Highbury a couple of weeks earlier. I forget what game it was now but I was driving to the ground in my black Range Rover Sports with Mum and my mate Jermaine Wynters. It were an evening kick-off and fans were milling around Blackstock Road as usual when we slowed up in congested traffic. That's when we heard the taunt. 'JOOOD-US . . . JOOOD-US.'

To the right side of my car, on the pavement, were a gang of Arsenal fans who had been stood outside a pub, and they were on the kerb, yelling at me; their faces twisted with hate. Stupidly, I thought I could reason with them. I wound down my window.

'You fuck off to Chelsea then you traitor!' yelled one of them, and before I knew it this gang was around the car, sheep following sheep. I tried to explain that they shouldn't believe everything they read in the papers.

'Come on, give us a break!' I remember saying, almost pleading for common sense.

'Just drive on Ash,' said my mum, sat beside me and getting more and more concerned. Not that it dawned on these idiots that there was a lady in the car; let alone the fact it was my mum. I wound up the window. And then they started up big time, banging on the windows, thumping on the bonnet. 'JOOOD-US . . . JOOOD-US!!' I drove away. In my rear view mirror, they were all stood there laughing and jeering, flicking Vs and giving the finger. A policeman was somewhere amongst them trying to calm them down, moving them back onto the pavement. None of us – me, Mum or Wynters – knew what to say. It was silent in the car for a few moments. I couldn't believe what had just happened.

'You alright?' Mum asked, and yet I knew she was the one who was shaken. 'The bastards!' she added.

It was a horrible experience and I'll never understand hostility like that. I know every club has a brainless minority but it was something I weren't ready for. Facing boos from a section of the crowd was one thing but that hostility in the street was vicious.

Even in the ground, there was no escaping the abuse. Especially for Mum. She'd be sat in her seat behind the directors' box and people knew who she was, and fans would start yelling how shit I was and how brilliant Gael Clichy was.'He's the man . . . He's the man . . . forget Cole!' one fan shouted loudly in Mum's direction. And there was the usual bile of 'traitor', 'Judas', 'Chelsea rent boy'. All credit to Mum, she never rose to the taunts and she kept her cool but it must have been hard for her to listen to, and why should she? What had Mum done to deserve all that?

Towards the end of the season, she'd heard enough.'Ash, you've got to move me from those seats. The lads behind me are being so abusive about you and it's doing my head in. I'm going to turn round and punch one of them if I'm not careful!' And Mum probably would have done because she's a fierce protector when it comes to her sons. I really felt for her because she loved her seat and made a lot of friends but some mindless idiots had made it unbearable. So, for the new season, I bought a box in the Clock End. I felt happier that Mum could get back to watching her beloved Arsenal and scream and shout her support as usual, instead of hearing people screaming and shouting abuse about me.

Mum was learning, like me, to keep her head down, blank it all out and just get on with life. Which is what I had to do that day when the Chelsea supporters started cheering my name. I kept my head down and pretended I was listening to my iPod. Having to contend with Damien Duff was enough to think about for a day's work without getting bothered about the madness of Chelsea fans being kind! All I could do was knuckle down to the job in hand. We needed to win that day to maintain even the faintest hope of pegging back the leaders. There was an irony to the occasion, too, that illustrated the shift in supremacy that season: Chelsea were protecting an unbeaten home record of 22 matches, so we knew, more than anyone, that their self-belief was akin to having a twelfth man running around in a blue shirt. We'd closed the gap from 13 to 11 points and needed to reduce that margin to 8.

In the tunnel before the match, I saw Mourinho and that was an awkward moment. All my team-mates milling around on one side, the opposing manager on the other, about to go into a huge game. The last thing I needed was to come out with something stupid like 'Hey, what's happening man!' So I looked at him for a second, he looked at me and we said nothing. Probably for the best. God knows, if we'd have dared say 'hello', the FA Premier League might have seen it as illegal approach number two! The Chelsea tunnel is not a corridor like at Arsenal, it's more of a wide avenue, so it's not as if we were close enough to talk. I stretched against the wall instead. I looked around at the blue shirts and saw my challenge for the evening: Damien Duff. Then I saw my England team-mates John Terry and Frank Lampard, and they were both hungry to turn us over that night and go on to record two 'firsts': first league title in half a century and first league win over Arsenal in ten years.

Nothing would have been sweeter for those two, and I wouldn't have heard the end of it. Both of them are quality footballers and quality people. People can rave all they want about how Abramovich's billions have bought foreign imports to lead the revolution, but those two English boys have been instrumental in turning around Chelsea's fortunes.

I've been playing against John Terry since the age of 12. He played as a midfielder back then for Senrab FC, along with J Lloyd Samuel, Bobby Zamora, and Ledley King, and I was a nippy little striker with Puma FC. But once, in a district game between my team, Tower Hamlets, and his side, Dagenham and Redbridge, he scored a hat-trick from free kicks in a 6–6 epic. Seems crazy now, I know – but he was the Beckham of our adolescence!

Even though he's a solid central defender these days, he's still got a good shot on him. In Portugal, he was mucking around on the training pitch, taking free kicks with left and right shots, and he was whipping them in. He's not lost his touch, let me tell you. John trains like he plays. I'm one of those players who doesn't train as well as I know I can play because I don't want to run the risk of injuring someone else or myself. But John means business whenever he puts his boots on, like a Martin Keown or a Patrick Vieira, and his desire is something else.

Frank 'Lamps' Lampard used to get hammered by the Arsenal fans when he played for West Ham. They used to call him 'Feedback Frank' because he'd always give the ball back to the keeper. But he's shut up a few thousand people now. His game has improved beyond measure – he scores sensational goals, he's got a great range of passing and he's a workhorse who can run all day.

Before the game at Stamford Bridge, the boss had made a joke to reporters about it being impossible to match Chelsea's financial clout unless Arsenal drilled and found oil at London Colney. But we matched them in every department on the pitch, and a tight match with few clear-cut chances ended 0–0.

And I won the Sky Sports man-of-the-match award. Point proven.

Afterwards, the boss described Chelsea as 'worthy champions', even if we hadn't had to endure the humiliation of handing over the champions' belt that evening. They would have to wait another ten days before clinching the title. We would go on to record four more victories, including the 7–0 demolition of Everton, before ultimately finishing second with 83 points – 12 points off the deserving champions.

I felt I'd had good games right up to the finishing line. Whether I had made a strong enough point to the Doubting Thomases who still remained in the stands and on the board, I've no idea, but it was almost becoming immaterial what kind of talking my feet were doing. Soon enough, I would have to take the witness stand and speak up for myself, and so my days were being spent at training in the mornings and with my legal team in the afternoons, sometimes spilling into the evenings.

By the end of April, it had been announced that the matter of the

'Football Association Premier League and Ashley Cole, Jose Mourinho and Chelsea Football Club' was set to be heard at Marble Arch Tower in central London on Tuesday 17 May and Wednesday 18 May.

The irony of the timing jumped out at me, like so many ironies that season. The FA Premier League and Arsenal Football Club had banged on ever since January about the critical need for such rules to be enforced to prevent under-contract players being distracted and destabilised by off-the-field events. Like the boss had said, the timing of the 'hotel meeting' was 'atrocious' coming before the 4–2 league defeat against Manchester United. Never have a heavy one-to-one with any player before any big game. That was, and still is, his belief, and David Dein and the FA Premier League had agreed.

So what does the league do?

It decides to hold its tapping-up inquiry in the glare of the media spotlight – just a few days before our FA Cup final against Manchester United on Saturday 21 May.

It was to be both Arsenal and Manchester United's 17th FA Cup final. It was to be my fourth, having been part of the 2001–02 and 2002–03 winning Gunners teams (I tend to forget the 2001 final). If I'm honest, apart from the odd moment or two, I managed to store all thoughts of the league inquiry in a locker in the back of my mind. There was no mental space to think about anything other than how to grab our only chance of silverware that season, avenge our worst enemy for two league defeats and the Carling Cup quarter-final and repeat the Community Shield victory. Let them have the six points, but let's make sure we take the trophies. Just the thought of walking out at the Millennium Stadium once more was enough to bring me out in goose bumps; the thought of taking the witness stand beforehand brought only a shrug of the shoulders. Not that the press was ever going to let me forget the hurdle before the final. All it could ask the boss was, 'Will this be Ashley's last match for Arsenal?', 'Do you think he'll be found guilty?', 'Do you think he'll be unsettled for the final?', plus a load of other questions.

It must have got to the boss, because he came up to me for a quiet word on the day before the inquiry and said, 'You know, you do not have to go. You do not have to put yourself through it.' I could have sat it out and attended only to give my evidence, but I wanted to be there for the entire thing, to listen to every word. I'd already had my eyes opened and stumbled across a few home truths by reading Arsenal FC documents disclosed to my legal team. I sat with my brief, Graham Shear, in his offices near Chancery Lane, and it was like discovering private diaries I was never meant to see. Nothing pricked me sharper than knowing that the boss asked if it was worth risking me for an extra five grand a week and knowing his words made no difference. Nothing removed my blinkers to club politics more than that. What do they say about not getting too close to the club you support because you learn too much and it ruins the mystery essential to blind hero-worship? Believe me, even as a player you can learn too much and it can be equally as damaging to the heart and soul. Having seen it all with my own eyes, I wanted to go to the inquiry to hear it with my own ears, to see it coming from the same mouths that had told me everything would be okay. I also wanted to be there in person to clear my name.

My FA Cup preparation began with training as usual on Tuesday 17 May. While I ran up and down the left flank in a yellow top and grey shorts at London Colney, my barrister, David Pannick QC, was explaining to Sir Philip Otton, the inquiry chairman, why I was missing.

'Mr Cole will be arriving very soon, after training.' David Dein, Jose Mourinho, Peter Kenyon and Jonathan were already there at football's court of law.

After training, I took the Aston Martin for speed. As I drove, Mr Dein, the first witness called, was getting himself all mixed up – Jonathan and I would laugh about it later. Jonathan filled me in on what I missed. Apparently Mr Dein said that the hotel episode impacted so badly on the club that Arsenal's 49-match unbeaten run was ended in the match following the *News of the World*'s story. But the unbeaten run had ended the previous October, not in the January. From what I was told, the vice-chairman was all over the place with his facts. He wasn't half milking the drama either apparently, talking of 'a dark cloud hanging over the club' and describing how I only had 'a walk-on part in the whole drama'. He also said he felt sorry for me, thought I had been silly, and added, 'We like Ashley. We love Ashley.' And he went on to value me at £20 million. It all got a bit sparky between my barrister and the vice-chairman, it seems, but I missed it all. I was too busy at the front gate, messing round with the paparazzi and panicking like mad that they were going to scratch the car. I'd have had more luck driving straight into Buckingham Palace that day instead of Marble Arch Towers. I ran into a wall of television cameras, photographers and reporters. Bulbs were flashing, grown men were jostling and camera lenses were bumping and knocking the windscreen.

'Mind the car!' I screamed, but might as well have been screaming to myself. I know, I know. I'm overprotective of that car. There are only two babes in my life: Cheryl and the Aston Martin. Just ask the missus – I won't even let her loose behind the wheel. So to see these idiots having complete disregard for it, just for the sake of getting a shot of me, made my blood boil. Bang. Whack. Flash. Flash.

'Don't touch the car!' I screamed again. Eventually, the gates opened and let me in. The first thing I did when parked up was get out and check for scratches and dents. 'Pricks!' I muttered under my breath. It was not the most chilled, coolest of starts to my day in court. I decided to walk in the next day.

Graham Shear met me at the bottom of the stairs and we got the lift to the second floor. I started to sweat a little. More nerve-wracking than going to the vice-chairman's house, it was. I walked in as Mr Dein was walking back to his chair after an adjournment at the end of his evidence. He smiled. I nodded. Jose Mourinho stood up to walk to the witness stand. It was so quiet: just the scraping of chair legs, the sound of coughing, papers shuffling. The sound and atmosphere of people being all formal. My barrister was first to speak up, saying that I had just arrived. I sweated big time after he said that; my clammy hands refused to dry. Jose Mourinho, looking as dapper as ever, fiddled with the dodgy microphone in front of him. The inquiry chairman told him to keep his voice up, to imagine that he was on the training ground. I liked that.

I looked around me. It was not like the court I had imagined. It was just a big white room with tables. There was the chairman sat with two other men either side of him at a table facing us all, but it weren't raised on a platform or anything like that. There was a woman tapping away in the corner to our left – a stenographer. Across the other side of the room, to our right, was the witness stand.

Then each side faced the panel from separate tables: the FA Premier League (the prosecutors), Chelsea and me (the defendants). Arsenal, in the form of Mr Dein and a lawyer (victims), sat on two chairs at the back.

Each table had files and folders stacked high. None of the barristers wore wigs and when one of them called the chairman 'My Lord', the chairman got all modest and replied, 'Please, call me sir . . .'

It looked like I had brought a team of real big guns with me as I sat at the table with Graham Shear to the left of me and David Pannick QC to the right. It was an impressive three-at-the-back defence, I joked.

Jonathan was sat behind us with another lawyer, Alison Green, who was scribbling down notes. I was busy watching Jose Mourinho's performance so I could see what Mark Gay, the lawyer for the league, was like with him. The Chelsea boss skilfully negotiated his way through it all. Like the best of his front men. From a tactical point of view, he was fascinating to listen to.

He talked about me and Jonathan both being unhappy. He listed as reasons the contract I had, the way the negotiations had gone and said I was generally frustrated with how things were being handled. He then said something like, 'After that, Ashley spoke . . . by saying a few things. If you want me to tell, I can tell.'

I grew more and more agitated in my seat as he continued by saying that I also weren't happy with the relationship Arsene Wenger had with some of the French players and that they were in control of the dressing room.

Next up he compared the situation at Chelsea, saying that I had contact with some of the Stamford Bridge boys in the England team and they had told me how happy they were with the set-up in the Chelsea camp and with Mr Mourinho himself. That made him feel good he admitted.

He then suggested that he had gathered 'intelligence' on the Arsenal dressing room from me, and that was the best thing to come out of the meeting.

A couple of times as he spoke I looked across at him, unsuccessfully trying to catch his eye.

The only thing he did say that I wanted Mr Dein to note was this: that I was to Arsenal what John Terry was to Chelsea, and he added that no-one can touch a home-grown player like JT because the club respected him and paid him the most.

The rest of his evidence weren't good for me. Nor was the evidence of Peter Kenyon, who was next up. He said Pini Zahavi made the approach on our behalf. I didn't have time to think about it all at that point because my barrister stood up and said:

'We call Ashley Cole.'

Don't get bogged down in detail. Keep it short. Don't tie yourself in knots. Just answer the questions. Keep it simple. Don't try to be clever. That was what Graham Shear advised me, because I was potentially a nightmare witness: not good with long words, not good at remembering dates off the top of my head.

Thinking on my feet with a right-winger coming at me is easy. Thinking on my feet with all that legal mumbo-jumbo flying at me was something else. My back started sweating the moment I was asked to check if there was a certain piece of evidence in front of me, a volume containing an official interview I had given to the FA Premier League on 14 March, around the same time I'd met David Dein at his house. As I opened up the volume, and was asked to keep up my voice, I felt the dampness of my shirt as I leaned back into the chair. I was well nervous. I told the inquiry that everything that had been said about the hotel meeting was rubbish. I ran them through the whole thing from start to finish: how a brief meeting with Pini Zahavi was interrupted by a knock on the door, in walked the Chelsea manager and chief executive, there was general chit-chat and then we left.

Then came the cross-examination. The Chelsea barrister wanted to check out my ambitions to play in Spain and asked if I knew David Beckham. Yes, I said. He then started banging on about why I hadn't called Becks about Spain and his lifestyle.

'Because I don't have his number,' I said. And it's none of your business. I thought.

For me, Becks is a big star and I'm just another player from Arsenal. I wouldn't want to hassle him with my questions.

Then he asked if I'd got advice from Reyes.

'He can't speak English,' I replied.

'So how do you call for the ball on the pitch, Mr Cole?' and with that the room burst out laughing. Barristers can be as bad as reporters for trying to put words in your mouth and then twist them. This bloke was determined to try to tie me in knots. Especially when it came to Mr Mourinho's 'intelligence' from the Arsenal dressing room. He did my head in for the next 15 minutes, trying – and failing – to confuse me.

'Do you agree that you admired the togetherness of Chelsea?' he asked.

'It's good,' I replied.

'Did you say, whilst on England duty, speaking to friends like Frank Lampard and others, you admired the team spirit?'

He was trying to suggest that Chelsea had started the whole motivational team-hug thing and that I was jealous of it. What got my goat was that it was a trend we started at Arsenal and had been followed by others. Even Spurs.

You'll see Arsenal, before every match, gather in the centre circle, hug each other, high five each other, shake each other's hands. I think it started after a Leeds game and went on from there. It does give the lads a boost and revs everyone up for the match. It wound me up big time that he was trying to make something out of this, and I could feel myself getting warmer and warmer with anger.

Then he tried to get me on whether there was a French clique in the Arsenal dressing room.

I knew he was stabbing in the dark. 'Look,' I said, 'there's more Spanish than French, so how can there be a French clique?' I impressed myself with that one. I remember looking at the panel, hoping they'd noted that one down as a point to me, but then, and on other occasions throughout my evidence, I got a bad vibe about them. It didn't seem to me, when I glanced over, that they were really listening or under-standing. Each time the chairman stepped in with a question of his own, it focused on me being fed up at Arsenal or the extra £5,000 I wanted. As much as I had repeated that it was never about money, it was about principles, I'd have had more joy banging my head against a brick wall than getting my message across to that bunch of suits. Each barrister who had a pop at me suggested I had taken my bat and ball home and run off to Chelsea when negotiations with Arsenal had broken down. Did it not occur to anyone that the whole 'tapping-up' story was nonsense anyway? The way it was played out in the media and that courtroom, it was as if I could desert Arsenal whenever I wanted, have a sneaky meeting with Chelsea and join them at will. But the transfer market doesn't work that way.

Chelsea would have needed Arsenal's consent, and it was a consent that would never have been given. One more reason why I'd never have sounded out Chelsea for a move: because it was an unlikely scenario. But people forgot all about consent in all the fuss. I do understand that it was their job, but from where I was sitting it just felt like the Chelsea and FA Premier League barristers lined up to take pot shots at me during cross-examination until it all came to an end.

'Thank you, Mr Cole, you are free to go now, no need to come back tomorrow,' said the chairman as the grilling came to an end. 'I think we're impartial and we hope you have a good game on Saturday,' he added.

David Pannick QC, my barrister, stood up: 'I think Mr Cole will come back tomorrow. I think he has a close interest in the matter. He has a free afternoon. Nothing would give him greater pleasure than to spend it with us.'

'Well,' said the chairman, 'we are flattered.'

I must have been sat in that chair for a good hour and I thought I'd done good. I was sure things were going to get even better when the boss took the stand. After Jonathan, he was my next best character witness. He knew me, and he knew my game and ambition were never about money.

Then the inquiry hit me with the biggest blow. Arsene Wenger was not being called, because it was Cup final week. The FAPL decided it had no interest in calling the boss to the stand and the chairman agreed. Mr Dein's evidence would stand alone as the Arsenal view. Coupled with the evidence of Mr Mourinho and Mr Kenyon, I think I knew I was dead at that point.

Jonathan gave his evidence at the start of day two and was a lot more talkative than I had been. You couldn't shut him up. He said Chelsea's recollection of events was completely different from ours. He even had a go at the league's man, Mark Gay, suggesting he didn't really understand football.

The barrister countered that by saying Jonathan didn't understand English and the definition of what was a 'meeting' with Chelsea. Jonathan accused the barrister of not being able to read as his statement clearly said there was no 'meeting' with Mr Mourinho and Mr Kenyon. 'They just came in,' he said.

Mr Gay got all dramatic on us again. He reckoned that when the Chelsea manager and chief executive walked in, it was the same as if Princess Leia and Luke Skywalker were having a meeting and Darth Vader walks in. I almost burst out laughing.

The panel chairman didn't seem too impressed either. Everyone in the room looked confused.

That's when Mr Gay rephrased his question asking whether his natural reaction hadn't been to get out of there.

I thought Jonathan was brilliant with his response. He said he thought it was wrong of Mr Gay to assume that because we had been in a room we had been going to be talking about business. He said he thought it was important to establish that we are talking about human beings, who are allowed to sit and talk. That's all there was to it. The league would be sitting every week if it was reported every time someone from one club happened to bump into someone from another one. I loved that.

So my case was made, the closing statements were given and we awaited a ruling, but it was decided that the panel would not give any decision until after the FA Cup final. 'Strong representations' were made by Arsenal, who wanted to avoid big headlines going into the match. Protect the club, it seemed to me, not the player. It was consistent, if nothing else, but I couldn't allow it to bother me. I had to mentally prepare for Cardiff, and I went into the match not knowing if I even had a future with Arsenal.

*

Sometimes in football, nerves of steel can overcome style and technique, and sometimes football isn't fair.

I remember when we lost 2–1 to Liverpool in the 2001 FA Cup final. We battered them in terms of football, skill and dominance, but nothing went our way. I had a shot cleared off the line, so did Thierry, and Henchoz handballed a goal-bound shot on to the post only for the referee to award a goal kick. We protected a 1–0 lead brilliantly until the last ten minutes when we were sunk by a quick Michael Owen double against the run of play. We missed a hatful of chances and Liverpool took their two and won.

Sometimes, there is no making sense of football and, on FA Cup final day 2005, there was no making sense of our performance. Manchester United were all over us. They battered us – they absolutely battered us – but couldn't finish. Van Nistelrooy couldn't hit a barn door. He was bang out of form and missed some unbelievable chances. He was hopeless. The final at the Millennium Stadium became more of a psychological battle and our nerves held firmest. The more chances United missed, the more we began to think it could be our day. As the minutes ticked by and they squandered more and more chances, we grew in the belief that they would not score if they played till midnight against five men. Dominance only counts when it is converted into goals.

I remember being physically wiped in that game; the heat was a joke. I also got booked for sending Wayne Rooney flying in a crunching tackle. We were up against it the whole match, but were determined to hang on, determined to survive until penalties. We were on the rack and knew we weren't going to score so we fought like dogs for each other, defending desperately at times.

Patrick did a great block from Roy Keane and Freddie saved the match in the 85th minute when he cleared a van Nistelrooy close-range header off the line. I don't think the United players could believe he'd kept it out, and I think that was the moment their bubble burst. As we gathered around for extra-time, I remember thinking, 'This is meant to be our lucky day . . . we can win this,' whereas Rooney, Ronaldo and van Nistelrooy seemed mentally beat. After another half-hour of deadlock, and after Jose Antonio Reyes had been sent off for a second bookable offence, the game went to penalties, and United's dominance meant nothing any more. We were suddenly equal to them again and had a massive psychological advantage. Nerves mattered more than ever. It was Portugal and Sheffield all over again.

I kept standing, socks rolled down, mouth desert-dry, but I had to keep standing as the boss took down my name as one of the five penalty-takers. I looked up into the stands to find Mum. There she was, sat next to my cousin Donna Brown. I waved to them and they urged me on. Cheryl wasn't there because she had commitments with Girls Aloud, but I visualised her face: that was enough encouragement. I saw seven friends – Reece Weston, Paulo Vernazza, Andrew Douglas, Greg Lincoln, Lee Docherty, Danny Boateng and Terry Bowes – standing in T-shirts, each one with a letter on its front, spelling 'ASH COLE', three on one row, four on the row below; red letters on a white background. I'd played with those boys since I was 16 years old, and there they were, supporting me when it mattered most. As the shoot-out started, Arsenal stood in the centre circle as a team, arms interlinked around shoulders. And as the fans held their breath, we held our nerve.

Lauren, van Persie and Freddie all stepped up and scored. Then Paul Scholes missed, his shot saved by the brilliant Lehmann. Then came my penalty. On that mile-long walk to the penalty spot, I knew that if I scored and Patrick scored, we'd won. Patrick said to me afterwards that he'd worried about whether I'd buckle under the pressure because so much was on top of me. Everything I had been through since January boiled down to this one moment of judgement before the Arsenal fans. Miss, and I'd be the player whose heart had deserted the club and should never have been allowed the responsibility. Score, and I'd claw back some credit. Friends would say to me afterwards, 'You had some arse to stand up and take that penalty!' Weeks later, I learned from Wes Brown that even the United players had me down as a banker to miss. 'We all thought you'd never score with everything that had gone on,' he said.

Other friends were listening to the match live on radio and the commentator said, 'Next, it will be Ashley Cole who's had such a troubled week off the field, with a disciplinary hearing over the alleged tapping-up by Chelsea and his part in all that. He's put it all behind him today in terms of his performance during the 120 minutes of the match. Now one last contribution from him . . .'

I remember the whistles of the United fans, the cheers of the Gooners. Now, they were singing my name.

I crossed that white line to walk into the penalty box and picked up the ball. The noise was deafening but, as I placed the ball on the spot, I knew I was going to score. It was as if the United fans all became a blur in the background and the noise was drowned out by my own thoughts and focus. All I could see was a yawning gap between the sticks. Roy Carroll, their keeper, bouncing around on his line, might as well have been invisible. Nothing was in my head apart from one thought, 'Put it in that left corner.' I ran up, side foot, hit it high. Goal! The relief that went through me was like nothing else. Look at pictures of me that day – I went mad. I sprinted back up that pitch, elated.

I looked up to the stands. Mum raised both her hands in the air and was being hugged by Donna. I kissed my finger and blew it up to her. I saw all my friends celebrating. 'ASH COLE' warped in the jubilation, as letter 'A' jumped up and down with letter 'C' and the 'H' went mental with 'C' and 'L'.

It was fitting that it came down to Patrick to slot home the winning goal. It would be his last match for Arsenal before his sudden move to Juventus, but it was a tremendous way to put a seal on a superb stint and captaincy with the club. It was Arsenal's tenth FA Cup win and my third medal. When Patrick lifted the trophy into the air from the pitch podium and the fireworks crackled and the red ticker-tape fell, I've never felt such joy and emotion at the same time. Lauren and Dennis were jumping up and down behind me, van Persie was spraying me with champagne. It was a tremendous atmosphere for both the players and the fans. I caught the boss stood behind us as the photographers ran around taking pictures; he was stood back, clapping, but he, too, was looking into the stands for the people that mattered. We were still champions of a different kind thanks to him, and his modesty has never accepted the due credit. As for me, I was so happy that I had scored a penalty to help win a trophy for the club and fans that had doubted me.

We lined up to hold aloft and kiss that trophy, showing it off to our friends and family in the stands. When my turn came, I held it up to Mum and that choked me up. It wasn't just because the lid slid off and smashed me in the head that my eyes were watering. That victory meant so much to me for so many personal reasons. In the team celebration pictures, I made sure I was right next to that trophy. I didn't want to let it out of my sight. I wanted every moment to last because, sometime during the parade around the pitch, the thought had hit me like a smack in the face that this could be my last match for the Arsenal.

The newspapers were full of the same speculation the next day. In the *Sunday Times*, Andrew Longmore wrote, 'If this was Ashley Cole's last action in the red shirt of Arsenal, he might well want to erase the tape except for the last, decisive minute, at least.' He poked fun at my 'dinner date' with Chelsea, but was also kind when he wrote, 'There is nothing wrong with Cole's spirit. Anyone less resilient would have been broken by the pressure readily inflicted on him . . . it is a tribute to Cole's equable temperament that throughout one of the more tumultuous weeks of his career, he never missed a beat in training, nor gave Wenger a moment's cause for concern. He is a clockwork player . . .'

I'm glad someone had noticed.

On the pitch, when the thought hit me that this could be my last match, I was noticing everything. I stopped jumping around and screaming and concentrated instead on taking it all in. I got all nostalgic, looking back on the season and the ordinary days at the training ground.

Kolo Toure came rushing up behind me, jumped on my back and said, 'Jesus, Ash! We just won the cup, we didn't lose!' As I laughed, he ran off and jumped on to some more team-mates. When we got into the dressing room, everyone was hyper and all I could do was rush around, grabbing the club photographer, getting him to take pictures of me and the boss, me and the trophy, me and Dennis, me and van Persie, me and Patrick. Oh yeah, and me and the trophy in the bath. I was like an excited kid going round shouting, 'Picture, picture, picture.' If it was to be my final match, I wanted every memory to be captured. And the night was still young.

After flying back to London, the club had arranged for a celebration dinner at Sopwell House, and Mum and Donna were my guests. I remember seeing a beaming Mr Dein mingling with the crowd, shaking the hands of players' wives and relatives, and I wondered what he'd say when he came to greet Mum. He'd always been a charmer with her, always going up to say hello and telling her 'You must be very proud of your son!' Mum loved it. But she was in for a surprise that evening. Mr Dein walked by her without even saying a word.

On the way back to my table with some drinks, the managing director Keith Edelman stopped me to say, 'Sorry about everything that's happened, but we do hope you'll be staying. We really don't want to lose you.' And another director, Ken Friar, who is a top bloke, said to me, 'I don't want you to go . . . you'd be a big loss to this club.' They were all kind words, but I didn't want to dwell on my future there and then. I wanted to go out and get absolutely hammered, to tell the truth. So I did – at the Embassy Club in Mayfair.

And because I hadn't wanted the day to end, I was out in my Tommy Hilfiger Arsenal suit until 6 a.m. the next day, led astray by Stuart Taylor and Sol Campbell! It was a great night with the lads, and I drank to remember the FA Cup win and to forget the imminent decision of the FA Premier League 'tapping-up' inquiry.

I was never going to be found innocent. In the back of my mind, I'd already accepted that I might as well have given my evidence to the FAPL tribunal from behind a thick glass wall.

I turned up at Marble Arch Towers on 1 June to hear the verdict in person, having flown into London from New York on the back of England's 3–2 friendly win against Colombia the previous day. I had just stepped off the plane and was knackered. My agent and solicitor joined me there.

We sat and listened as they pretty much hammered us all. Guilty as charged. As expected.

The commission's conclusions felt like one of those shocking referee's decisions which you cannot change. It was a 15-page judgement that concluded: 'We are satisfied that every individual was fully aware that a prearranged meeting was to take place and that its purpose was to discuss with Ashley Cole his future. We reject Peter Kenyon and Jose Mourinho's explanation that they merely went to listen. They played an active role. We safely infer that there was an active discussion between all those present on the basis that Cole was going to be up for sale in the near future. Chelsea were exploring the prospect of acquiring him. We infer that Jonathan Barnett contacted Pini Zahavi and explained the position and, in all probability, the two agents discussed the possibility of a transfer deal for Cole . . . we had grave difficulty giving credence to Cole and Barnett's account.'

So they didn't believe a word I'd said. For me, the judgement was one mass assumption – it seemed they'd filled in the gaps for themselves with a form of justice based on there being no smoke without fire.

If Arsenal had banked on the league backing up its bark with a bite, it was to be disappointed. Chelsea were *not* docked any points. Instead, they were handed a *suspended* three-point deduction and fined £300,000. Jose Mourinho was fined £200,000 and I was fined £100,000, despite the inquiry conceding that 'the arrangements of the meeting were not of his direct making'.

What got me was that I was fined £100,000 based on 'probabilities' and yet defender Christian Ziege got hit with a mere £10,000 fine in 2002 when he was actually caught being tapped-up by Liverpool behind the backs of Middlesbrough – and that was an open and shut case!

Where's the fairness in hitting me with a fine ten times greater? Were they just trying to make an example of me? What bothered me more than anything was the stain that the word 'guilty' left on me. 'THE DAMNING' is how the *Daily Mail* reported the verdict, while Simon Barnes in *The Times* wrote about my 'blatant disloyalty', providing more ammunition for the Arsenal faithful. People weren't going to remember the fine, they were going to remember me as being guilty. Looking back at everything that happened then, and has happened since, everyone will look at my arguments and go 'yeah, yeah, yeah – he was always wanting to go and we were right to call him disloyal'. But that weren't the case and I've almost become bored of pleading my innocence because no-one is prepared to believe me anyway. History will always remember me for going behind the back of Arsenal to encourage interest from Chelsea.

But one man's version of history is another man's different account. It all depends on where you were and what your perspective at the time was. From my viewpoint, sat on the *inside* of that room with Peter Kenyon and Jose Mourinho, I know what weren't said. From the fans' and the league's point of view, sat on the *outside*, with only suspicious minds to rely on, they seem to think they know what must have been said.

And for forever and a day, all of us are going to have to agree to disagree.

Arsene Wenger came out publicly after the judgement and said he felt sorry for me. Mr Dein issued a statement saying that he 'hoped' I would stay with the club. Maybe he thought I had a short memory.

On the steps outside, the press couldn't wait to hear our response and my agent Jonathan was as robust and defiant as ever. 'We are not prepared to accept what has happened and we will do what it takes to clear our names. We will not stop. We feel so strongly about this that we will appeal and fight on. I have always maintained that Ashley is innocent of any wrongdoing,' he said.

Ultimately, Jonathan and my lawyer Graham Shear would work tirelessly to overturn the decision and, on appeal that August, my fine was reduced to £75,000, 'bearing in mind the level of Mr Cole's culpability and his then financial position', in the words of the commission. Jose Mourinho also had his £200,000 fine reduced to £75,000 and we were both landed with the legal bill, to be split between us 50–50. But there was no taking back the guilty verdict against me. So we took our legal fight to Europe and the Court of Arbitration for Sport in Lausanne, but failed to get the verdict overturned in January 2006 because 'the Premier League's regulations do not contain any reference to a right of appeal to CAS'.

As for the relationship between me and the club, I thought it was fractured beyond repair following the initial verdict. I was boiling mad. All I could think was that Arsenal had been hell-bent on revenge against Chelsea and hadn't given a toss about my welfare, and I'd not just been hammered with a hefty fine, but also with a bill for the FAPL expenses. I couldn't hide my anger for Mr Dein and gave him both barrels in an article which allowed me to have my right of reply. I chose the very newspaper that had broken the story: the *News of the World*.

I blamed him for wrecking my Highbury career. And I did blame him. And still do. This quote from me still stands today, as much as it did back then. They were not words fired from the hip. They were words that summed up how I felt: 'It's no exaggeration to say they have broken my heart. I'm more upset than angry. I feel like they have hung me out to dry. I still love the Arsenal fans, players and backroom staff. But, for the first time, I am having to think whether there is a future for me there. I love Arsenal. I have been there since I was nine but I don't really know what will happen now . . . They have left me feeling that there is no way back, that they don't want me to put on my beloved Arsenal shirt ever again.'

There was so much red mist in front of me that I couldn't see me playing in red and white ever again. I was disillusioned and didn't know what to think.

I remember going home to Cheryl that night and telling her, 'I want to leave, babes. I've had enough.'

I told my Mum and agent the same thing. It was an emotional reaction, but I really did fear that my Arsenal career was over, even if the club had high hopes. 'Everybody wants him to stay and we'll talk to him face-to-face,' said chairman Peter Hill-Wood.

William Hill was even taking bets on my future, offering 8/11 odds-on that I'd stay and even money that I'd walk away. It was speculation gone crazy, and I didn't know if I was coming or going, let alone staying or leaving.

All I knew was that I needed a break. I needed time *not* to think about it. My agent was due to meet with Arsenal, and my lawyer, Graham Shear, would be starting the appeal process but I was mentally exhausted after four months of the whole thing and couldn't wait to escape. Once I'm away from a situation, I can forget about it and put it to the back of my mind, and I'd gone through so much anger, rage, hurt, sadness, disappointment and stress that I couldn't wait to get on a plane and disappear.

A holiday with the missus to Dubai was just what the doctor ordered. Arsenal, Girls Aloud and back-page scandals would be forgotten for two weeks in the isolation of the desert.

Not that I'd be able to chill straight away, because a different kind of stress was occupying my mind. I was about to face one of the biggest and scariest moments of my life, something even more nerve-wracking than a penalty shoot-out . . .

Proposing marriage to Cheryl.

7

The Fame Game

I remember them getting out the dictionary and thesaurus at the tapping-up inquiry.

It was time for final submissions and the chairman and barristers wet their index fingers and rifled through the pages to find the *Oxford English Dictionary* definition for an 'approach'. Another phrase for it was, apparently, 'sounding out'. It's why the league went on to make a big deal about me 'sounding out' Chelsea as part of an illegal transfer approach.

Nicking a rare good idea from the league, I thought I'd borrow a dictionary to look up the meaning of the word 'fame', because I've been asked about it a lot and I'm not sure what it means myself. It's a strange thing to have pinned to your life, and it comes without warning and without definition. It can be both a pat on the back and a slap around the face all at the same time.

The dictionary just says: 'fame – renown, being famous' and 'famous' means 'well known, celebrated'. The thesaurus lists similar words such as 'celebrity and notoriety', and it's those two words that sum up the flip side of the fame game that surrounds me and Cheryl; a footballer-popstar combo that automatically attracts attention wherever we go, whatever we do. We've both enjoyed the rough of notoriety and the smooth of celebrity. Whether it's the highs of scoring a winning goal for Arsenal or winning 'Pop Stars: The Rivals' to become Girls Aloud; whether it's facing flak from the media over an FA Premier League charge or a CPS charge for assaulting a nightclub toilet assistant, we've both learned the hard way about having a love-hate relationship with that thing called 'celebrity status'.

Here isn't the place to go into what we say actually happened but it is a matter of record that Cheryl was sentenced to 120 hours' community service in 2003 for 'occasioning actual bodily harm' on a toilet assistant at a nightclub in Guildford. That's what the record states. I think we've both resolved that what doesn't kill us, makes us stronger. So Cheryl's had to deal with her moment of 'notoriety' and I've had to deal with mine. Maybe that's why she's been such a solid support for me, because she's faced the media shit-storm.

Fame doesn't half distort people's image of you, though. It gives off a wrong first impression. If you believed the newspapers, Cheryl's a stroppy, aggressive, party-animal Geordie lass who falls out of bars more than van Nistelrooy falls down on the pitch. Nothing could be further than the truth. About Cheryl, that is. She is the most gentle, sensitive, warm and quiet person I've ever met. Don't get me wrong, she knows how to be fiery, have fun and enjoy life, but the media image of her is about as false as the media painting me as some kind of aggressive, trouble-causing rebel who clubs for England.

We sometimes read about ourselves and think we're reading about somebody else. I wouldn't mind if the articles were true, but it's the rubbish that's written that pisses me off. Even the small stuff can be irritating, because people on the street just believe what they read. Like the time I was 'in Selfridges with Mariah Carey', despite having never met the woman. Or the nonsense that I'd 'bought a £20,000 diamond-encrusted PSP games console', so now everyone thinks I'm flash and reckless with the cash. Or the time a magazine said I was 'feeding Cheryl strawberries' at a fashion show, even though we were sat in the front row for everyone to see, holding hands at a venue with no food. Where do these journalists get off? What makes me laugh is that they call it journalism. It's like me calling Subbuteo real football.

I never thought for a million years that, as a footballer, I'd have to put up with so much crap, and it's a good job we understand how it all works and how poisonous some newspapers can be. Once, a newspaper tried suggesting Cheryl had been having an affair with a guy in Newcastle, even though she hadn't been to her home town for months. Trust, therefore, has to be like the best of the Arsenal defences, and the trust and understanding between me and Cheryl are rock solid. The snide remarks, the gossip and the innuendo get beyond a joke at times, and it's a constant drip, drip, drip of unnecessary hassle and stress.

Our attitude to the fame game is different. Cheryl needs the papers on her side because the pop industry needs a positive image. Her career demands that she is loved, mine doesn't. If I run out on to a pitch and get booed, it's no big deal. Well, by the opposition anyway. If she went out on stage and got booed, then she'd be in trouble. Cheryl understands she needs to co-operate with the press to help promote and shift records. I don't. I would gladly go through the rest of my life without ever speaking to them again. I don't need them to score goals or defend well.

I'd probably define 'fame' as something that can be both amazing and sickening, and it's hard to adjust to, especially when I didn't ask to be famous. Fame is the knock-on effect of what we both do, and we've both been lucky enough to get public recognition for our separate careers. One of the many things I love about Cheryl is that she has done amazingly well, is superb at what she does and yet she remains a normal, down-to-earth person, unaffected by the whole thing.

We both went into our careers because we loved doing what we do, not because we wanted to be famous. And we fell in love because we found something special, not because we wanted to be a footballer-pop star cliché. Our independent fame has fused together to make an even bigger fame, or some would say an even bigger monster. We became a 'celebrity couple' overnight and have had to get used to being a couple in the spotlight, which means the focus is more intense than it normally would be. I mean, you don't see Dennis Bergkamp and his missus or Thierry Henry and his missus being trailed by the paparazzi around Tesco, Bluewater or the West End.

And I didn't get followed before Cheryl. The press weren't bothered about me. It was all about my football and my performances and that was it. But there's no helping who you fall in love with, and I wouldn't have my life any other way because Cheryl is key to it all. She's the one person who makes sense of all the madness, and she's helped me understand it more and made me more patient and tolerant. She has always been there for me: after bad games, during tapping-up scandals, during the tribunal and during injury lay-offs. It don't really matter in the scheme of things whether I'm loved by the Arsenal fans or not. I've got the love of Cheryl and that's all I need.

The press attention has been a bit mental since we got together. I'd never been someone who had been on the front, middle or news pages before I met Cheryl (or before the day I happened to meet Jose Mourinho in a hotel). I was back-page news only, and was more than happy to stay there. Even if there was the odd occasion when I'd get wrongly fingered as the prime suspect in certain cases of flying pizzas at Old Trafford!

But with Cheryl, I've crossed over into that 'world of showbiz' and that's brought with it the shadow of a constant stalker called the paparazzi – on our doorstep, at the gateway to our home, outside the clubs we go to, the restaurants, the shops, the airport. The body language you display as a couple gets scrutinised and, even when you're happy, 'observers' are looking for cracks, for tension and for moods. It's been a steep learning curve, this fame game, but it's all part of the journey we're sharing together.

We know that however fierce the whirlwind gets around us, be it a transfer scandal or gossip about our private lives, we'll be fine so long as we're holding on to one another throughout it all. Maybe I'll just have to learn to treat the press like Spurs – as a necessary evil in life.

What we do get fed up with is the 'new Posh and Becks' label the media gives us. It's such rubbish, and we don't really know what it means. It's something made up by lazy journalists who want an easy label to slap on to any footballer-showbiz couple. It's been applied not just to me and Cheryl, but also to Jamie Redknapp and Louise, Gavin Henson and Charlotte Church. Even Wayne Rooney and Coleen. And, in the build-up to the 2006 World Cup, we even had 17-year-old Theo Walcott and his girlfriend Melanie Slade as the new golden couple of soccer. It's become a joke. And if the press isn't looking for the next Posh and Becks, it's looking for the next Pele.

Footballer and pop star get together? Must be the new Posh and Becks!

New wonder-kid with the ball and world at his feet? Must be the new Pele!

The newspapers can be as simple and unimaginative as that sometimes. In the same way there will only ever be one Pele, there will only ever be one David and Victoria. They are a great couple who have enjoyed, and deserved, phenomenal success, and they've both worked damn hard to achieve it. They've also proved a lot of people wrong about the strength of their marriage and their resolve as individuals along the way. But seeing what has been thrown at David and Victoria has served as a warning to the likes of me and Cheryl, and it is frightening how intrusive and vicious the press can be.

David is right when he keeps saying that as long as he has his wife and his boys around him, nothing can touch them. It's how Cheryl makes me feel. She makes me happy when I'm sad, and her support through the whole tapping-up saga was massive. We know what matters is our private world and how we are together at home with family and friends. The artificial bubble of fame and the perception of us as a couple is not important.

Within the four walls of our home, we're an ordinary, private couple – me slouching around in shorts and T-shirt, Cheryl pottering about without make-up in her tracksuit and pink fluffy slippers, both of us cleaning the shit off the wooden floor left behind by our dogs Buster and Cocoa. When Cheryl stepped bare-footed in some poo one day and was hopping on one leg to get to the toilet, believe me, she didn't look glamorous!

But she had me rolling around the floor, doubled up with laughter. 'Celebrity' and 'image' don't belong in our gaff because we know the fame game isn't real, isn't glamorous and, sometimes, isn't much fun. But we also know that we have to play the game if we're to promote Arsenal, England and Girls Aloud. We've also learned that fame is a beast best tamed, and that means 'handling' news that concerns us as a couple – choosing a magazine to tell our story in our own words to take the sting out of the hunt for gossip. It is why we chose to tell the story of our engagement to *OK!* magazine in July 2005, and that of our wedding one year later. We ensured the truth was put out there, in our own words, with no room for bullshit. Life has become a balancing act between maintaining our privacy, keeping the press at bay and handling the stories as they happen.

But even then, shit still happens and stuff is still made up. It always will be. Understanding that is what keeps us strong. We're a young couple enjoying a journey together, and we're determined to keep our feet on the ground. There's not a day that goes by when I don't look at my life, look at where I've come from and then pinch myself. And Cheryl does the same. We've come together at an exciting and amazing time in our lives, and it's made better by being together. I've come from nothing and am living a dream, and she's come from nothing and she's living her dream, and we reckon we're lucky people. But some newspapers have seemed intent on ruining our happiness from day one, and the sickest, biggest lie was yet to come, courtesy once again of the *News of the World*.

None of the press stuff entered my head when me and Cheryl first met. All I knew was that I'd found the future Mrs Cole within minutes of chatting with her at the tennis courts of the complex of flats where we both lived in north London. As luck would have it, she had a flat on the same floor as me, but our paths never really crossed before that day. I used to spot her when I was round at the ground-floor flat of my friend and former Arsenal team-mate Paulo Vernazza. Cheryl, a face I'd got used to spotting in the papers and glossy magazines, often walked by his front window with the rest of Girls Aloud, and I'd be sprinting to the window to check her out.

We met on a sweltering day in August 2004. I was playing tennis with Jermaine Pennant who knew her band-mate Kimberley Walsh. That day, the two girls were driving up the road out of the complex to buy a cooling fan when 'Penno' shouted at them to stop. They came over, we stopped playing and I started chatting to Cheryl through the fencing surrounding the courts. Sweat was pouring off me, but she just played it cool (even though she later confessed that she was as nervous as hell). We spoke and laughed, and I had this weird sense she was right for me; here was someone on my wavelength. I knew it there and then.

Can't explain it. Just knew it.

She left to drive to the shops and returned to find me messing around with the Aston Martin: its battery had gone flat. She wound down her window to ask me what was up and we chit-chatted for a bit. Then, for someone normally so shy, I surprised myself when I asked her outright for her number. But she blew me out there and then. 'I can't. I can't. I'm sorry,' she said.

So much for being brave. The next time I saw Cheryl she was walking around the front of the complex. She later said she was mortified to see me that day because her hair was a mess, she had no make-up on and she reckoned she looked awful. Around that same time, I'd just appeared in *Zoo* magazine and I remember her shouting out across the road to me, 'See yourself in the magazine? Looking good!'

I didn't know whether she was taking the piss or being serious. I didn't know what to say, got all shy, said nothing and scuttled off.

What I didn't know was that she then went to see a male psychic who gave her a private reading. She was told there was a footballer in her circle, she'd seen a picture of him in a magazine, the signs were good and she'd be married by the time she was 24. I'm not into any of that spiritual stuff, but it's what brought Cheryl to me so I'm not going to knock it.

It was one week later when she acted on the 'signs'. Penno's mobile received a text message. It was Kimberley passing on Cheryl's number to forward to me. One ex-Arsenal team-mate and one member of Girls Aloud had acted as match-makers (with an assist from a psychic). I toyed with that number for about a week because I didn't want to come across too keen. Then, one night, in a hotel room before a match, I texted her. It was late, about 1 a.m., and, like a coward, I sent a text at a time when I thought her phone would be off. 'Fancy meeting up?' I tapped out.

Seconds later, my phone lit up with a reply: 'I'm still awake. So how are you?'

That caught me on the hop, that did. Cheryl was still up because Girls Aloud had done a gig in Scotland and I guess performing live on stage is like performing live on a football pitch: it's hard to come down afterwards with all that adrenalin going on. We must have texted each other for another 20 minutes. We knew we'd get on from the tone and humour of our texts. Everything with Cheryl – talking, laughing, texting, silence – has seemed so effortless and easy, right from the moment we first met.

Our first date, a few days later, weren't the most romantic of affairs: round at my place for a bite to eat and a few drinks. But, from that day on, we saw each other nearly every day when our schedules allowed. We both knew early on that our feelings for each other were powerful. I'd never met anyone I've connected with more than Cheryl.

When the Arsenal dressing room got wind of the new woman in my life, they weren't going to let me off lightly. At training, I'd come in and find sexy magazine pictures of Cheryl stuck to my seat. Jens Lehmann, who knows how badly I sing in the team shower, kept joking about me doing a duet with the missus. And Dennis Bergkamp was a real tormentor. I'd be in the treatment room with him and he'd be lying back reading a copy of *FHM* or *Loaded* and he'd suddenly start going, 'Mmmmmmmm . . . Mmmmmmm . . . Look at this woman in here!' and, of course, it was Cheryl. Then he'd look at me, act all surprised and say, 'Sorry Ash, didn't see you there!'

Good banter is part of a healthy dressing room.

Meeting Cheryl has brought me to the happiest time of my life and, as we neared the end of the 2004–05 season, I knew that at least one future was worth sealing: the one with Cheryl. I bought an engagement ring four weeks before the end of the season. It was a posh single diamond: a champagne diamond. And I knew exactly when, where and how I wanted to pop the question: on holiday after the FA Cup final.

When we went on safari, about an hour's drive from Dubai, I had it all planned out in my head. It was going to be quiet, romantic – sand dunes, sunset, champagne and just the two of us (if you ignore the camel and the guide). I should have known the signs weren't good when we got to our hotel villa, looking out across the desert, and this sandstorm whipped up out of nowhere. We quickly got away from the veranda and went back inside. Outside, it was like a tornado scene from a movie. There were these twisting funnels of sand breaking out everywhere, the wind was howling, the rain was pelting down and our wooden sun beds were airborne and flying off God knows where. It was quite scary.

I used the noise as a cover so I could nip to the toilet and make a phone call to Cheryl's dad, Garry. I wanted to do it all traditional, so when he answered the phone in his native north-east, I said, 'Hi, it's Ashley Cole. I want to ask for your permission to ask your daughter to marry me.' Cheryl hammered me later for introducing myself to the future father-in-law as Ashley Cole. 'Why didn't you just say, "It's Ashley"? How many Ashleys do you think he knows?!' she mocked. It does sound stupid now, but take it as a sign of how nervous I was.

Anyway, he said yes and that's what mattered. There was too much planning going on in my head – not to mention the long speech to Cheryl I had been rehearsing. Outside, the storm went as fast as it came; like someone had flicked channels from storm to complete quiet. It was baking when we stepped outside. The ring was hidden in a little bag I carried over my shoulder. We found our guide and clambered on to a camel; me at the front, Cheryl behind. Then it all started to go wrong. There was me thinking we'd be the only couple and the only camel, but when we get there, I see about ten more people, six more camels and loads of kids. I cursed under my breath.

'Can't do it now. It's all ruined,' I thought. Last thing I needed was an audience.

But Cheryl was clueless as to my dilemma. She was more bothered about the 'cruelty' to the camels, who were tethered together by a rope strung through the rings in their nostrils. She was behind me, moaning and clutching on to me for dear life, going on and on about how our 'cute' camel was suffering, how its nostrils must be hurting, how it was too hot for him. Too hot! For a camel! She said when we'd climbed on the camel, it had made a groaning noise, so it must be fed up, she reckoned.

'It's a camel, Cheryl! Camels groan!' I said, getting more and more frustrated that my big romantic moment was not only being shared with a crowd, but was also turning into a complaint about camel welfare.

'But what if we're too heavy for him and he really is suffering?' she said into my ear, her arms wrapped around my front. I bit my tongue.

'What about his feet! His poor feet treading on all those prickly bushes, Ashley,' she went on.

'BABE! Is there any chance of you just shutting up!'

It just came out, and I wanted to take it back as soon as I said it. Cheryl went quiet and blanked me from then on as we wobbled on the back of a camel into the desert.

Brilliant. On top of everything else, my potential fiancée was blanking me. How am I going to propose to someone who isn't even talking to me?

Ten people, six camels, a bunch of kids and a girlfriend with the hump. It could not have been any worse.

It was at the halfway stage of the camel trek that I decided there was no turning back. We'd all climbed off and sat on the sand dunes with champagne and strawberries to watch the sun setting. Cheryl's mood had mellowed and she was talking to me again. Just. We were sat a little way away from the others and so I decided to grab the moment. We were sat side by side, looking out towards the red, orangey sky.

'Can you stand up please?' I said to Cheryl, 'I want to ask you something.'

'What's the matter?' she asked, 'What are you going to do?' She didn't have a clue what was coming next.

'Please, will you just stand up?'

She stood. I got down on one knee. The big speech that I had planned went to pieces with my emotions and, with a voice that hardly got to the end of the sentence, I asked her, 'I love you so much. Will you marry me?' She started crying. I started crying. She said yes. We stood there hugging each other. And the crowd, when they realised what had gone on, started clapping. So it all went well in the end. She even managed to forget about the camel.

That night, back at the villa, we just kept reminding ourselves that we were going to get married. Cheryl was fantasising about the day. Big wedding, big dress, horse and carriage, lots of bridesmaids, the works.

She became the wedding planner, together with the experts at Banana Split. We looked at our diaries and saw gigs and football fixtures everywhere, and Cheryl was set on a summer wedding. So it would have to come after the 2005–06 season, after the 2006 World Cup, after the Girls Aloud UK 'Chemistry' tour that same summer and before the new 2006–07 football season. We had a three-week window to get married and go on honeymoon, and more than any World Cup and any Girls Aloud tour, our wedding was to be the most important event of our year. We couldn't wait to become Mr and Mrs Cole.

*

It was while I was on holiday that a deal was done to keep me at Arsenal, brokered by my agent and Mr Dein. It was a compromise. We agreed that I'd stay for one more year, extending my contract until June 2008, and the club finally paid me the £60,000 a week I'd asked for in the first place.

That was the 'official' deal as sold to the Arsenal fans.

But it weren't the only agreement made between club and agent.

There was also a secret, verbal agreement that propped up the written contract.

It was agreed, as witnessed by a third party, that I'd only be expected to stay at the club for one more year – despite the contract's official expiry date.

The idea was that it would give Arsenal a twelve-month period to repair bridges, to discuss my future and, as my agent told me, 'hopefully persuade you to stay'; a year to allow the dust to settle. If, in that year, relations between club and myself did not improve, Mr Dein agreed that Arsenal would let me leave after the 2005–06 season.

It was an unwritten escape clause, if you like, to allow both sides to review the situation after a year.

Of course, Arsenal came out of it smelling of roses; they pay £60,000 a week, or £3.1 million a year, and get to sell me for at least £15 million if things don't work out.

I remember putting pen to paper in my agent's office and thinking, 'If only they'd done this at the very start, none of this mess would ever have happened.' That's what bugged me – it was all so avoidable. And the more I dwelled on that, the more it simmered inside me because it had tainted forever a very special relationship. So the signing of the new contract was a bitter-sweet moment, and I reckon there were regrets on both sides of the table.

But I was happy to do another year because I was with the players and fans I loved. I'd also just got together with Cheryl, so it wouldn't have been a good time to face the sudden upheaval of a move to

Europe. At that time, we needed a little stability. I think Cheryl was happy I was staying for a year. Mum certainly was. We'd all spoken about a move to Europe, but felt the timing wasn't right. Everything had been happening too fast and we needed a period of calm and security. What was funny was that there I was making a lifetime commitment and proposal to my new love Cheryl, and yet I couldn't see beyond another year with my first love – Arsenal.

I think the new deal saved Arsenal's face, because if I'd left and the story I'm telling in this book had come out back then, with the truth about the politics I was up against, Arsenal would have been crucified by the fans. Or I'd like to think they would have been. But, by giving themselves a year's extra breathing space, they've been able to smooth things over on the PR front, give me an increased salary and say, 'Well, we gave him the money he wanted.'

Whatever unfolded in the future would all be down to me; that's what they wanted the fans to think I'm sure. Makes sense. It was going to be interesting to see what charm-offensive tactics they'd use over the following year to re-build bridges with me. Especially when my future and that of Thierry Henry were up in the air at the same time. We were, apparently, two players that the club were 'desperate' to keep. Time would tell.

And time would expose the massive differences in the treatment received by a striker viewed as a god at Highbury and that received by a left-back who'd been cast as a traitor.

The newspapers learned of the new deal just in time for pre-season training. It was reported as me and Arsenal 'patching things up' and 'reaching a compromise'. We were all smiles again in public.

For me, though, there was no getting away from the damage that had been done. As a schoolboy, I had put pen to paper believing that my entire future would be at Arsenal. As a 24-year-old, signing a one-year extension, there was a cold reluctance to look further than a year. I'd gone from 'forever' to 'day by day'.

It's funny, but I've grown up a lot since February 2005, and grown a thick skin, too. I'm less trusting and, I'd like to think, a little bit wiser. I think I've grown out of the illusion that Arsenal is a 'family' and that, as one of its adopted sons, I'd be treated as someone special. I'm an asset, not an adopted son; an asset they valued at £20 million but wanted to pay on the cheap. And I'm an asset that is part of a ruthless industry, not a family. I've learned that if nothing else.

Me and Cheryl had set the date and named the venue for the wedding. All eyes were on 15 July 2006 at Highclere Castle, Newbury, Berkshire. I remember when Thierry and his missus Clare got married there and it was an amazing day, so we paid our deposit and started on the wedding plans. Lord and Lady Carnarvon's castle was going to be our dream setting. Or at least, that was the *original* plan. Until September 2005 when everything had to be hastily rearranged.

I was sat in the bedroom at home, flicking through the channels, when news coverage came on about Jordan and Peter Andre's wedding. At Highclere Castle.

'Oh shit!' I thought.

I sat there with my mouth open, not believing what I was watching.

I scrambled for the phone and rang Cheryl straight away. 'Babe, you are *never* going to believe where Jordan is getting married today . . .'

I remember Cheryl's exact reaction. 'NO WAY!' she screamed, and then she added, 'Right, Ashley, we're changing venues!'

Every bride wants to be unique and original and Cheryl was no different. It would never have been 'Ashley and Cheryl getting married at Highclere', but 'Ashley and Cheryl getting married at the same place as Jordan and Peter Andre'. Sure enough, the *News of the World* and the 3 a.m. Girls in the *Daily Mirror* ultimately found out and reported their 'exclusives' along those lines. In the world of celebrity, our big day would forever have been linked to that of another couple, so it left us with no option but to think again. It was a bit of a panic finding another venue at that late stage, when there was no flexibility on our date, but the planners at Banana Split pulled out all the stops, and we got what we thought was an even better, more romantic venue.

We'd managed to get over that unexpected snag and Cheryl gave a massive sigh of relief. Our special day was back on track and we weren't going to be following in the wake of nobody. And the press would still think that Highclere was the venue. Right up until the morning of the big day. Clueless to the end.

You'd think people would be happy for a couple in love, that it'd be celebrated or something, especially in the year of the actual marriage. But the biggest drawback to being part of a celebrity couple is the media's microscopic scrutiny on the relationship, and its search to find the cracks behind the smiles – even when those cracks don't exist. Me and Cheryl couldn't be happier. She is the best thing that has ever happened to me. I love her to bits. Yet the *News of the World* doesn't seem interested in happy-ever-after stories, and its thirst for scandal – true or false – weren't going to be satisfied simply by the tapping-up saga it drummed up and the wrecking of my relations with Arsenal. It felt like it wanted to ruin my personal life as well. I'd go as far as to say that there seemed to be a deliberate 'let's-get-Ashley' agenda; some kind of sad attempt to ruin my happiness. However much they may choose to deny my suspicions, their actions speak louder than their words.

In the February of 2006, me and Cheryl had to deal with the sickest load of crap ever invented at a time when we should have been busy planning our dream wedding.

We'd got wind that something was bubbling in Fleet Street weeks before it actually happened; a reliable grapevine had tipped-off my lawyer Graham Shear that the paper was 'looking to do a number on Ashley'. There had also been an age-old rumour flying around football circles that 'there was a big gay Premiership scandal brewing'. You hear this kind of thing from time to time and dismiss it as tittle-tattle that will come to nothing. Graham is razor sharp and great at his job, so he was across it all anyway. If there was a legal England team, he'd be John Terry or Rio Ferdinand – always keeping out the opposition, and heading off trouble outside the box.

'They can't be doing a number on me because I've done nothing and been nowhere,' I remember telling him. It was probably another made-up kiss-and-tell story or some other malicious gossip about me being with a girl; another attempt to destabilise me before the marriage.

Get this for a disturbing fact. There have been *ten weekends* in the past year where my legal team have had to deal with shit from the Sunday newspapers, having to respond to a reporter's call on a Saturday afternoon that they're running a story about me with a girl, me being spotted with a girl, me flirting with a girl, me and a girl in a hotel. There has been other rubbish, too, about my lifestyle and things. None of it true, as my legal team proved on each occasion. I tell you, this is the kind of crap that goes on; this is what it's like to be a 'celebrity' in a tabloid generation. You can't rave too much about being happy or in love because there will always be someone going to a newspaper somewhere to try and claim otherwise.

I'm bored of receiving a text message from Graham saying 'Call me'. It's like a tabloid alarm bell going off and I'm like, 'Shit! What now?'

2006 was just a few days old when I got my first 'Call me' text message of the year.

I had been celebrating the New Year with some friends at a hotel in London while Cheryl was with her mum in New York. I'd met my mates in the hotel, we'd had a good night out and a couple of girls had latched onto the group before I went home. I remember speaking with Cheryl on the mobile in the cab because she was five hours behind UK time. Then I stopped off for a Chinese by myself and went home.

A couple of days later, I get a call from Cheryl, ringing me to say her PR with Girls Aloud has had a call from the *News of the World*, putting the allegation to them that 'Ashley spent the night with another woman in a hotel room'. Now, Cheryl trusts me but you can imagine her reaction when she's thousands of miles away and she gets news that some girl has gone to the papers and the story is 'running tomorrow'. She rang wanting to know what was going on. Or words to that effect . . . Soon after, I also got the 'Call me' text from Graham. I was straight on the phone to the Girls Aloud PR to get the full SP.

I knew it was bollocks but needed to know what I was up against. You end up having to fight fires that don't exist half the time. So I find myself in this ridiculous situation where the *News of the World* are planning to run a story that I've been cheating behind Cheryl's back and I've got to *disprove* a lie to stop the story from running. Graham rang the Chinese restaurant and they found the CCTV footage of me sat in the restaurant alone, and we tracked down the cab company to confirm I'd been picked up and dropped off alone – at the exact times when this stupid girl was saying she was with me. We had the evidence to clear me, and the story was never published. But, even as I write that down, it's insane to read back. My lawyer shouldn't even be wasting his time having to 'clear me' from something that isn't even true in the first place! But if you don't have an alibi, the danger is that the press will run a malicious story that upsets not just me but my family, and facts tend not to get in the way of a good tale in my experience. Papers print stories that aren't true. And, if proof of that sad fact were needed, the *News of the World* provided it just two months later when, this time, it published a story that got way out of hand. It was to be the most poisonous yet.

I'm sure the paper's 'showbiz' department laughed like naughty little children when they published this particular crap. But they'd ultimately end up laughing on the other side of their face by the time my legal team had finished with them. Because they went one step too far and I weren't going to let them get away with it. The person responsible for the article was their main showbiz reporter Rav Singh. Now, if he were a footballer, he'd play punt, hope and pray. He'd also score a few own goals if his reporting and fact-checking on my story was anything to go by.

This ugly episode all unravelled – conveniently for the media – on the weekend before Valentine's Day, the weekend of 11–12 February. It was the Saturday when the rumour gathered pace that the *News of the World* was publishing its big gay Premiership 'exposé'. The word that 'something was going down' didn't come from my lawyer this time, it came from Mum. She'd been in the back of a cab in London and the driver had been telling her that he'd picked someone up from the *News of the World* who'd said that 'there is going to be a gay Premiership footballer story breaking tomorrow' and that he should buy the newspaper.

The cabbie threw the names of two footballers into the hat who he reckoned were at the centre of it all. Mum flagged it up with me as soon as she got home and I rang the players concerned. It turned out that their lawyers were already aware of something but couldn't nail it.

I remember speaking to another player about it that evening because, let's face it, we were all curious.

'Don't worry about it Ash, it'll be a pile of shit anyway,' he said, and we had a good moan about the press.

That night, when Cheryl came back from rehearsals, I told her all about this story and how two Premiership footballers were supposedly in the frame.

'GAY AS YOU GO!' was the page seven headline the next day; a headline sandwiched between two anonymous silhouettes of two footballers, each one with a question mark plastered on their blacked-out faces to heighten the mystery of their identities. '**Premiership stars romp with mobile . . .**' added the headline. The text said 'Player

A' and 'Player B' were 'caught on camera cavorting with a pal well known in the music industry in a homosexual gay orgy that will shock soccer . . .' This 'exclusive' told how Rav Singh had actually seen footage of two players and a DJ putting a mobile phone down their boxer shorts, using it as a sex toy and making it vibrate before having an orgy. 'It was like something out of a hard core porn film . . . and the sordid sex session took place in the flat of one of the players . . .' he reported.

I remember reading it and thinking, they can't be that sure about these players otherwise they'd have named them. Cheryl also read it and, like me, didn't believe a word and we tossed the newspaper to one side and thought nothing more about it.

I've since learned that behind the scenes my name was already being linked to the story. I was the source of giddy gossip in the bars of London where Fleet Street's reporters share tit-bits of information. Someone had already dropped a match in the outback and wild rumours were spreading like wildfire. I was being wrongly identified as 'Player B' and my DJ mate Masterstepz, who works for Choice FM, was supposed to be the man in the music industry. The Chinese whispers had begun . . .

What had happened, and how it all came about, almost beggars belief. If it weren't so sick, it'd be funny. Rav Singh seems to have told people, and I presume also his editor, that he had seen actual snapshots of video footage of this incident, filmed on a mobile phone. As his first article said, he was 'still wincing after seeing the photos'. Now, I'm not convinced what he saw. Because the footage didn't exist. Not of me anyhow. It was pure invention and it seems as though someone had sold the *News of the World* a dummy. How and why my name was thrown into the mix, I'll never know. But the paper must have felt it was safe to fly with a rumour-story for a bit of fictional entertainment so long as they didn't name names. Real journalism used to be about having evidence, publishing stories, naming names and proving it. So I've been told. But not this time. The *News of the World* couldn't prove it because it weren't true. But they thought they'd get away with it by keeping everything anonymous. If only someone had bothered to tell its sister paper, the *Sun*, that was the play-it-safe strategy.

Because word filtered down to the *Sun* reporters that 'Ashley Cole was Player B', and the newspaper's executives must have been wetting themselves over the mischief they could have in the following day's paper, on Monday 13 February. The *Sun* tried to be clever. My lawyer calls it 'innuendo by juxtaposition' – two stories side by side which drop hints, nudges and winks to the identity of the player without actually naming him.

So, on page fifteen that Monday, the *Sun* repeated the *News of the World* story with the headline: '**SO WHO BUMIT? Riddle of gay soccer stars**' and it added: 'Football fans were left guessing the identity of the Premiership players – said to have been pictured using a mobile phone as a sex toy.' That article was printed next to a colour photo of me and Cheryl leaving the Embassy nightclub; my image side by side with the 'gay soccer riddle'.

Three days later, the *Sun* couldn't wait for another pop. Me and Cheryl had gone out for a romantic dinner on Valentine's Day, and the paparazzi were onto us as usual, following us through the street. We'd been photographed many times so it weren't unusual but I remember noticing that the paps' activity was more intense than usual. It was a constant flash, flash, flashing in my eyes; the guys were in my face and wouldn't let up. It seemed more aggressive. I got pissed off but Cheryl, as always, just kept smiling. 'What was their problem tonight?' I asked her afterwards, still unaware of the Fleet Street gossip. Unaware, that was, until I saw the comments that went with the photo they'd taken. '**Ashley's got a good taste in rings**' was the loaded headline, and everything about the words was designed to mention mobile phones, rings and vibrations: all signposts to the earlier *News of the World* article. The *Sun* picture caption read: 'Arsenal ace Ashley Cole enjoys a Valentine's night out with his lady – Girls Aloud babe Cheryl Tweedy. Fiancée Cheryl, 22, got her £50,000 engagement **ring** out again at London Fashion Week. England star Ashley, 25, looked like he was waiting for a **ring** as he held his **phone**. It must have been on **vibrate**.'

Just in case the reader didn't get it, it added an arrow to the photo, pointing out my phone with the words: 'Waiting for a **buzz**?'

Bastards. I clocked it straight away. I knew what they were doing. I was so angry at reading it that I could hardly get the words out. No matter how much Cheryl tried to calm me down, she failed.

'How can they be saying it's me?! What the fuck are they playing at?! Why are they doing this!!' I yelled.

I was livid. I got my lawyer on to it straight away. I texted a friend. I told him what the papers were doing. He texts me back: 'I know mate, and it's all over the Internet as well . . .' he replied.

The Internet! I couldn't believe it. I've never felt so powerless in one moment.

Overnight, one wild rumour had become a newspaper innuendo had become a Chinese whisper had become gossip in Internet chat rooms and websites. It was snowballing out of control, and going nationwide as everyone seemed to gossip and snigger about the identity of 'Player B'. It was like I'd been thrown into someone else's nightmare by mistake.

It got worse before my lawyers could nip it in the bud. On Sunday 19 February, the *News of the World* came back for me with 'The truth behind the story that VIBRATED the nation'. Under the headline '**NUMBER'S UP!**', it published a photograph which I instantly recognised. It was of me and DJ Masterstepz with our faces blurred out to obscure our identities. Two arrows pointed to 'The DJ' and then 'Player B'. It was the final confirmation that my name was, inexplicably, being linked to the story. The final straw came a couple of days later in the street. I was in north London and had just got out of the car to fill a parking meter when this complete stranger came right up to my face, said 'You're gay you are!' and walked away laughing at me.

Not much bothers me. It takes a lot to get under my skin. But that got to me. I started worrying that the more people who read it, the more would believe it. I remember saying once to Cheryl that there can never be smoke without fire but this episode taught me that there *can* be smoke and not even one burning ember. Can you imagine if Cheryl weren't so understanding, weren't so trusting? Can you imagine the kind of hell this could have caused?

I was angry for me, angry for Cheryl in the year of my marriage and angry for Mum. I didn't come into football to put up with all this crap, and if this was the price of fame, they could hang up my football boots and I'd go away and live a quiet life with Cheryl. That's what I was thinking at the time. None of it seemed worth the shit I was having to deal with. The real scandal was that I was having to deal with it in the first place.

I tried to rise above it all but it was impossible. Each day brought a new phone call or a new text message. My phone didn't stop ringing, and I'll never forget one mate ringing up in hysterics and saying: 'Shit Coley, it's YOU!' and he started pissing himself laughing.

Cheryl pissed herself laughing, too. It was that far-fetched, she said, it was hysterical. She was brilliant.

I kept telling her 'It's not true babe . . . it's not true' and started going into all sorts of explanations and justifications. And that was the mad thing. I was being made to feel shame, guilt and humiliation over something that weren't true, but the accusation put me automatically on the back foot. Cheryl couldn't believe what I was putting myself through. She bollocked me each time I tried to reassure her. In the end, I took strength from her and the rest of the family who rallied around me. 'Ashley, don't even worry about it . . . You? Gay? Don't make us laugh. I *know* it's not true. I *know* you,' she said, and she threw her arms around me. Her arms and her support were a refuge during that time. But, like me, she also got angry that we were having to face such bullshit from the papers. We both knew that we couldn't sit back and let it lie. Not this time. I mean, what straight man could take being ridiculed – and that's what they were doing – for being gay, knowing thousands of people nationwide were talking about it in the year of your marriage? Not that being gay is a bad thing. But the story suggested I was dishonest about my sexuality and, therefore, my marriage to Cheryl was going to be a sham. I weren't having that. I had two choices: do nothing and let a false rumour be whispered about for years to come, or stand up and fight it. With Cheryl right behind me, we decided to fight it. 'And once you've put it in the hands of the lawyers, we're not going to talk about it,' she said. 'We're going to get on with planning our wedding and we're going to forget it!'

The ridiculous thing was that the *News of the World* had tried to say I'd been cheating behind Cheryl's back in January. So, one minute I'm a love cheat; the next, I'm supposed to be up to homosexual tricks with a mobile phone. It couldn't make its mind up let alone get its facts straight.

I rang Graham my lawyer and said to him: 'If they've got this video, tell them to go ahead and print it. Put it on the front page. Tell them to publish it. Go on, tell them to publish it!'

I knew they never could because I knew the 'footage' of me didn't exist.

My legal team issued legal proceedings on 20 February against the *News of the World* and the *Sun*. I sued them for libel and breach of privacy. Everyone asked me afterwards how it could be a breach of privacy if the allegations weren't true? What they didn't realise was that I'd had to discuss my sexuality with my agent, my lawyer and their assistants to help them build a case. So the fact I had to discuss that intimate stuff with them all – even though the allegation wasn't true – was an invasion of my privacy brought about by the newspaper. There was a similar case to mine fought on those grounds. Test case law, Graham called it. And he also said something about a number of false newspaper articles counting as harassment. So we sued the *Sun* on those grounds too. I was back in the legal arena for the second time in a year. Of course, me taking legal action meant that I was bringing it all out into the open, away from the rumour mill and the Internet chat rooms. But that was the risk I had to take, and I had to sit back and allow the *Sun* to print on its front page this headline: '**Ashley's fury over gay orgy claim**'. But at least everyone knew that I was fighting it.

I spoke to Thierry about it at Arsenal and he couldn't believe that the press could do such a thing. The story weren't even mentioned at the club – it was too raw for that, and everyone knew how upset I was; the dressing-room silence on the subject was support itself in my eyes. The boss was a huge support as well. He knows what it's like to face the poisonous lies of newspapers. Nine years earlier, he'd faced a similar kind of shit from the press with false rumours about his private life. We had a chat about it all and his words, and experience, were a big help. He told me I needed to show mental strength. In public, too, he stood by me.

'**I STAND BY ASHLEY**' was the *Daily Mirror* headline on 4 March. '**WE'RE BACKING ASHLEY**' said the *Daily Express* back page. The boss came out fighting for me and probably remembered his own experience when he said: 'Nobody likes to read these sorts of rumours. But, unfortunately, we are in a job where sometimes you have to face that. Maybe he has decided that because he is going to be married soon, he cannot accept any insinuation on his private life. Ashley wants to clear his name . . . and I can understand that.'

I had let Graham Shear do all the talking on my behalf. In a statement issued to the press, he said I'd launched legal proceedings because, 'these newspapers published false and offensive articles designed to tell readers that Ashley had behaved in what the *News of the World* described as a perverted way with other professional footballers. The newspapers knew there was no basis to name Ashley but arranged the articles and pictures in such a way that readers would identify him. There is no truth whatsoever in these allegations, and Ashley Cole will not tolerate this kind of cowardly journalism or let it go unchallenged. It is disgraceful that he should be faced with this kind of unpleasant insinuation and innuendo at a time when he is trying to focus on this summer's World Cup and his forthcoming wedding.'

The newspapers were full of legal experts saying I was 'running a high-risk strategy' by bringing the action. But it was now me versus the newspapers, and if there was justice, the risk would pay off. All I could do was leave it in the hands of my legal team. Like Graham said, I had much more important things to deal with: one World Cup and one dream wedding.

One other person who was a constant support through the newspaper 'scandals' was Sven-Goran Eriksson. He kept seeking me out, offering words of wisdom to help me deal with the media shit-storms. He knew how much Arsenal and the World Cup meant to me and was always there for me. He'd come to the training ground or ring me up for a quick chat and he gave me a lot of one-to-one time. I don't know many national coaches that would do that.

If anyone knows about the down side of the fame game and how to survive in the eye of a media storm, it's him. He's had his private life raked over more than anyone. He must be the most photographed, most followed England coach of all time. In January 2006, it seemed to me, and to others writing in the press, that constant harassment of Sven brought about his downfall when the FA buckled under the pressure of a so-called exposé in the *News of the World*.

When the players saw the newspaper on Sunday 15 January, we couldn't believe our eyes. Not because of what we read or what

Sven was supposed to have said, but because an English paper had stitched him up like that to cause him grief ahead of the World Cup. Or maybe it was a deliberate attempt to get him the sack *before* the World Cup?

Many players thought it was a disgrace when they saw the headline **'SVEN'S DIRTY DEALS – £15m to quit England and he'll tap-up Becks'**. What got me was that it made this big thing about how Sven should be 'totally focused on vital team preparations' but 'tried to get an undercover *News of the World* investigator . . . to buy Premiership club Aston Villa and give him the manager's job'. As if it was Sven's idea to meet in Dubai! The only dirty deal we saw was Sven being lured to Dubai and being stung by people leading him on.

And what were the dynamite revelations? His own opinions, that's what – that he'd want, and would probably get, David Beckham to join him; that Michael Owen wasn't happy at Newcastle; that Villa was for sale; that Wayne Rooney was from a rough background; that Ryan Giggs would have preferred to play for England and Rio Ferdinand was lazy sometimes. As England boss, he's entitled to have his own private views about individual players, and he's aired much worse opinions than that on the training pitch.

But because he's said it to an undercover reporter, the *News of the World* starts screaming **'SVEND OF THE WORLD'** on its back pages after 'the shamed Swede plunged the FA into World Cup crisis . . .'

Sven's reaction was the same as that of the England dressing room: he couldn't give a shit what the papers said. It was a 'crisis' concocted by a paper that must have been wanting him sacked (why else would they do it?), and I don't for one minute think the players felt let down by him. He'd made it clear during 'the sting' that he couldn't do anything 'until the end of the season', so it's crap to say he went behind England's back and weren't focused. Sven is an honest, genuine, straight-talking manager who was focused on winning the

World Cup as much as Arsene Wenger is focused on winning the Champions League. But that one story seems to have cost Sven his job. On Monday 23 January, the FA decided to terminate his contract after the World Cup. Make no bones about it, he was sacked, regardless of all the talk of 'mutual agreements'. That's what I believe. I think it was terrible that a newspaper treated him like that and that the FA didn't have the balls to stand by its man until after the World Cup. All I saw was the FA rolling over and lying down instead of standing up and being strong.

The only good thing the FA said in its statement was this: 'Sven is definitely the man to lead us in Germany. Now is the time for everyone to get behind the team as we prepare for a tournament that presents us with a genuine chance of success.'

It was a sentiment that would have brought a roar of approval from the dressing room. All that mattered to us, as a team, was that we had an outstanding manager in charge of an outstanding team with an outstanding chance in the 2006 World Cup.

On the club front, there was no looking back once I'd signed on the dotted line and sealed the one-year extension.

I had a job to do and a new season to focus on. I'd be lying if I said there weren't no resentment in me, but I tried to keep a lid on it. I reported for pre-season training hungry for the next Premiership campaign, as eager as the boss and the rest of the team to snatch back the championship title from Chelsea. A central figure to that aim was Patrick Vieira, as much a crucial part of the Arsenal team and its success story as Thierry.

When we all turned up in early July at London Colney, none of us had considered the prospect of a season without him. In fact, neither had Patrick. He'd long since put behind him the temptation of a move to Real Madrid and had pledged his future to Arsenal. In the close season, while I'd been popping the question to Cheryl, he'd tied the knot with his Cheryl in a ceremony in Nice, France, before escaping to the Bahamas and then Miami, and neither of them had thought about a settled future anywhere other than north London. Not even when the newspapers started linking him with a move to Juventus.

I remember asking him straight: 'Pat, are you leaving?'

'No,' he frowned, 'no-one has mentioned anything to me,' and he dismissed it as paper talk.

Little did he know that Mr Dein and Juventus had already held initial discussions. So after nine years at the club, Patrick had first got wind of what was unfolding via Fleet Street.

And now my mind flashes back to the inquiry and the evidence of Mr Dein. Even though I missed his testimony, my legal team told me of the moment when he said there'd never be any attempt to sell an Arsenal player to another club without first informing the player.

According to what I was told Mr Dein said, it would be daft for the club to go behind a player's, or his agent's, back because in the end that player might decide he didn't want to go to, say, Juventus. That was the example he used, apparently. Funny that he picked 'Juve'.

Yet Arsenal and Juventus were already 'getting a transfer going' by holding initial discussions. So how the vice-chairman can give that evidence and then treat Patrick the way he apparently did is beyond me.

Patrick told me that the first he heard of the Juventus move, after the newspaper stories, was when Mr Dein called to tell him Juventus had offered a good contract and Arsenal were 'neutral' as to whether he stayed or left. Hardly the best way to make him feel wanted and special. I know the feeling. Such a couldn't-care-less attitude made up Patrick's mind there and then. Which is why it pisses me off when some fans question his loyalty. That man's heart was in Arsenal and he was as loyal to the club as any player can be. Until he was given no option, dressed up as a choice. In the same way they didn't fight tooth and nail for me, they didn't fight tooth and nail for Patrick either. And the fans wonder why a team once bonded by spirit and camaraderie begins to fall apart.

Within the space of 24 hours, Patrick went from knowing nothing about a transfer approach to sitting down with Juventus in a meeting in London.

'Do you want to go?' I asked him, knowing how much he loved Arsenal.

'No, but they're not bothered whether I stay or go and so . . .' and he shrugged his shoulders.

The next day, the deal was done and Patrick told us he was leaving. It was a shock to all of us, not only because he was such a great player, but because he was such a good friend to so many in the dressing room. His departure sent shockwaves through the squad and we were all asking ourselves, 'Why are they letting someone like him go?' We needed to be buying players, not selling them, if we were to have a realistic shot at knocking Chelsea off the Premiership pedestal. It was hardly a shot in the arm for a squad that had already lost the influence and talent of Edu.

Every great Arsenal side has been able to boast a strong and experienced central midfield, a powerful engine that gets up and down, defends and attacks: Vieira and Petit, Gilberto and Vieira, Gilberto and Edu. The midfield that remained for the new 2005–06 season lacked strength and experience. Gilberto is always outstanding, but he can't run central midfield on his own. With all due respect to lads like Fabregas and Flamini, who attempted to plug the gap, we were to go into the new season with a gaping hole left by Patrick's departure and a lightweight midfield that lacked punch, physical presence and experience. Opposing players weren't scared of us no more.

It needed the likes of John Terry to remind the Arsenal board of the madness of the decision to sell Patrick and not replace him. In an interview with the *Daily Mirror* before the season started, he compared it to Chelsea losing Frank Lampard and replacing him with a youngster. 'I'm not quite sure what impact it will have on Arsenal,' he said.

He might not have been sure, but there were a few predictions within the Arsenal dressing room, let me tell you. In time, the impact would become all too clear, as the destabilising effect of tearing out the heart from our midfield set in. The decision to let Patrick go would backfire. Such madness would lead to our worst ever domestic season under Arsene Wenger and crisis talks in the dressing room that left us all thinking about uncertain futures.

The Final Salute

'We're the Clock End... We're the Clock End... We're the Clock End, High-bu-ree...'

'We're the East Stand... We're the East Stand... We're the East Stand, High-bu-ree...'

That spine-chilling territorial chant from the Highbury faithful bounced around the stadium, sweeping from stand to stand in wave after wave of support.

'We're the North Bank... We're the North Bank... We're the North Bank, High-bu-ree...'

They seemed to sing it louder than ever before, and maybe it was because all of us – fans, players and staff – kicked off the new 2005–06 season knowing it would be the last 'first game of the season' that the iconic stadium would witness.

Arsenal versus Newcastle United on Sunday 14 August was the

beginning of the end of the Highbury story before the switch to the Emirates Stadium, and so every match, every goal and every moment over the following nine months would be a little bit more special. Signs of the approaching end were everywhere as I warmed up on the pitch. There was a billboard on the middle tier of the North Bank: 'Highbury 1913–2006'.

And another one which commemorated '93 Years of Memories'. There was a giant digital clock in the corner – the 'Highbury Countdown' had begun: day by day, hour by hour, minute by minute, second by second, we'd all be able to watch time running out before we faced the wrench of the move to the new stadium, its skeleton structure, in mid-development, visible through the gap between the West Stand and Clock End.

What I didn't realise at the time was that this also spelled the beginning of the end for me as an Arsenal player. The same clock counted down my time left as a Gunner. Not that any of that entered my head on that sunny summer's day. Far from it. I ran out determined to win the fans over again. I'd heard the snide remarks that I'd only stayed for the money, but that was never the case. I was 100 per cent committed and would give 150 per cent on the pitch. As soon as I stepped out on to that turf and heard those chants of old, I was up for the new season.

Looking back, maybe I was naive to think we could bandage up an old wound and play on like nothing had happened, and certain episodes over the ensuing season would open my eyes and make me realise the scars were permanent. Maybe the *Mirror*'s football correspondent John Cross was right, in hindsight, when he asked about me in an article on 1 August, 'How could he rekindle his love affair with Arsenal after such a public show of spite?'

But at the time, I was confident of putting the tapping-up saga, the guilty verdict, the lost appeal and the whole sorry episode behind me. No-one wanted Arsenal to get back on track and regain the

Premiership more than me, except maybe Mum. Then there was the elusive crown of Europe to go for. Then the World Cup in June 2006. Not to mention the historic significance of the final season at Highbury. Once I'd signed that new deal, my Arsenal heart and professional head were as much in tune together as me and Thierry working down the left.

Not that the press would let me forget so easily. I'd gone from 'Judas Cole' to 'want-away Cole', which wasn't much of an improvement, and my season would be dogged by transfer speculation about my 'likely departure'. All that did was weaken people's faith in me. So the new season had started as the old one had ended: with me running around the pitch with the same question mark hanging over my head. The days of the halo – similar to the ones forever hovering above the heads of Thierry, Dennis and Freddie – were long gone. But I was going to bust a gut to prove people wrong.

We had a new captain in Thierry who had taken over from Patrick. We had new shirts to wear – more of a redcurrant colour than the traditional red and white. It was time for fresh starts and it felt like I was flying in that first game, forging forward and creating chances for both Thierry and Freddie before we broke Newcastle's stubborn resistance with goals from the skipper and Robin van Persie in the 81st and 87th minutes.

The fixture list hadn't assisted my attempts to put the previous season behind me. Either side of the Newcastle match, we'd played Chelsea in the FA Community Shield at the Millennium Stadium and again in the league at Stamford Bridge. We lost 2–1 and then 1–0. In both matches I noticed that the ironic cheers of the previous season had gone. This time, Chelsea fans booed me. I was suddenly the money-grabbing Judas in both north and west London.

I suspect the boos from the Arsenal fans this 2006–07 season will be savage. However much I plead my case, I'll never lose the tag of traitor. Just ask Sol Campbell about his transfer to Arsenal from Spurs, where he was hero-worshipped. Or Alan Smith about Leeds United and his move to Manchester United. Or David Beckham: villain of the 1998 World Cup in France one minute, national cult figure the next. Reputations and adulation are the illusions of football. It's a funny old game and fans can be even funnier with their fickleness. I suppose that's why I've learned to put things into perspective. Or maybe it is the reason for writing this book – to at least *attempt* to make people understand that being a player is not just about kissing the badge; it's about politics and internal relationships, just like any other workplace.

Did David Beckham ever dream of leaving Manchester United? Did Alan Smith ever think he'd walk away from Leeds? Did I ever think I'd see the day when I'd quit Arsenal? None of us did, because, for each of us, those clubs were as much a part of us as they were the fans. But maybe fans need to ask start asking themselves 'How did it reach this stage?' and 'What led to this?'

At Arsenal, we spent a lot of the 2005–06 season doing our own soul-searching. By mid-October, we'd lost 2–1 away to Middlesbrough, drawn 0–0 at West Ham and lost 2–1 away at West Brom, and we went on to draw 0–0 against Spurs. Sides that we'd turned over for fun in previous seasons had found us out.

We'd fallen from the summit, going from 'the Invincibles' to 'the Beatables'. Especially away from home. Our supremacy in the league was replaced with hesitant, stuttering, unsure performances. We were not the same Arsenal and weren't playing the Arsenal way. We were suddenly faced with unfamiliar headlines such as '**DARK DAYS FOR GUNNERS**', '**WENGER: WE'VE NEVER BEEN SO BAD**'. Commentators such as Simon Barnes in *The Times* asked:

'Where did it all go wrong . . . for Arsenal and Wenger. Arsenal's falling away has been the more dramatic and the more rapid. For a team that were unbeatable, Arsenal have become uncertain, tentative and self-questioning . . .'

In the *Daily Mail*, Matt Lawton observed, 'Arsenal supporters must worry about who will follow Vieira. Thierry Henry? Ashley Cole? Robert Pires? Failure leads to itchy feet . . .' and he went on to describe a 'terrifying view of a possible future . . . an Arsenal side not even capable of matching an upwardly mobile Tottenham'.

Outside the dressing room, the 'experts' we hate agreeing with had hit the nail on the head. Inside the dressing room, the self-analysis was constant. We knew we'd been unlucky with injuries, with me, Thierry, Sol, Pires and Dennis all sidelined at different stages but our bad form ran deeper than that. We had crisis meeting after crisis meeting at the training ground, called by a worried Thierry. He's forever hungry and has high standards and he couldn't stand the fact that we'd slipped. He'd mull over a defeat for an entire weekend and call a meeting when we were back in training. We knew teams had worked out how to play us – give us no room, niggle at our heels, get physical – but our overall machine weren't clicking or running smoothly, and as a team we had to sit down and sort it out. We'd analyse, discuss and try to put things right, but we'd end up having the same meetings again and again.

Thierry hates losing – absolutely loathes it, whether it's a Premiership match or a game of cards. He, like me, has a winning mentality and winning had become an addiction for a lot of us from the 'immaculate season'. So we searched for answers to our form; we wondered out loud whether this younger Arsenal had that same mentality. We asked because there were times last season when you'd see certain players come into the dressing room and wonder how much defeat hurt them. Because it should hurt. It should hurt like hell. But it seemed like some were happy if they'd had a good game individually, regardless of defeat. Many times last season, I felt the dressing room needed a rocket, but I can't remember the boss ever kicking anyone up the arse, even when they'd been rubbish and made big mistakes. Sometimes, maybe, the boss was *too* nice, *too* fair. That's what I felt anyway, sat there.

So where did it all go wrong? Well, football is all about opinions and this is my opinion.

The brutal truth is that too many people played for themselves and not as a team. I spent a lot of the season injured, and watching games from the stands gave me a different perspective on matches, and I saw too much rubbish being played too often, lazy players who didn't pull their weight and schoolboy errors. Without Jens Lehmann and Thierry Henry, I don't know where Arsenal would have finished in the table, but those two kept us in games. I said all this one day to Pat Rice, 'They're not playing the Arsenal way, Pat! They're not running for one another and not defending as a team.'

Some people seemed to think that if you play for the Arsenal first team, you're automatically the best, but that's not it. When you pull on that jersey, you have to *become* the best. And it was so frustrating for me to see people taking five, six, seven touches on the ball. In the immaculate season, we were slick and fast and taking no more than three touches before passing and moving on. It was like the boss said at times – we were starting from scratch all over again.

Another thing was the silence in games. I think back to my time playing alongside a screaming and shouting Tony Adams. He weren't the quickest of players and always wanted me next to him to cover his arse. As a result, I learned a lot from him about communication on the pitch. He talked, bellowed and shouted non-stop, whether it was a match or training. I didn't need to check if there was a man behind me because he always let me know –'Left shoulder','Right shoulder','Man coming', 'I'm just to the left', 'I've got him', 'Push on', 'I'll cover' – and that gave me so much experience in backing up my team. Even today, I'm bellowing and screaming – it's the influence of Tony Adams. But last season, senior players started to notice how the atmosphere within the team was 'dead'. There was nowhere near as much talking going on. Even training was quiet, and that's weird. I train with England and there's a vibe, an energy, a rapport and banter; like being back with 'immaculate' Arsenal. But London Colney don't have that same atmosphere no more which means it don't have enough people pulling together.

I'm from the Tony Adams/Martin Keown school of thought. It's never enough just to pull on the Arsenal shirt. It doesn't mean you've suddenly arrived, as some new signings thought. As a new recruit, I was given no time to bask in the glory of making the first team. Once there, I had to earn my place, keep fighting for it and prove myself, and the senior players were on my back all the time. Don't just wear the jersey, earn the right to wear it, they said. I even had to earn the right to sit in the back eight seats of the team coach.

'You can't sit there, that's John Lukic's seat.'

'You can't sit there, that's Bouldy's seat.'

'You can't sit there, that's Tone's seat,' and on and on the rejection went when I climbed aboard the team coach for the first time. It was like being back on the school bus at Bow All Boys' Secondary.

You earned your stripes when you had won trophies as part of a winning team. That was the unwritten rule that seemed to go out the window last season.

In our 'invincible' year, we had household names in the team – trophy winners, international caps, World Cup winners. Experience was the life blood of that team and the youngsters can learn from it. Just like I did under Tony and Martin. Just as I was eager to learn from the likes of Nigel Winterburn.

Which is probably why I could never understand the attitude of some of the young ones who chirped up a little too much for their age and experience, acting like leaders saying, 'Come on! Come on! We've got to win!' or 'We must fight, we must tackle!' I'd sit there, look at the likes of Freddie, Sol, Thierry, Gilberto and Jens being urged on by these new recruits and cringe. They'd pipe up before every game and then give the ball away or miss a crucial tackle. Tony Adams would have put them in their place, let me tell you. Concentrate on your own game, improve it and then – and only then – come back and tell me what to do, he'd have said. That's why one of Arsenal's big problems last season was too many big heads on young shoulders.

The key ingredient for a successful team is the ability to walk out on that pitch and know you'd go to war for your team-mates. Ask the great Arsenal teams under George Graham or Arsene Wenger. Ask Chelsea under Jose Mourinho. Just don't ask the Arsenal team of 2005–06. It's like I told Sol one day, I wouldn't go to war with these guys because they're not fighting for one another, not tackling enough, not being verbal enough, not being physical enough. Some players were letting us get kicked and allowing team-mates to get bullied. In the old days, I'd have been able to speak about it and get it off my chest. But, in the new era, too many people took constructive criticism way too personally and wouldn't talk to you for a week. So I learned to say nothing to keep the peace in the dressing room.

'The young guns', in my opinion, were not prepared to listen or learn.

Take, for example, when Martin Keown, now 40 years old, was invited down to spend some time with the lads at training. The boss wanted someone who was a winner to spend time with the younger players, to push them through and work quietly with them. He knew the culture of the club, said the boss. The man is a legend, and he was a player's worst nightmare to come up against – always pinching, elbowing, niggling and barging; making his presence felt in a game. He was a great, rugged defender. No wonder the boss felt his experience was needed on the training pitch. We needed to defend more as a team. But I was stunned when I saw him speaking to Philippe Senderos, advising him to get tough, do this and do that. And Senderos just looked at him, blew his cheeks, and walked off. That showed disrespect in my book to an Arsenal legend from an Arsenal player with one season under his belt.

Success has so much to do with attitude and how a team gels and everywhere I looked last season, I saw a well-oiled, proven winning machine breaking down. We used to be so tight as a team; a strong camp made for strong performances, and that's what made the Arsenal family. In 2005–06, we became just a team, no longer a family.

When training finished at 12.30 p.m., some players were up and out the door by 12.40 p.m. The old Arsenal would hang around until two or three. In hotels, on the eve of matches, players had their meal and went straight to bed. With the old Arsenal, there'd be a gang of us playing cards, having a coffee, sharing a laugh.

Last season, out of an entire squad, it'd be only me, Thierry, Sol and Pires sat around after dinner.

I remember feeling how fragmented we'd all become when Robin van Persie spoke up at training about Freddie Ljungberg. 'He doesn't even talk to me. Why doesn't he talk to me?'

Social occasions used to be a big thing, but last season we stopped going out as a team. I couldn't tell you a thing about Kolo, Eboue, Reyes, Cesc or Senderos. I don't know whether they have girlfriends, a family, what they do or where they go in their spare time. The days of card games at a player's house or going round to Patrick's to play snooker tournaments disappeared when he went to Juventus. It's sad, because last season, the team felt detached from one another and I felt like a stranger in the Arsenal dressing room. There was many a time when I didn't feel a part of it any more.

This wasn't the all-for-one-and-one-for-all philosophy that had made us such a tight unit in the past. As the boss himself said in 2003, 'To build a great team is not all about money. First you have to create spirit and togetherness in the squad, and that's not easy.'

There was another contributing factor. The purse-strings were being tightened, the effects of those cut-backs also affected team morale, and we felt the Arsenal lifestyle was being constricted perhaps as another knock-on of the new stadium. I can't remember a time when Arsenal has counted its pennies so carefully, and I've wondered if that's why the team has not seen much investment.

It got to the point where the finance men wanted to know who ate what, who ordered this, who ordered that after the team's visits to hotels. We had to start writing down our orders like children on a school trip. An extra coffee or a cappuccino is now duly noted.

I swear, if it was down to some of them, we probably wouldn't have stayed in hotels before games. We'd be on the coach on the morning of the match and travel back the same night. Thankfully, the boss digs in his heels because he is a big believer in players being relaxed, comfortable and treated well in the run-up to games. But it's another sign of how life changed for the worse at Arsenal.

Of course, then there was the decisive Vieira factor. There was only one player, other than Thierry, whose name dominated conversation in the Arsenal Tavern and Gunners Pub before matches, and that was the player who was no longer part of the team. The impact his loss has made cannot be overstated. I think the boss and the board tried, at first, to shrug off his departure and deflect attention on to the emergence of Cesc Fabregas, but, with all due respect to Cesc, he's no Patrick. It's like putting the gloves of a heavyweight champion on the hands of an unproven featherweight and telling him to go out there and knock out the opposition.

In his match programme notes at the start of the season against Newcastle, the boss had written, 'This is the first time I have started a season at Arsenal without Patrick Vieira, but I believe we can begin a new positive era. A club doesn't die when a player leaves. Football is not like that.'

But losing a man of Vieira's stature and presence from the pitch, dressing room and club was always going to have a negative effect. A lot has been said about the hole his departure left and there will always be a difference of opinion among management and fans about its impact. All I can say, as a player, is that his exit pricked the bubble and the midfield didn't seem as strong. His loss, I think, was immeasurable.

I can't argue with the words of Dennis Bergkamp when he said, back in February 2006 in an article in *The Times*, that the team had become 'lightweight'. And it had. No club could afford to release a powerhouse like Patrick and not at least attempt to replace him. It is insane for both the football and business side of the club.

When they let Patrick go and didn't re-invest in the team, the club didn't die, but our chances of supremacy did, because football *is* like that. We weren't going to win, and senior players had predicted that much in the last few months of 2005.

But there was an even worse scenario looming as the season went on: we'd win nothing and finish behind Spurs in the table. *That's* how depressing the season was getting.

Our dip in form did my head in more than most because I couldn't do anything about it. I was sidelined through injury for most of the season, reduced to the role of a frustrated spectator in the Clock End alongside my mum from October through to April.

I'd played in the 0–0 draw at Upton Park and had travelled with the team for our away match at Ajax in the qualifying group of the Champions League on 27 September 2005. It was while I was training in Holland that I felt this ache in my right foot. At first, I thought it was my ligaments, but then it got to a point where I couldn't take the pain no more. 'My foot's killing me, there's something not right,' I told physio Gary Lewin. A scan in Holland didn't pick up much and it was put down to bruising. So I soldiered on against Ajax, played well in our 2–1 win and returned home to play my part in the 1–0 home win over Birmingham the following Sunday. It was after that game that the pain suddenly kicked in again. It was excruciating, and I'd obviously made matters worse just ahead of England's two crucial World Cup Group 6 qualifying matches at Old Trafford against Austria on 8 October and then Poland four days later.

An accurate scan this time picked up a stress fracture in my fifth metatarsal bone. It must have happened in training or during the West Ham game and it hadn't snapped, it had just cracked. It was the least famous case of the 'curse of the metatarsal'. Just like Beckham. Just like Rooney. But minus the hype, sense of urgency and prayer mats. It was only October and the World Cup was the following June, so there was plenty of time for me to recover, but I was still gutted to be missing the two qualifiers, and I was going to miss three months of domestic and European football.

Come December, we'd lost two back-to-back matches, away at Bolton, 2–0, and then at Newcastle, 1–0. It was the first time we'd lost two games on the bounce in three years. Shearer taunted us over the loss of Vieira when the boss complained about Newcastle getting physical and roughing us up. 'Well,' Shearer responded, 'I never saw Patrick Vieira pulling out of challenges.'

Add to the scoreline: Shearer 1 Wenger 0.

We'd also clawed a point away at Spurs, 1–1. Martin Jol's team were third in the Premiership then and there was a lot of talk about the balance of power shifting in north London. Thank God Robert Pires came off the bench to grab the equaliser in the 77th minute because, in truth, Spurs dominated for large parts of that game.

We went into the home game against Chelsea on Sunday 18 December with the boss saying defeat was 'unthinkable'. Before kick-off, he said he'd every confidence in the team and we were still the best out there. He was trying to paper over the cracks. There was a crisis of confidence and everyone felt it.

We were no longer the most powerful team in the Premiership. We'd shrunk in stature and belief, however hard the boss tried to make us believe otherwise. And cometh the hour, Chelsea tore us to shreds, winning 2–0; the first time they'd won at Highbury in the league since 1990 and the first time they'd done the league double over us since 1970. Where once we used to set records, others were now setting them at our expense.

Chelsea had the Premiership title pretty much in the bag, just in time for Christmas – going 20 points clear of us as we languished in eighth place behind the likes of Bolton, Manchester City, Wigan and Spurs.

At the after-match press conference, the boss effectively conceded the title. He then got mocked in the press for suggesting that there wasn't much between Chelsea and Arsenal. Except 20 points. '**HE'S LOSING THE PLOT!**' screamed the *Daily Mirror*.

I remember being at training the following week when he told us that it was 'the worst Chelsea team' we'd played since he'd been at Arsenal. He said they were reduced to playing the long ball because we'd matched them in the middle of the park. For the first time in my Arsenal career, I looked at the boss and thought to myself, 'Get real!' They may well have put balls over the top, but they must have had time to do it, which means we weren't shutting them down quick enough. For Lampard to get the ball, turn and have time to chip it over the top means we weren't that hot in the centre of the park. We weren't a match for one of the best Chelsea sides for years – *that* was the painful truth. Some senior players gave the boss puzzled looks that day. We'd been at the top with him, we'd shared the most unbelievable journey with him, we'd set records with him and we knew what it felt like to match Chelsea. So there was no kidding us. Or the rest of football. Chelsea had become the dominant, deserving, unbeatable force in the Premiership and we were streets behind.

Reality got harsher three days later at Doncaster Rovers' Earth Stadium in the quarter-finals of the Carling Cup when we almost went out to the Division One side who played the game of their lives. I don't know how we got through that night, because we were 2–1 down with two minutes of injury time in extra-time left. Then Gilberto rescued us with an equaliser that took us to a shoot-out which we won 3–1.

By the end of January, we were out of all domestic cup

competition. In the FA Cup, we were dumped out by our bogey team Bolton, 1–0, and in the Carling Cup semi-final, Wigan – the team of the season for me – drew 2–2 with us over two legs, and went through on away goals. With a 1–0 away defeat to Everton to add to the mix, it was the worst I'd ever known our form under the boss, and our best end-of-season target seemed to be fourth place, the last finishing position that guaranteed qualifying for the Champions League for the new season. But if we were to do that, we'd need to dislodge the long-time sitting tenants of fourth spot – Spurs.

I was surprised when my comeback from injury was pencilled in for the home match versus Middlesbrough on 14 January; surprised because I didn't feel match-ready, and I felt the boss was rushing me back. But they were dire times, so I wasn't going to argue. Anyhow, I was told not to worry, that I'd be eased back and would probably come on for the last five or ten minutes. Good job, because I was knackered. I'd trained intensely for five days as part of my recovery, not thinking I'd be picked. Normally, you wouldn't do more than three days on the trot ahead of a match. When Pascal Cygan went down injured in the first 30 minutes, with the lads already 3–0 up, I didn't even look at the boss. He'd put fellow substitute Flamini at left-back.

'Ashley, warm up,' said the boss. I sat there motionless, stunned. 'Hurry up!' he added.

Before I knew it, and after a quick run up to the corner flag as my only warm-up, I was on the touchline, waiting to come on after 34 minutes. Knackered and, in my eyes, not ready for 56 minutes of Premiership football. But when the PA announcer read out my name as the sub, the cheer was unbelievable. It was a night full of surprises. I'd not heard the Arsenal fans cheer my name like that for almost a year. God, I'd missed that. I thought I'd lost that kind of support in a London hotel in 2005, but, as I ran out on to the pitch that night, it was as if the whole stadium was behind me again. What a rush! I think it was the adrenalin burst that made me forget the pain I was feeling in my thigh. I put it down to being a bit rusty.

It was one hell of a match to make my reappearance in. We went on to win 7–0. It was one of those sublime Arsenal shows, full of pace and rhythm, and Thierry scored a hat-trick that took him level with Cliff Bastin on 150 goals as the club's leading scorer. That night, the man was unbeatable. As for me, the final ten minutes were almost unplayable. The adrenalin had worn off and I knew something was wrong. I could hardly run, let alone kick the ball, and it was a good job Middlesbrough were out for the count because I couldn't do nothing. I was hobbling and passing the ball a few yards. I'd worked too hard, too quick after a week rammed with training and my thigh had gone. I'd made a comeback too soon and I think the boss accepted he'd made an error of judgement. I was out of action with a thigh strain for another five weeks.

I've never trained as hard to get fit again. It was tough when the sun was shining outside and all the boys went to play a match on the training ground, leaving me in the gym for two hours. All the time, I kept thinking about the Champions League and the World Cup, imagining the games, because the battle during physio is to keep focused. After four weeks, I was back running outside, but I couldn't shake this weird sensation: it felt like there was a little ball in my thigh muscle and it kept clicking as I ran. One day, I wouldn't feel it, the next day I would. If you have a problem with the thigh, it can sometimes be that you can jog, but the moment you sprint, spring or kick a ball, that's when the sharp pain stabs the leg and it feels like the muscle is about to rip.

It was that injury and that sensation that led to a bizarre conversation that, in my mind, proved to be a turning point regarding my future with Arsenal. It was one doubt and one criticism too many.

I'd just come in from training, having worked with some balls, doing some gentle kicking and passing. Fitness coach Tony Colbert was stood near the doors as I walked inside to go to the changing rooms.

'You okay, Ash? Feeling okay?' he asked.

'Yeah, yeah, yeah. Feeling good,' I said, because I was.

But, like I've said, one minute this thigh sensation would be there, the next it would be gone. In the physio room these twinges came back. I turned to Gary Lewin and winced. 'I'm feeling it a bit now,' I said.

At that moment, Tony walked in and heard me groaning.

'So why didn't you tell me that outside? You said you were fine a few minutes ago,' and he looked at me like I was a kid looking to get out of class by throwing a sickie.

'It wasn't hurting outside, but this keeps happening. Maybe I should stop training for a bit, otherwise it's never going to get better,' I suggested, trying to ignore his accusing tone. I'd been telling them for weeks that it needed resting, but they said it would be best to keep working at it, which made no sense to me.

That's when he said it: 'What do you expect me to do, Ash, when you tell me you're okay and then come in here like you've just been shot?'

That was it. I blew my lid. 'Are you taking the piss? Who's acting like they've been shot?!' I yelled, and he stormed out. It was a good job he did, because, after that, we both needed to calm down. But the matter clearly still rankled with Tony and, when all the lads had left, he came back in. It was just me and him in the changing room and he wasn't finished with his inquisition.

'Be honest with me,' he said, 'are you just making out that it's worse than it actually is because you've got an eye on the World Cup?'

I could sense he was nervous asking the question and his nerve left me staring at him, making him squirm. He dug his hole that little bit deeper. 'I was just wondering, that's all,' he went on. 'I wondered if you were just holding back a bit?'

'What!' I shouted, barely able to keep a lid on it, 'I NEED to play for Arsenal to go to the World Cup, so why the fuck would I hold back . . .'

'Nah, nah, nah . . . I didn't mean it like that, Ash . . .', but I weren't letting him finish. He'd said enough.

'The MORE I hold back, the LESS chance I've got of going to Germany! And YOU are insulting me,' I said. 'I'm no wuss who comes in here with a little injury and folds. I TRAIN through my injuries and TRAIN through the pain as much as I can, so don't you dare question my commitment to the club!' I'm not one for confrontation, but he'd pushed me too far. I'd worked my nuts off to get match-fit and now some guy was saying I was chucking one in.

My anger echoed around London Colney that afternoon and I told Gary Lewin that I refused to train with Tony. 'He more or less said I was putting it on to save myself for Germany. I'm not working with him again,' I said.

I was so pissed off. Then I started wondering whether what was being aired was the collective thinking of staff. Is that what the boss thought? Gary Lewin reassured me that weren't the case and I believed him. But, for me, it was one more person at the club doubting my loyalty. And it was the final straw.

I'd had a vice-chairman and board who, to me, had thrown my loyalty back in my face, fans who'd questioned my faith for a year, a dressing room I didn't recognise anymore and now someone seemingly doubting my professionalism.

'Why am I even bothering? What future have I got at a place like this?' I moaned to my agent and family that evening. Neither agent, Mum nor fiancée could provide an answer any more.

My comeback was the reserves' north London derby against Spurs at Barnet's Underhill ground on the night of 27 February. If I came through the match okay, I'd play in the Champions League quarter-final second leg against Real Madrid at Highbury the following week.

It was a hope that lasted all of seven minutes.

In a tackle, one of their players came over the top of the ball and the pain was excruciating. Desperate to run it off, I tried to play on, but it was impossible. I'd sprained my left ankle, badly bruising it on the talus bone which connects to the foot. I sat there on the pitch as the physio treated me and I could have cried. First the broken foot. Then the thigh. Now the ankle. It was like I was cursed, destined to miss the Champions League, the last match at Highbury *and* the World Cup. That night, I was back on crutches.

Sven-Goran Eriksson was in touch with Gary Lewin that night, asking for an assessment. I was asked to go for a scan the following evening as a matter of urgency and those next 24 hours were almost as painful as the ankle itself. Because I knew that the World Cup depended on the outcome of the scan.

Specialists spoke of floating bones and operations. I saw experts shaking their heads as they looked at the scans behind a thick glass wall in a consulting room. And my imagination and paranoia played tricks on me. Eventually, after much discussion, it was decided no operation was needed. But the bruising of the talus was so bad that it could have cracked under pressure, so I had to rest for a month and keep the weight off my foot. It meant not being able to resume training until the start of April, so I wouldn't be match-ready until the end of that month. That immediately raised questions about my fitness for Germany.

Would I be sharp enough? Would I get enough games under my belt?

I'd not played a full 90 minutes since October and the media started talking up 'a race against time' which, in turn, made me worry about the timetable. I desperately needed to get back playing for Arsenal.

As we neared May, and the end of the domestic season, word reached me that Sven had called the boss and said, 'All Ashley needs is five minutes and he'll be in the squad.'

I'd needed to hear that, because the press had been getting on the coach's back and there were doubts about me everywhere.

At one point, Sven publicly said that if I wasn't playing with two weeks of the season to go, then I might well be struggling to make it. He'd even come to the training ground in person to check on me.

'When do you think you'll be playing?' he asked, and there was concern in his voice.

'I'm getting there, I'm getting there!' I told him, not letting on that I was shitting myself about cutting it fine. The 'race' to get fit – to *prove* to Sven that I was ready and sharp for Germany – was telling on me. I went to Arsene one day and said I was ready for the Champions League semi-final against Villarreal. He disagreed. He said I needed one more week of training. Then I'd play in the reserves at West Ham.

I think he could tell I was frustrated. And then the previously unmentionable history came spilling out. A season of simmering frustration on both sides proved too much for me.

'You seem angry. Are you angry at me? The club?' he asked.

'Angry? I'm not angry at the club or you, boss. I'm angry at one man – Mr Dein.'

None of this had anything to do with my fitness or comeback but we were talking about it now.

'Come on, Ashley, we've been patient with you. I've let you get fit, we extended your contract, gave you more money and we said that you can leave at the end of the season if you still want to go,' said the boss, referring to the secret arrangement between club and player.

You can leave at the end of the season. 'Bet he's not said that to Thierry Henry,' I thought.

You can leave at the end of the season.

'Boss,' I said, still thinking about what he'd just said, 'all I'm bothered about at the moment is playing. Until I play, I'm not going to be happy.'

No player is happy being sidelined. It's miserable. Especially with a fourth spot in the Premiership to fight for, a Champions League final still a real possibility and a World Cup campaign around the corner.

'Well, I've spoken with Sven and he said that all you need is five minutes. I might give you more than five minutes, or even a game, so keep your head up,' said the boss.

Everything hinged on the last three Premiership matches of the season in May. I couldn't afford one more injury, set-back or twinge. The World Cup squad was going to be announced on Monday 8 May. And Arsenal couldn't afford one more slip in the league. They had 270 minutes of football in which to leap-frog Spurs into fourth place and guarantee Champions League football for the 2006–07 season. Club and player were going to take it down to the wire.

Sunderland away was the scene of the comeback: take three.

We won 3–0, but it was an awful game. Afterwards, Dennis came into the changing room and said, 'Lads, I'm not saying it was down to you, but that was the worst game of football I've ever seen in my life!' He wasn't wrong. It was rubbish. We couldn't pass the ball that night. But it was three crucial points in the bag. We'd narrowed the gap to four points with Spurs – still sat fourth – and had a game i n hand and I'd come on as a sub to play 30 minutes. Job done. No after-effects.

Our next game was Manchester City away, and I got in a full 90 minutes as we won 3–1, putting us a point shy of Spurs going into the final game of the season. They had West Ham away. We had Wigan at home. Our last match at Highbury was going to be filled with 90 minutes of unbearable tension and 93 years of memories.

On that Sunday afternoon of 7 May 2006, not even the Champions League or World Cup seemed to matter. Highbury – in the final dramatic act before the curtain came down – was the only football stage to be playing on.

*

Even as we got ready at the team hotel in east London, the day felt surreal, as if it shouldn't really be happening. We'd been sat around watching television when a news bulletin mentioned it was the 'Final Salute to Highbury', and it hit me there and then that we were about to make our last coach trip to the stadium. It was an afternoon loaded with emotion and expectation – no-one wanted to say goodbye, we had to win and Spurs had to lose. Simple as that. And if it panned out, they'd be talking about a fairytale ending to the Highbury story.

'I can't believe this is the last game here!' said Robin van Persie, as the coach pulled up by the steps leading to the Marble Hall.

'I can't believe this is going to be my last game in England wearing an Arsenal shirt,' I thought.

There was no future left for me at the club any more. I knew that. Cheryl knew that. Mum knew that.

Nothing that season had convinced me anything had changed and the club had done nothing to build bridges with me. If anything, being sidelined had made me feel even more detached. My head had accepted my time at Arsenal was over, even if my heart hadn't quite caught up. In the week before that final match, me and Cheryl had moved from our flat to a new house in north London. It was a time for packing up boxes and memories and moving on.

We stepped off the coach and climbed those marble steps for the last time. Every final moment was intensified. I'll miss that brief walk from coach to stadium when you say to yourself, 'I'm at Highbury. I'm home.'

That was a special feeling that can never be transferred to the Emirates Stadium.

I'll miss that walk through the Marble Hall. I'll miss the walk down the narrow, red and white corridor to the dressing room. I'll miss the banter and rapport that used to exist in the dressing room. Then there was Paddy, a character who had been part of the furniture at Highbury for around 30 years, the club's odd-job man whose little room became the ref's room on match days. Paddy is an ageing, white-haired, wiry Irish bloke with a heart that is red and white. He was stood in the Marble Hall on my very first day at Highbury and, when I got off the coach, he was there on my last, with a tear in his eye. He used to help me with the kit I'd have to collect and take to the training ground when I was a YTS boy. He'd seen me grow from boy to man, from youth-teamer to first-teamer, and he'd always had good banter with me. I'll miss that man, but not as much as he'll miss Arsenal because he was also parting company with the club that day. The board couldn't find a role for him at Ashburton Grove, not even as a gesture.

We left our sentimentality and emotions outside the dressing room door and got down to the job in hand: a must-win match against Wigan. Paul Jewell's team had played without fear all season and it was going to be a tough game, as our bitter Carling Cup semi-final exit reminded us. What we didn't need reminding about was what the stakes were over the following 90 minutes: Champions League football at the expense of Spurs.

If results went our way.

Even before kick-off, there had been drama on that front. On the coach we'd heard from one of the masseurs that half the Spurs team had gone down with food poisoning and had called for the West Ham match to be postponed for 24 hours. We thought it was some kind of wind-up until the story popped up on Sky Sports News on the coach TV screens. The team had eaten something dodgy at their hotel and some players were genuinely ill, but you can't call a match off like that. It would set too much of a dangerous precedent. The police and Premier League rejected the request and so, even before kick-off, the odds had tilted in our favour. We had a fully fit team. Spurs had ten players with dodgy guts whose bodies had been suffering. Not the best big-game preparation.

As we ran out on to the pitch, we couldn't have felt better.

The atmosphere was pure electricity and flames shot into the air either side of the tunnel. The fans wore alternating red and white T-shirts in blocks, so when massed together they formed giant stripes of Arsenal's colours. I think Thierry had heard a lot of the lads talking about how brilliant and special it all was. So he gathered us round into a pre-match huddle to give us a pep talk.

'The atmosphere *is* amazing,' he said in his French accent, 'but let us not get sucked in by it, let us not be overawed by it. We're here to do a job and we're here to win a game. They can party now. We can party when we win.'

The game itself was full of twists and turns and tension, as results swung for and against us. The match tipped and wobbled and teased our fate. Goal Arsenal. Goal West Ham. Fourth spot Arsenal. Equaliser Wigan. Second goal Wigan. Equaliser Spurs. Fifth spot Arsenal. Fourth spot Spurs. Then we equalised through Thierry before half-time. 2–2 at Highbury, 1–1 at Upton Park.

In the second half, no-one could have written the script better for Arsenal or Thierry. He scored two more to say farewell to the stadium with a hat-trick and give us a 4–2 lead, and he kissed the turf in celebration.

Then, four minutes later, just as we were bringing on Dennis Bergkamp and Robin van Persie, the Highbury crowd went berserk and we knew instantly what it meant: West Ham had scored in the 80th minute. Thierry spontaneously rushed over to me during the on-going substitution, hugged me and screamed. His pre-match pep talk went out of the window. Ten minutes later – victory, and fourth place and Champions League football was ours.

'We did it! We did it!' screamed Thierry, as he joined me and Jens Lehmann in a dancing circle of three. We'd nicked fourth spot from Spurs after they'd been in possession of it for nearly the whole season. They couldn't finish in front of us even when we were at our worst!

I found the boss, raced over to him and gave him a hug. The crowd was singing and partying all around the ground. 'Well done boss! You're the man!' I shouted. And he is. What he has done for Arsenal and me over the years has been incredible. Even during a season that had looked disastrous at the end of January, he managed to steer us to fourth place. We'd salvaged something, and still had a Champions League final to play.

We sat in the dressing room as the 'final salute' ceremony took place on the pitch. A podium was set up in the centre circle and the crowd was reminded of the Arsenal greats spanning 93 years, as players from every generation walked around the pitch: from Liam Brady to Steve Bould, from John Lukic to Anders Limpar, from Frank McLintock to Malcolm Macdonald, Kenny Sansom to David Seaman, Bob Wilson to Ian Wright. Then, after about an hour of memory lane stuff, it was our turn to walk around and say goodbye to Highbury. I kept at the back of the group with Kolo Toure as we walked the touchline, looking up into the stands, acknowledging the fans. I've never seen so many people with tears in their eyes. That was how much Highbury meant to them. I remember wanting to hang back to make that procession last longer. I remember thinking, 'This is the best pitch, best stadium, best atmosphere.' In front of the Clock End, I looked up to the box – there was Mum, my agent, my friends. Mum waved. I waved back. And then I had to look away. I saw the boss shake the hands of the fans behind the goal and a wide beaming smile had replaced the trademark frown.

'Take it all in, take it all in,' I kept saying to myself. I wanted to pick up the atmosphere and take it home.

In that moment, I didn't want to leave Arsenal. In that moment, in that atmosphere, I could so easily have stayed; the fan within me didn't want it to be the end.

One thing I didn't want to do was leave that pitch. And neither did Thierry. We'd spoken the night before about how we wanted to soak up the atmosphere and savour every moment. So at the end of the party, as the crowds reluctantly walked away, we decided to stay out there. We went to the podium where all the presentations and speeches had taken place and we sat down. Just me and the captain. We watched all the other players head to the dressing room. A lot of them had not been at the club long and the significance and emotion of the day was probably lost on them.

The media would make a lot of me and Thierry staying out there, saying 'it was impossible to escape the conclusion that they were saying farewell to the club'. But it weren't anything to do with that. We just wanted to soak it all up. It weren't about futures at that moment. It was about memories. Far too often, as a player, you rush through occasions and don't appreciate them. But not this time. We'd actually expected the crowd to have gone by then, to be on the way to the pubs to party. But hundreds of them stayed, as we stayed, and we were determined to be the last ones to leave as dusk fell.

Neither of us could believe it was all over. 'This is a special place,' said Thierry, looking around – he's an emotional guy. And so we sat and recalled our memories – certain matches, certain goals.

'You're the man here, you've had some unbelievable moments,' I said to him. He smiled modestly.

At that very moment, it was as if the crowd had heard me, and they started singing his name and chanting:

'Sign him up! Sign him up! Sign him up!' and then 'Four more years! Four more years!'

He waved to each side of the ground. 'Hey, Ash, they'll sing your name next. Wait for it,' he said.

And as his chants faded away, we waited. And we waited. And there was nothing, and Thierry rocked backwards, falling about laughing. I shrugged my shoulders. 'They're not bothered about me,' I said, resigned to the fact.

As the crowd began to trickle away, Robert Pires walked across the pitch to join us, wheeling his travel bag behind him. He sat down next to Thierry. His name echoed back from the stands, he waved and they started singing again. 'Four more years! Four more years!' It was like I was the invisible man.

If ever there was an illustration of how my relationship with the fans had broken down, that was it. I smiled and put on a brave face in front of Thierry and Robert but, privately, I was gutted.

I think Thierry knew it had got to me. He put a hand on my shoulder. 'I love this place,' I said to him, 'but I can't do this no more. It don't feel right no more.' In a way, Thierry was the first person at the club that I'd told this to. 'It'll never be the same again for me at Arsenal,' I added.

I was proud of my contribution to the club and what I'd achieved, and no-one could say I'd given less than 150 per cent in every game. The people that matter – family and friends – know how strong my love is for Arsenal. The club will always be in my blood and I don't need the fans' approval to know that. Because I know it myself. In the same way I knew it was time to move on to a new challenge and start afresh.

Physio Gary Lewin walked out to say goodbye. Then his mobile phone rang. It was a call for me. 'Are you gonna be sat out there all night? Some of us have homes to go to!' It was Steve Jacobs, ringing from the box, where he'd been stood watching with Mum and my friends. I heard their laughter echoing from the Clock End. There were only a few hundred people left in the stadium. All of a sudden Highbury was as empty as a reserve fixture. Thierry patted me on the back. It was time to go to make way for the bulldozers. I got up, followed by Thierry, and we walked to the tunnel for the last time. Before leaving the ground, I gave Paddy my shirt and signed it.

That night, I went out and got hammered at the Embassy nightclub but, unlike other years, no other Arsenal player joined me. Instead, I found myself at the end-of-season Premiership bash with John Terry, Joe Cole, Carlton Cole, Damien Duff and a few of the other Chelsea lads. The champions were out on the town, celebrating and sticking together; the kind of camaraderie that used to bind Arsenal together.

By the time I woke up the next afternoon, Sven-Goran Eriksson had already taken to the stage at London's Cafe Royal and announced me as being part of his 2006 World Cup squad. All eyes were on Germany.

But before that, there was Paris – and the small matter of a Champions League final.

9

The Elusive Crown

'You are the best players, you deserve to be here – now go out there and win this!' said Arsene Wenger, his words piercing the silence of the dressing room; his trademark frown illustrating the determination and passion in his message.

We all stood as one, puffing out our chests. 'COME ON LADS!' everyone yelled.

This is it, I thought, this is the final. That one surreal thought kept going over and over in my head. *This is the Champions League final. Versus Barcelona*. Club football don't get bigger than that. It was the boss's biggest dream; his sole aim is to become the first Arsenal manager to lift that trophy. There's a quote from him that sums up his thirst for European glory: 'Even when we were walking around the pitch in front of all those happy people, my first thought was the European Champions League.'

He said it in May 1998 when not even the league and cup double was enough for him, but he could easily have said the same thing after the Leicester game when we'd won the domestic title with the unbeaten run.

Because no matter the scale of achievement, there's only one trophy he craves: that one jug-eared trophy that has eluded him and us since he took over.

As we heard the noise and atmosphere building in the Stade de France above us, it seemed almost too good to be true. Football, even at this level, can still make me have to pinch myself. Players can talk of the magic of the FA Cup and all that but the Champions League final has a different edge; it's the diamond-encrusted final.

Win the World Cup with your country; the Champions League with your club. They're the ultimate aims in football. And what heightened the rush I got from the occasion was that I'd never expected to be in the starting line-up because of all my injuries. The horizon in Europe I'd been focusing on was Germany in June, not Paris in May. But there I was, limbering up and lining up with the rest of the boys, and I can't remember ever feeling as proud to be wearing an Arsenal shirt.

We would enjoy our biggest and proudest night in Paris on the evening of Wednesday 17 May 2006, after what had been a long, winding and frustrating odyssey across Europe over many seasons. We'd struggled to even reach the quarter-finals in previous years, but suddenly that trophy was within reach. I remember seeing a photo in the papers a day or two before the final, showing the boss stood next to the gleaming trophy on a plinth, eyeing it up like a kid eager to unwrap the Christmas present he'd always wanted.

Ninety minutes of football was the only barrier that stood in his and our way. And it had been a remarkable story that had led to what would become a dramatic night of football and controversy in the Stade de France.

*

So, okay, in the Premiership, you've got crunch games like Manchester United, Chelsea and Liverpool. Or an intense London derby versus Spurs and some niggle versus West Ham. But fixtures in Europe are in a different league of football glamour, with a never-ending list of the magnificent and the mighty: Inter Milan, Juventus, AC Milan, Real Madrid, Dynamo Kiev, Bayern Munich, Ajax, Barcelona, Valencia, Benfica, FC Porto. Imagine all those teams in the Premiership, and how exciting matches would be week in, week out.

That's what Europe is all about: pitting the best against the best and seeing who comes out as Kings of Football. The boss must, must, must win the Champions League, and he won't be satisfied until he does.

In 2006, we thought we were going to do it. We really did. The boss had predicted as much in October 2005, before our group away match at Sparta Prague, saying Arsenal *will* win the Champions League. Even I raised my eyebrows at that one. I mean, by then, we'd gone down 2–1 to both West Brom and Middlesbrough and drawn at home with West Ham. I could hardly see Real Madrid or Juventus quaking in their boots. It's as the boss would later say, everyone thought he was crazy. Me included. But maybe we were going to mirror Liverpool's 2004–05 season: inconsistent away from home, but worthy champions of Europe?

I'd missed most of the campaign through injury, but desperately wanted to be back for the first big fixture: Arsenal versus Real Madrid – nine-time winners of the competition. We'd drawn them in the first knock-out stage, having won our qualifying group, and I was desperate to be sharp again to come up against the likes of Ronaldo, Robinho, Zidane and, of course, my England team-mate David Beckham. My mind was fixed on at least travelling to the Bernabeu Stadium on 21 February 2006 for the first-leg, and the thigh was feeling good. No English side had ever gone to Madrid and won, so it was one hell of a game to be involved with. I'd been buzzing on the training ground and certainly felt worthy of a place on the bench if nothing else.

Then, one week before the game, the boss pulled me to one side. I wouldn't be going to Madrid. Instead, he'd picked me for the reserves against Barnet at the training ground. My heart sank. From the cathedral of the Bernabeu to barren London Colney; from a capacity crowd of 80,000 to about one hundred die-hard spectators. The contrasts were grim. I couldn't help but feel gutted, but I understood – the boss didn't want to rush me back like he'd done in the league against Middlesbrough. We'd both learned from that mistake, so his decision made sense, even if it was tough to swallow. There was always the return leg at Highbury to focus on. So I played at unglamorous Barnet in the day and went round to Mum's that evening to watch the Real Madrid match on television. I remember the words of ITV commentator Peter Drury that night: 'Arsenal *are* swaggering!' and they were.

It was to become the best result in the club's European history, as Thierry slotted home the only goal to secure a 1–0 victory. Arsenal were slick and attacking, but also well organised, which you have to be in Europe, and we cut through Real Madrid as if they were West Brom in disguise. We outplayed, outran and outfought them. Jens Lehmann denied Beckham twice and a young Arsenal side seemed to brush aside an ageing, less athletic Real Madrid. 1–0 to the Arsenal in the Bernabeu was a brilliant result and I ached at not being a part of it; reduced to being an armchair spectator back home. But everyone knew there was a second leg and that Real Madrid were capable of coming back at us, so the match on 8 March was going to be massive and it became my new focus. If I came through the next reserve match against Tottenham, played at Barnet's Underhill ground, I'd have a good chance of being in the team.

But as I've already said, it only took seven minutes of that reserve match to dash my hopes.

That's when I was crocked in a tackle and was subsequently back on crutches with a badly sprained ankle. 'ASHLEY'S NEW BLOW' reported the *Evening Standard* the next day, and I could have cried with frustration. It was then that I started to worry about whether I'd make the World Cup, let alone another match in Europe. So I found myself hobbling to Highbury for the Real Madrid second leg, one among 35,487 other fans, and we witnessed the most pulsating and exciting of 0–0 draws. It was typical of our journey on the road to Paris – we didn't half ride our luck at times. Without the heroics of Jens Lehmann, I think we'd have crashed out, but he kept us in it, and his defiance summed up the team's performance as we went through to the quarter-finals, 1–0 on aggregate. He fully deserved the next day headlines: 'JENIUS' and 'UNBEATABLE'.

Whatever Real Madrid threw at us, he had an answer for. For me, he was not just the man of the match, but our man of the 2006 Champions League campaign. In a week when Liverpool and Chelsea were dumped out of the competition, we became the last men standing for England and that fact alone made the club swell with pride after an unforgettable night of football. I can't remember a night of such tension and excitement at Highbury.

After the game, I saw Becks wandering around, and he was still catching his breath. He shrugged his shoulders as if to say 'What more could we have done?' We had a little chat and there was a funny moment when we spoke about our different positions. I looked around at his team and said to him, 'You know what, I'd love to be over there with you!' – my eyes were still fixed on a future in Europe.

As quick as a flash, he grinned and said, 'You know what, I'd love to be over here with you!' and we both fell about laughing. It was light-hearted banter that ended a superb night, but the truth was that none of us at Arsenal would have swapped places with any of the Galacticos. We were in the quarter-finals. And our dream run got better and better even though I remained sidelined through injury. We beat Juventus 2–0 on aggregate and then Villarreal 1–0 on aggregate to reach the final against Barcelona. The boss's belief in the team had come off. We'd also set a new Champions League record by keeping ten clean sheets on the trot, a run that stretched back to that Sparta Prague first-leg away match. In fact, we'd only conceded two goals in the entire competition: one at home to FC Thun, one away at Ajax in the group matches. Come the final, I was back from injury, with three league matches under my belt, ready to take on the champions of La Liga, the conquerors of Chelsea.

Arsenal versus Barcelona almost seemed to dwarf Arsenal versus Real Madrid. Mainly because Barcelona are considered to be the best team in Europe.

My England team-mates had, that same week, travelled to Portugal for a pre-World Cup get-together with their families but the likes of me and Sol Campbell couldn't afford to look ahead to Germany. Not then. We were focused on Paris, and it was a medal we both desperately wanted. I'd said an emotional farewell to Highbury. I now wanted to say goodbye to Arsenal with a Champions League-winning medal clutched to my chest. Because, as I travelled to Paris with the team, I *knew* in my heart of hearts that this was going to be my last match for the Gunners. Win or lose, this was it. Not that I knew which club I'd be joining at that time, but the departure was inevitable, even if the destination was unknown.

If I'm honest, I couldn't believe we'd reached the final with the team we'd got. On paper, and on league form, no-one would have backed us. It's odd that when we were at our worst, we got through to the final, but when we were at our unbeatable best, we couldn't get beyond the quarter-finals.

I'd been buzzing from the moment the boss had picked me ahead of Gael Clichy and Mathieu Flamini. As soon as we turned up at the team hotel in Paris, the butterflies started. I looked out of my room and saw the Eiffel Tower in the distance, and the sense of occasion hit me. Time to take deep breaths.

I rang Cheryl and described it all: the sights and the nerves. She was manic doing rehearsals for the Girls Aloud 'Chemistry' tour of the UK, but I had to ring and share the moment with her. She knew how nervous I'd be, she knew how low I'd been with all the injuries and she knew this was one of the biggest games of my career. It's funny how a few words with Cheryl can put me at ease when the jitters start.

Normally, I'd ring her from the team coach en route to the match, but I'd told her I wouldn't be ringing her because I needed to put the mental blinkers on. She understands where I'm coming from on that score more than anyone. Before her gig in Manchester later that same month, she knew I'd be among the 17,000 people at the MEN Arena, but didn't want to see me back-stage or speak to me beforehand because that would have made her more nervous and she don't need that distraction. Sometimes, be it a Champions League final or a UK tour, it's enough to know that other person is rooting for you and cheering you on. And Cheryl has cheered me on since the moment we met. I knew she'd be watching the final on a television somewhere, screaming as loud as my mum, and she'd text me – like she always does – at the end of the match.

Come the big day, Wednesday 17 May, I couldn't have felt better. We might have been the underdogs, but the boss reminded us that we'd earned our place in the final. In the team hotel, he'd had one of his inspirational moments and it was quite funny really. He'd gathered us all together to watch one of his psychology videos. The lights went down, the boss stepped back and we were suddenly watching a formation of geese flying through the air. When one of the geese got tired it dropped back and another moved up front, but they always moved in formation. It was all about sticking together and working as a team. But there was one point when all the geese started quacking (if that is what geese do) to each other; it's how they communicate to slow down or speed up. How we laughed. Because all the lads started honking and quacking and asking the boss if this is how we should talk to each other in the final! It even raised a wry smile from him.

Then it was time to set off for the stadium. In the dressing room, the boss had one final pep talk. Using golf speak, he urged us to follow through as a team. He's clever the boss, creating an image to get a point across. He told us to think of a golf swing and how a golfer concentrated on following through to strike the ball.

'You must do the same with this match – follow through!' he told us. 'If you stop halfway, you lose.'

He felt we didn't follow through in the semi-final, second-leg away match against Villarreal, which we drew 0–0 to secure 1–0 on aggregate. 'We won, but we didn't come out and attack and we played within ourselves. You must now go out there and follow through all your hard work of this season. Follow through and attack. Follow it through and you win,' he said.

After that pep talk, we were all soaring. Once again, some quietly delivered words of wisdom had injected further belief into us. You only have to watch the opening minutes of the game and see how we tore after the ball and attacked Barcelona to notice the effect his words had on us.

The tunnel at the Stade de France is as wide as an avenue and both teams lined up side by side for the 50th European final of champions. Beneath my studs, weaved into the blue carpet, were the words 'Finale 2006 Paris – 50 Years of Champions'. I kept focused, staring straight ahead as we trotted out onto the pitch in front of 75,000 fans. I remember the deafening noise and the constant flashbulbs going off in the crowd; flickering white flashes from every part of the stadium. We lined up, and they played the Champions League theme tune – Handel's coronation anthem, 'Zadok the Priest'. Its stirring sound drifted in and out of ear-shot, because my focus blanked it out. In big games like that, I concentrate so much that I block everything else out, picturing the game in my mind, keeping in my head the image of the player I've got to mark. That night, I had to mark one of the quickest in the game – Ludovic Giuly. Jesus, that man is quick! He's so hard to mark because he just hovers on the touchline. As a defender, that's hard to deal with because you've still got to cover your centre-back; one long ball from their left to right can potentially kill me. I'd studied his game and knew I'd have my hands full. As it turned out, I thought I did good because every time he tried to run me, I got in a tackle and restricted him to a couple of long shots from outside the box.

Ronaldinho was someone else I was going to make sure didn't get one over me, like he had in the 2002 World Cup, when England lost to Brazil in the quarter-finals. It's an embarrassing memory that one. We were 1–0 up when he got the ball 25 yards out, ran at me down the centre of the pitch, did a step-over which caught me off balance and I almost fell over. That allowed him to go inside and pass to Rivaldo on the right, who slotted it past Seaman. Going into the Champions League final four years later, all my friends were saying, 'Don't get too tight, don't let him do that to you again!' A player might do a trick on me once if I'm not ready for it, but he'll never get away with it a second time. Ever. And against Barcelona, Ronaldinho didn't get one over on me. Eboue, who had the task of marking him, did an excellent job and had a great game. Tactically, I thought Barcelona got it wrong in the first half, putting Ronaldinho up front and Eto'o on the left, because Eto'o is strongest up front, holding people off, turning and shooting on goal. It was only when they finally swapped it around that Barcelona suddenly started putting pressure on ten-man Arsenal.

We'd gone down to ten men after 18 minutes, in a drama that weren't part of the dream plan. In what became the talking point of the match, our keeper Jens Lehmann walked after bringing down Samuel Eto'o just outside the box. As Eto'o tumbled, the ball rolled on into the path of Giuly, who slotted it home, and the Barcelona fans went crazy, thinking they'd gone 1–0 up. But it wasn't going to count because the ref, Terje Hauge, who had a stinker, had already blown for a free kick.

The moment he blew, he knew he'd done wrong. I looked at him and saw him cursing himself. 'Sheeeet!'

Had he waited just a couple more seconds and not been so whistle-happy, advantage could have been played, the goal would have stood, Jens could have got a yellow not a red and we'd have had an evenly fought final of 11 versus 11 for the next 72 minutes. Instead, the ref buckled and sent Jens off, egged on by the Barcelona players who surrounded him, sticking their hands in the air, screaming, 'Red card! Red card!' Jens won't forgive the Barcelona players for that. When the red card was held above the melee, I felt for our man. He'd been unbelievable all season and, for me, his performances against Real Madrid, Juventus and Villarreal were the very reason we were in the final. His face when he realised he was being sent off said it all: he was broken. The face that is normally twisted with passion or rage was suddenly empty of all emotion. He couldn't believe what was happening. It weren't even his fault. He'd gone to get the ball, Eto'o had nicked it round him and he'd been beaten for pace. As it was, Barcelona failed to score from the resulting free kick so it remained 0–0. But we had to sacrifice Pires to make way for our replacement keeper Manuel Almunia and it was definitely 'advantage Barcelona' from that moment on.

We'd have probably chosen 1–0 down with 11 men still on the pitch than 0–0 with ten men and Jens and Pires off the pitch, especially because we'd started so brightly and surprised Barcelona with how quick we came out of the starting gate.

But we ten men dug in and kept battling on with a team spirit that defied the odds, and defied much of the previous season. Then the imbalance tilted back in our favour. Eboue won a free kick down the right, Thierry whipped in a cross and Sol rose as if he had springs on his feet to power home a header and take us into a 37th-minute lead. From where I was stood, near the halfway line, all I saw was Sol jump and then the net bulged. Me and Eboue roared in celebration as Sol was mobbed by the other lads. What a moment that was, and what a moment for Sol.

He'd been through some heavy shit all season, both personally and professionally, and you've got to admire the way he bounced back to show Sven-Goran Eriksson that he was back in business just before Germany 2006. That night, he was our best player on the pitch.

With us 1–0 up, Barcelona switched Ronaldinho and Eto'o and stepped it up a gear. Eto'o almost had an immediate impact, crashing the ball against the post, aided by the fingertips of Manu. They were coming at us, but nothing seemed to be going right for them. They'd had a decent goal disallowed, we'd taken the lead despite being down to ten men and they'd just hit the post. Maybe – just maybe – it was going to be our night. Luck seemed to be on our side, even if the ref weren't. Mind you, half-time couldn't have come quick enough, because Barcelona were coming at us with wave after wave of attacks. I remember feeling relief when the half-time whistle went.

In the dressing room, we found a disconsolate Jens waiting for us. Who knows how much self-berating he'd done in his own company, but the moment we all walked through the door, he wasn't having any pity.

It's a mark of the man that he got up, went round to each player, apologised and then rallied us.'Come on, you can win this!' he said.'You can win this!' The fire and passion were back in his face.

The boss was calm and assured, geeing up each player along with Pat Rice. All he said was that we needed Thierry to stay up more, because we were getting the ball at the back, but there was no-one up front to feed.

The captain had been back helping us defend, making up for the lost man. He was everywhere that night, running his socks off. But the boss felt that if he stayed up, we'd get the ball over the top and he'd be through.

In the second half, having continued to keep Barcelona at bay, it almost went to plan. With about 20 minutes to go, we sent the ball over the top, Thierry found himself one-on-one with the keeper and half the Arsenal fans were rushing to put their mortgages on him to score. Had he done so, it would have been game over, but he fired straight at Valdes. I think Thierry's legs were knackered from being up and down, up and down all game. But his chance gave us renewed hope as Barcelona piled on the pressure without penetrating us. They seemed to be getting more desperate and frustrated as me, Kolo and Sol flew in with the blocks and the tackles, keeping them out. In one break of play, I looked across to the dug-out and saw the boss stood in his sky-blue shirt in the technical area, getting drenched in a rain that had turned from drizzle to downpour. He was pacing and as restless as ever. He knew how close we were. I remember looking up at the stadium clock. It had just counted down into the 75th minute.

'We're going to win this . . . we're going to win this,' I told myself. I was feeling tired and I'm sure Sol's legs were as heavy as mine, but that whiff of victory was like potent smelling salts.

'COME ON!' I bellowed in the rain.

The Arsenal fans gave incredible support that night, all through the game. They were way better than the Barcelona support and were getting behind us big time. The atmosphere was just unbelievable.

Then, the game turned on its head.

Barcelona's pressure and two substitutions – Larsson on to support Eto'o and the nippy Belletti on for Oleguer at right-back – eventually told and Eto'o got the break they needed. In my view, he was definitely off-side; that was the injustice. I looked across the line, saw he was off-side and my arm went up, but when I looked across to the linesman his flag was down. I've learned my lesson not to hammer linesmen because you'll only ever get a yellow card for your trouble. From where I stood it was one of countless poor decisions that night and all I could do was pick the ball out of the net. That was the 76th minute and we knew we'd be under immense pressure from that moment on. Now, their extra man was going to tell.

It took four minutes for them to score the second. Belletti steamed into the box to collect a through-ball from Larsson and he powered in a shot that ricocheted off our keeper's legs. It was a cruel deflection on a cruel night of football. There was nothing left in our engine after that. We'd run ourselves ragged, but fatigue had grabbed our ankles, and those last ten minutes felt like a last period of extra-time. When that whistle blew, it was one of the worst feelings I've experienced in football. Fifteen minutes from winning.

That's all I kept telling myself. Fifteen minutes from winning. It's hard to keep your shoulders back and your head high after a sucker punch like that. Drenched and deflated, I stood there, trying to take it all in as the Spanish party started around us. To my right, there was a dancing scrum of blue and maroon shirts, getting bigger and bigger as Barcelona subs and staff raced to pile into the melee of celebration.

We felt cheated. Not because Jens had been sent off; we felt it because to us the ref's performance throughout the whole match weren't even-handed. He'd been yellow-card shy with Barcelona all match. Eboue did one tackle and got an instant yellow. But van Bommel did about five fouls, Oleguer ten and Marquez was booting and treading on Thierry from start to finish. And only Oleguer got booked when he reached double figures. Van Bommel and Marquez got away with murder. Then, when Thierry made a crunch tackle from the side and *won the ball*, he got an instant yellow. You can't have zero tolerance for one side and lenient second chances for the other. Maybe the ref was trying to make up for the fact that he'd robbed them of a decent goal? Soft on them, tough on us?

Thierry spoke for us all afterwards when he said, 'It was hard enough without the ref helping them . . . he should have worn a Barcelona shirt.' I've never seen him so animated and angry.

The killer was going up to collect the silver runners-up medals from the podium in the middle of the pitch, earning sympathy as the also-rans, instead of bathing in the jubilation of champions. As I traipsed up to collect my medal, Thierry saw my head was down.

'Ash! Put your head up, man! You've done really, really well. Be proud. We didn't lose to Barcelona, we lost to the ref!' he shouted, and he didn't care if the official heard him.

The worst bit was walking past the Champions League trophy, knowing it wasn't ours to hold. I couldn't even look at it. There was a picture in the papers the next day that captured the pain of that moment. It showed the gleaming trophy in sharp focus and me covering up my eyes with one hand as I walked past it. The caption read: 'Cole can't look at the trophy'.

Then I went to swap shirts with Ronaldinho. If I weren't going to come away with a champion's medal, I was going to come away with a champion's shirt.

We all went over to the Arsenal support, clapping them as they clapped us. What they couldn't have known, because the boss didn't even know at that point, was that I was saying a quiet goodbye. Nine years at the club had ended with the Champions League final in Paris. The shy boy from FC Puma with an Arsenal dream would probably have settled for that, to be honest. I stood, looking up at the fans in the tiers, taking it all in, looking at that mass of red and white and thinking, 'I'll always be an Arsenal fan, even if I'm not an Arsenal player.' I raised my hands above my head and applauded them one last time and then turned on my heels as the emotion of the night – the nerves, the defeat, the occasion, the goodbye, the fact Mum was watching all this – caught in my throat.

In the dressing room afterwards, there was silence. I took off my boots and rain-soaked shirt and sat there, leaning forward with my head in my hands. Kolo and Sol said nothing either side of me.

A thousand thoughts must have been racing through Thierry's

mind as he sat there, shaking his head. I looked across to Gilberto and he was absolutely gutted. Then Thierry did his best to dispel the air of gloom. Like a true leader, he didn't want us to forget we had reached the final, and matched Barcelona with ten men.

'Come on, lads,' he said. 'Keep your heads up. We didn't deserve to lose like that and you've done the club proud.'

We left Paris firmly believing that we were as good as the champions on the night, but it had happened and we had to accept defeat. Selfishly, I didn't dwell on the post-mortem; way too many Arsenal memories were overwhelming me at the time. Not that I had much time for sentimental nostalgia either.

I had a World Cup to concentrate on. Germany 2006 was 22 days away.

Speculation was the story of the season for me and Thierry and the media had already got our passports stamped in Spain. It was done and dusted, apparently – we were both leaving Highbury for Europe.

'WE ARE SCARED HENRY WILL GO – **Wenger fears Barca move**' said the *Daily Mirror* in October 2005. '**COLE'S £8M REAL DEAL**' said the *Sunday Mirror* one month later. Then the *Daily Express* piled in with '**REAL DEAL DONE – Cole agrees summer transfer to Madrid**' in February 2006. Other newspapers threw in Juventus and AC Milan as other clubs we were off to. The irony wasn't lost on me. My very defence at the tapping-up inquiry, the defence no-one had believed – that my eyes were fixed on Europe not Chelsea – was now being given credibility. But it got to the stage where every question at every press conference focused on whether we'd be staying or going.

It went something like this. Reporter: 'So what about your future at Arsenal, Ashley? Are you staying?'

Stock, non-committal answer: 'I've not even thought about it, to be honest.'

Next day headline: 'COLE STAYING AT ARSENAL'.

I reckon that even if I'd have farted and said nothing, reporters would have taken it as a firm quote about my future. Sadly, it was only reporters who ever asked whether I was staying. No-one at the club thought to ask the same question.

By the time we'd reached the final in Paris, my patience with the endless media speculation was wafer-thin as we did the usual pre-match interviews, sat at a table surrounded by reporters, their tape recorders whirring in front of me. I wanted to talk about the final. They wanted to talk about my future.

'Look,' I said, 'I don't want to talk about this anymore. I'm bored with it. What do you want me to say? What do you *expect* me to say? I can't be bothered no more. We just keep going round in circles and I don't see the point in answering the same questions week after week.' Not that it stopped them. But I think that was my frustration speaking, the frustration of not knowing where I stood with the club, at the stalemate no-one seemed bothered enough to break. Or maybe the boss and vice-chairman just took it for granted that I'd be staying and concentrated all their time, energy and efforts on wooing and keeping Thierry, thinking that if he stayed, then I'd stay?

We ran out at the Stade de France with observers debating an uncertain future for us both. The *Mirror*'s back-page headline was 'THE PRIZE' and it showed a picture of Thierry, half in a Barcelona shirt, half in an Arsenal shirt, suggesting the ultimate prize for winning the final was his signature. Truth be told, I think Thierry had made up his mind to stay before the final. Fourth place in the league and another season of European football was already in the bag and the club's ambitions and vision for the future matched his. But let's face it, if Arsenal hadn't secured that fourth place, Thierry wouldn't be there, no matter how much he loves the club or the fans. Anyone who thinks otherwise is kidding themselves. A 4–2 victory against Wigan and West Ham's 2–1 defeat of Spurs kept Thierry at Arsenal. He stayed for the

Champions League football which fourth place had earned the club.

Two days after Paris, word leaked out that Thierry had agreed a new four-year deal. 'HENRY TO STAY' announced the back page of the *Daily Mail*. 'STAYING – Thierry answers Arsenal's prayers' added the *Daily Mirror*. I bought the *Mirror* and read how Thierry was described as 'the loyal Gunner'. Then my eyes went down the page and spotted a smaller article, only about eight paragraphs long, with my photo and this headline: '**Cole offered a new deal**'. It reported: 'Arsenal have made Ashley Cole a last-ditch £80,000-a-week contract offer that would make him the second-highest paid player at the club behind Thierry Henry. Arsenal are now making a final attempt to make peace with a player who seems never to have forgiven the club in the wake of the Chelsea tapping-up scandal . . .'

My blood boiled. Someone had planted a misleading story on the back of the Thierry announcement, making the club look like it was pulling out the stops to keep players like me, so that fans would read it and say, 'Look what they've offered Cole – he's got to stay now.' And if I didn't, I'd be greedy, rejecting the club and £80,000 a week. Make Arsenal look good, make Ashley look like the bad guy.

No-one had mentioned a word about a new deal, nothing had been put before me or my agent and no-one had bothered to set a date to discuss futures. I was furious over a lie that reflected well on Arsenal 'as the Gunners try to hold on to one of their prize assets'. The truth is that I felt the Gunners had done jack-shit all season to hold on to me.

I got on the phone to the club press office. 'Can you please tell me why this is in the paper, because they've not offered me no new contract, no nothing?'

They seemed as much in the dark as me, but rang the *Mirror* reporter John Cross to find out more. He apparently said the information had come from someone inside the club. Now if that's correct, then to me that article was deliberately designed to put pressure on me and cast Arsenal in a good light. My complaint probably never even registered in the scheme of things, because, the next day, Arsenal, the boss and Mr Dein were parading Thierry around the Emirates Stadium where he was to lead out the lads for the new 2006–07 season. Mr Dein made noises about 'the words that won Thierry' when he'd said to him, 'Here you are king. In Spain, you may only be prince.'

How I'd have loved it if Thierry had replied, 'Well, it's about time you started buying players fit for a king then!'

Because the truth is that Thierry is a winner and he deserves, and expects, to be playing in a side that doesn't finish 24 points behind Chelsea in the league, that doesn't battle with Spurs to scrape fourth place, that *will* win the Champions League next time around and that has a board that will put its money where his ambition is, that will invest in a team as well as a stadium. Arsenal might not have the budgets of Manchester United and Chelsea, but that handicap didn't stop Arsene building an unbeatable team that dominated the Premiership. If there is to be a new, exciting era at Ashburton Grove, the boss needs the finances to build another great team. Experience and proven talent must now be mixed with the 'young guns' of the future.

I was dead pleased for him when his deal was announced. I sent him a text message as soon as it was official. It read: 'Congrats on signing, hope all goes well for the future.'

He texted back almost immediately. 'Man, it's your turn next. I need you here with me!'

My mind flashed back to our conversation on the podium at Highbury and it did pull on me that someone of Thierry's calibre was saying that he wanted me to stay, that he saw me as part of his vision. I'm not going to lie, that was flattering. My problem was never with him, other players or the fans. It ran much deeper than that. It's like Thierry said when he justified his decision to stay: the fans wrongly think the game is all about money, money, money when it is actually about 'real love and real emotion'. And this is where there was a massive difference between his relationship with the club and mine.

For him, that real love and real emotion is still as strong as it ever was – his adulation grows and grows and he found that love impossible to walk away from. For me, the real love and real emotion came to an end when Arsenal went back on all that stuff discussed with David Dein and then let me be dragged through an inquiry. Also, the club made Thierry feel wanted and special, wooing him, wining and dining him, speaking in public about how much they want him to stay, going on a deliberate charm offensive to win their man. But me? I didn't have one dinner, one meeting or one phone call from anyone. No-one took time out to discuss the club's ambition and vision with me. That's not sour grapes, it's just a sad truth. All I had was the boss's reminder, ahead of the Villarreal semi-final, that I could leave at the end of the season, and a coach who asked whether I was feigning injury. It's no wonder my real love and real emotion for Arsenal was soured by what I see as neglect and resentment. I loved the club as much as Thierry, if not more so because I'm a Gunner born and bred. But if a club isn't treating me right then I'll leave, like most players. So when people asked me, as they did, about whether Thierry's decision made me think about staying, I'd reply, 'No, it didn't. Not for a second.' Because, for me, the love weren't there no more. More importantly, after the Thierry deal had been sorted, Arsenal still didn't approach me. The silence was telling and it led to an inevitable final act.

On 24 May 2006, while I was away with the England team preparing for a pre-World Cup warm-up game against Belarus at Reading, my agent Jonathan Barnett called a meeting at his offices with Mr Dein. And that was the moment when the vice-chairman was told about my wishes.

'Ashley wants to leave Arsenal,' said Jonathan.

My impatience and frustration was put across in Jonathan's usual robust way. He'd told Mr Dein, 'Ashley loves Arsenal to madness. Arsenal is his club and he is an Arsenal fan, and yet here I am telling you that he wants to leave and you've not got a clue why because you've not even had a conversation with him all season.'

He then added, 'And I suggest that, before you start blaming the agent for all this, maybe even now, at this late stage, you may want to speak with Ashley personally.'

Mr Dein apparently held his hands in the air and said, 'Point taken.'

Two days later, after an England B side had lost 2–1 to Belarus in an experimental match, I found myself sat at London Colney with the boss and he asked me, 'I hear you want to tell me something?'

I didn't think I'd be nervous meeting the boss until I was sat opposite him in his office. I'd played out the speech in my head a dozen times and thought it would be easy, but it was way harder than I'd imagined.

I've enormous respect for him as a person and a manager and I've so much to thank him for. I wished I could turn back time as this voice in my head kept asking, 'How the hell did it get to this?!'

I'd called the meeting because I wanted to speak to him face–to–face. He deserved an explanation even if the board didn't. It was a difficult but honest meeting. I never thought I'd be sat with Arsene Wenger telling him I wanted to leave Arsenal. He said that the new stadium had put a lot of pressure on the wage structure, but then he spoke the words I'd waited 18 months to hear, the words of someone who was taking responsibility.

'Ashley,' he said, 'both sides could have been accused of being petty, but maybe the club should have handled your situation better and I'm sorry it ever reached this stage.'

'Boss, it shouldn't be you telling me that. It's not because of you that I'm leaving!' I replied.

He then told me he didn't want to see me go, that he wanted me to stay. 'It will be sad to watch you in the World Cup knowing that you are not coming back to us next season,' he said. Jesus, the more he spoke, the harder it became.

I was choking up, because he was thanking me and telling me I was a winner and I was thanking him for everything he'd done for me. Then the rehearsed speech kicked in: 'Look, boss, I'd like to keep playing for you. I just can't see myself playing for this club – they've ruined it for me. Thanks to the board, my own fans still hammer me. I don't want to be at a club where I get booed, where everyone thinks I'm greedy, where everyone doubts my loyalty. I want to play football and enjoy my football and I've become miserable here and that's so hard for me to accept because I love this place. I've not even made up my mind where I'm going to go, but I know, in my heart of hearts, that I can't keep playing for Arsenal.'

He listened like no-one had listened since February 2005 and he took in every single word.

Both sides reached a reluctant understanding. He saw how upset I was becoming. 'It's hard, Ashley – it's like a divorce, I suppose,' he said. Just like with his team talks, the boss found the right words to sum it all up.

Then it was the turn for his speech. 'Look, I've heard from players before that they want to leave. But I will leave the door open for you in case you change your mind. In the meantime, thank you for what you have done at this club, thank you from the team, thank you from the fans and thank you from me. You've achieved a lot, you've won a lot and you should feel proud of your contribution.'

I couldn't speak when he said that. I nodded, we stood, we shook hands and he wished me luck.

I got in the car and felt absolutely gutted. Before turning the keys in the engine, I texted Cheryl. 'I've done it. I didn't know it was going to be this hard, babe.'

Cheryl knows that I'm a softie who doesn't like arguments or confrontation. On the pitch, I'm different and always up for a battle, but not away from it, and she knew how much I'd thought about that meeting with the boss. She'd listened to the speech enough times as well!

'I'm proud of you, Ashley,' she texted back. 'Time for new beginnings, babe.'

I'm going to need a thick skin on the day I return to the Emirates Stadium in colours other than an Arsenal shirt. I'm just glad I won't have to run out as the opposition at Highbury. That would have been way too weird. At Ashburton Grove, I won't know what it's like to be in the home dressing room and, as tough as it will be, at least there are no memories for me there.

Anyhow, nothing can ever be as bad as the abuse I received in Spain on 18 November 2004. That evening was my worst experience in football and Europe, and it came not with Arsenal but with England.

We were playing an international friendly against Spain in the Bernabeu and the entire stadium became this cauldron of racial hatred, with taunts and monkey noises hurled at me, Jermaine Jenas, Shaun Wright-Phillips and Jermain Defoe every time we touched the ball. It was as if the entire stadium was spitting its bile at us. As a professional, you've got to rise above it, play on and shrug it off, but I remember going into the dressing room at half-time and seeing how shocked everyone was. No-one more so than Becks – this was his home stadium with Real Madrid.

'I can't believe it. I can't believe it,' he kept saying, shaking his head. 'I've never heard it like this before.'

He was keen to point out to us that it wasn't Real Madrid fans. This was supporters from all over Spain. Not that it made it any easier to understand, because it weren't how I remembered Spanish people. Every time I'd been to Spain, and I'd had many holidays in Tenerife,

Marbella, Benidorm and Majorca as a kid, I'd only ever found them to be kind, courteous and friendly. I think that's why that night in the Bernabeu shocked me so much.

The Spanish manager, Luis Aragones, had lit the touch-paper a week earlier, making an abusive comment to Reyes about the skin colour of our Arsenal team-mate Thierry. When you've got an idiot like that leading his nation by example, then the racist venom directed at us is understandable, if not acceptable. Idiots follow idiots like sheep. It weren't nice being in that intimidating atmosphere; it was the worst abuse I've ever heard, because it was the whole stadium. No exaggeration, *the whole stadium*. As soon as I got the ball, the deafening abuse started and I remember feeling more and more sickened as the game went on. It didn't help that we didn't play well and lost 1–0. That added to our frustration and anger and at one point during the game, I almost came to blows with the Spanish manager responsible for whipping up the hatred. He'd picked up the ball after it had been kicked into touch near his dug-out. As I went to take back the ball, the whistling and monkey noises cranked up again, he came over to me, put the ball to my chest and shoved me away; the old man playing the hard man in front of the crowd.

'You ignorant pig!' I yelled. Or words to that effect.

He shouted something back, but the abuse from the crowd was so loud that I couldn't hear what he'd said. I just remember seeing red. I went right back at him. I wanted to knock him out. I found myself being pulled away by Bridge and Becks, as a linesman rushed in to get between us. And it was a good job they did because I was ready to lamp him. I almost lost it. I think we all lost our heads that night, and we struggled on many fronts. But I now know that whatever is thrown at me in terms of abuse from rival fans, nothing can ever be as bad as that night in Madrid.

At the end of the match, we couldn't wait to get in the tunnel, get changed and get the hell out of there. I remember walking off the pitch and Becks came over and put his arm around me and asked if I was alright.

'Jesus Christ, what is all that about!?' I said to him. It takes a lot to shock me, but that was unbelievable. I felt for Becks, because he had no explanation and he seemed embarrassed that his England team-mates had faced such shit at his home ground. My Arsenal team-mate Jose Reyes was so depressed about it afterwards. If Becks felt embarrassed, Reyes felt ashamed. We talked about it and he was worried what the outside world would think of Spain. The irony was that, before kick-off, both teams had unfurled an anti-racism banner as a united message. Sadly, it counted for nothing.

It is the ugly side of football that we must all stamp out. To be honest, it happens in a lot of foreign countries, even if it's rarely as rabid as the night in Madrid. In Slovakia, when England went to Bratislava for a Euro 2004 qualifier in October 2002, the stretcher-bearer came right up to my face and did a monkey impression as I went to take a throw-in. I've also faced it in Macedonia and Holland.

I don't get that mentality. Why do people have hang-ups about colour? I've a white mum and a black dad and I can't see the difference. In my mind, I was a black kid who grew up in a white family. I'm English. I'm an east Londoner. We're all human and we all have emotions, yet grown men and women are jumping up and down in football stadiums mimicking monkeys. Do they sit back afterwards and think they've made an intelligent point? I'm no stranger to it, because I grew up with it. I've faced it all: 'black bastard', 'you nigger'. But that was from kids who didn't know any better. I almost wonder if that's what the racist football fan is: mentally just a little kid, doing something and saying something just because everyone else is. In my opinion, we should ban every fan who makes a racist comment and every manager like Luis Aragones who stirs racial hatred like he did. FIFA should start getting tough on the European scene, as the FA has done in England, because Spain has a problem with racism at its grounds. The sooner it comes out of denial and starts doing something about it, the better. Then, like England, it can start to actually celebrate players who happen to be black, happen to come from Africa and happen to be blessed with an outstanding footballing talent. Like Eto'o. Like Patrick Vieira. Like Thierry Henry. Like Ronaldinho. When places like Spain can cheer, instead of jeer, such talent and concentrate on the feet, not the skin colour, then it will have matured as a nation and kicked racism out of football.

In my time at Arsenal, the road to Europe will be remembered for its frustrations, dead-ends and early exits, as well as memorable nights in the Stade de France. There were many brilliant nights in Europe and if the Emirates Stadium – a ground fit to house European champions – can capture half the memories that filled Highbury, then it will be an arena packed with excitement for years to come.

Not that Bayern Munich on 22 February 2005 was a fond memory. That first knock-out match, after we'd finished top of qualifying Group E, is remembered for me being ill, for us losing our bottle and losing 3–1 and for coming three weeks after my tapping-up scandal was exposed in the *News of the World*. February 2005 weren't the best of days of my life at Arsenal.

For two weeks before the match, I'd been laid up in bed with knock-out flu. The boss had taken one look at me and told me to go home and rest. I was on the mend when he selected me as a substitute for the fixture at the Olympiastadion in Munich. It was a bitterly cold night; a cold that brought on shivers that reminded me of the flu I'd just beaten. From the bench, I watched helplessly as we gifted them a goal with some bad defensive play and it went downhill from that moment. They scored again in the 58th and 65th minutes. Kolo Toure snatched one back for us in the 88th minute, but we went down 3–1. The boss described it as 'our worst performance in the Champions League'.

It meant that we needed to win the return leg at Highbury 2–0 to go through on the away goals rule. We gave everything that night, but, again, it wasn't happening. We won 1–0, but were shy of pressing forward for that crucial second goal. No wonder people called us 'bottlers' at times. We could dominate the Premiership, but seemed to have a crisis of confidence in Europe. We seemed scared, almost inhibited. We were strong in the qualifying group, but somehow unable to progress through the knock-out stages. Thankfully, all that changed in 2006, and I think we learned lessons from being too timid and defensive. Maybe Arsenal has cracked the code now and removed the psychological barriers by making it to the final. The Stade de France provided a platform for a new future in the Champions League.

The most disastrous start to a Champions League game actually led to one of our most inspired runs in the competition.

We'd gone down 3–0 at home to Inter Milan on 17 September 2003 in our qualifying group, leaving us rock-bottom in the table behind Inter, Dynamo Kiev and FC Lokomotiv. We'd been embarrassed by Inter in front of our own fans, who booed us off at half-time. It was our worst-ever home defeat in the Champions League and left us needing to win our remaining three games to stand a chance of qualifying. But if ever there was a time when Arsenal proved they had huge hearts, immense courage and a spirit few clubs could match, then this was it.

Inter were giving it to us big style after that Highbury result, saying we were rubbish and nothing special.

They'd tried to hammer me, saying the left side was our weakest link. I love the challenge of proving people wrong. Whether it's Arsenal letting me go on loan to Palace, or the Arsenal fans doubting my loyalty, or Mr Dein thinking my performance is affected by one meeting in a London hotel, I thrive on the pressure of others' doubt. I love going out to prove a point. And we had a massive score to settle in the San Siro. It was to become one of the greatest nights of football in my career to date. We swept Inter aside with some brilliant football and did what they had done to us: humiliated them in their own back garden.

Thierry was lit that night, scoring twice in a 5–1 rout, and I set up two of them as we handed Inter their worst home defeat in 47 years. That was sweet! It was even sweeter than being part of the 5–1 crushing of Germany in Munich with England in 2001. There are some results in football that go beyond dream status, results that leave even the players disbelieving the truth, and both Inter Milan and Germany took me into Neverland.

But, for me, the biggest buzz was the Inter result because we were already 3–0 down and beaten in so many people's eyes. It was a colossal team performance. That was a special night in an Arsenal shirt and I'll never forget it.

The one goal I'll always remember was the one I scored that kept our European campaign alive: a diving header in the 88th minute to beat Dynamo Kiev 1–0 at home in the group match before that night at the San Siro.

With the clock ticking down – and a 0–0 result looking like it was going to turf us out of the competition – Dennis got the ball. Their right-back was nowhere, I saw a gap and made a run from the halfway line.

Dennis chipped it in, Thierry flicked it on and I did a diving header into the bottom corner. Highbury went mad. The joke in the dressing room was that my larger-than-normal Afro hairdo that day could take the credit for the assist, not Thierry. We went on to beat Lokomotiv 2–0, winning the three games needed to qualify for the knock-out stages. We saw off Celta Vigo in Spain and then came up against Chelsea – still under the management of Claudio Ranieri – in the quarter-finals. We drew 1–1 at their place and lost 2–1 at Highbury, being suckered by a late 87th-minute goal by Wayne Bridge. It was the result that spurred us on to win the Premiership that year, it was said, although we didn't feel very invincible at the time. The boss said he 'beat himself up' after that result. He remains a man on a mission.

Until he completes that mission, his job won't be done. Me? I've walked away with some great memories from Europe and the best one is reflected in the silver medal from Paris. It will forever remind me of how close we came.

I'd played on the biggest stage there is in club football, but had little time to dwell on the memories, because it was time to play on the biggest stage in international football – the 2006 World Cup. Germany promised many more untold twists and dramas as I travelled with England to play in the biggest show on earth.

10

The England Camp

I never sleep after matches. I don't know many in the England squad who do. It's all that post-match come-down, the replaying of the game, the tactics or a near miss that go over and over in your head that keeps you bolt awake.

So it goes without saying that none of us got a wink after the quarter-final defeat and that penalty shoot-out against Portugal. The World Cup, Germany 2006 weren't meant to end with yet another bunch of 'if onlys'. I know that Wayne 'Wazza' Rooney was up chatting till 8 a.m. with Peter Crouch, still not believing his sending-off, still imagining what might have been had they played up front at the start of the 90 minutes. I know Becks was up all night writing his statement that he was stepping down as captain. And Sven would have been pacing his suite all night, beating himself up over a defeat that seemed unjust to all of us. He was the first to bed out of anyone but, like the rest of us, he don't sleep on match nights either. As for me, I went to the bar with the rest of the lads, drank and got wasted through till daybreak. I got to my room for about 9.45 a.m. I'd been last up together with Jermaine Jenas and Aaron Lennon. We even had a blurred kick-about in the hotel lobby around 7 a.m. I didn't want to sit there and dwell on all that post-match analysis stuff. We were out of the tournament. We hadn't played well enough. At times, we'd been shit. It was as simple and brutal as that. There was nothing else to know at that time. Had I stayed sober and allowed myself to think too hard, it would have done my head in.

There'd be the usual post-mortems in the press, questions about Sven's tactics and criticism about our performances. It was your typical World Cup script written for England – full of controversy and decided from the penalty spot. But even as I look back now, it's hard to believe that we stumbled and fell like we did when you think about the players, the talent and the belief we had.

We had a confidence like never before. We may have lost our way and rhythm at times, and the fans may have lost some patience and faith along the way; but we never lost our nerve, and never stopped picturing victory. Even when everyone was talking about us stuttering and faltering, our confidence was sky-high.

Defeat and an early exit was unthinkable in my mind. It really was coming home this time. That's what we all thought.

Which is why defeat to Portugal in a shoot-out felt like a kick in the teeth, stomach and nuts all at the same time.

We felt conned by our own belief. It lied to us and told us we were good enough. But belief as strong as that is what everyone needs – it's the psychological backbone of every winning team. Just ask the lads at Arsenal about the immaculate season. Or the England World Cup champions of 1966. Or the England rugby boys who tasted World Cup glory in Australia in 2003. Even when performances and the talent weren't the best, each player found a winner's medal around their neck on the back of belief.

As we set off for Germany under Sven-Goran Eriksson, I had never known such a superb team spirit running through an England camp. The feeling was hard to define but there was a binding conviction among the lads that topped anything we'd felt four years previously in Japan and South Korea. We felt there was no-one we couldn't beat. We felt no fear.

That was backed up by the knowledge that the England team of 2006 had that perfect blend of experience and youth, mixing the likes of Becks, Rio, Sol, JT, Gary Neville and Lamps with the new blood of Wazza, Lennon, Downing and Jenas. Not only that but the squad had matured since the last World Cup. I looked around the dressing room and realised we'd become a team of winners since 2002. No longer did you have to play for Manchester United to have known success. There was me and Sol with Arsenal; JT, Lamps and Joe Cole with the new Kings of the Premiership, Chelsea; and Stevie Gerrard and Jamie Carragher with the memories of Champions League glory still fresh in their minds. In fact, in the European Footballer of the Year Awards, Stevie Gerrard finished third behind second-placed Lamps. Two out of the top three – that'll do.

The England dressing room is like a family that has grown closer year by year. The spirit and rapport was brilliant among us. Sticking together and being there for one another was a big thing for Sven. In all his years, he told us, he'd never seen a tighter unit or better spirit.

With all those factors thrown together, we knew there was never going to be a better chance to win it. Sven's missus Nancy Dell'Olio even promised that she'd cook the lads her speciality pasta if we reached the final.

Mum believed this was the year, too. She'd bought a sparkly St George cowboy hat to wear at the final in Berlin on 9 July. Even Cheryl had plans. She was going to wear the full England strip. We had it all sorted. It was like Mum said: 'There's no point being here if you think you're not going to go all the way and win it. It's no good hoping. You've got to *know* you're going to win it.'

Arsene Wenger and Sven would have appreciated that pearler.

Sven is very similar in character to Arsene – it's as much to do with the mind as well as the body for them two. It must be the continental approach or something. I liked Sven a lot, and never did understand why the media battered him so much. Like his squad, he was a proven winner who has worked with top-class players over the years. He, like Arsene, inspires and encourages without the need to bawl and shout. He treats players as his equals, as men who know their job. It's that kind of respect that commands an equal respect and attention back to him. He earned my admiration over the concern he showed and advice he gave me during the tapping-up 'scandal'. He sat me down soon after the FA Premier League charged me with breaching rule K3 and I'd been dropped for the FA Cup game against Bolton. It was two weeks after all that nonsense when we played back-to-back World Cup qualifiers against Northern Ireland – beat them 4–0 – and then Azerbaijan – beat them 2–0. Sven took me to one side ahead of the Northern Ireland match at Old Trafford. He looked at me before he said anything. He looked worried and, unlike Arsenal – who seemed more obsessed about what had gone on, whether Chelsea had destabilised me, who did what, who said that – Sven was only interested in one thing: how I was as a person. Without any hint of doubt, he expressed confidence in me. There was no lecture, no patronising manner, no raking around for evidence. I told him what Arsenal had been paying me and he looked like I'd just asked him to play Sol Campbell up front. He couldn't believe it. 'That's not right, that's not right,' he kept saying. Here's a man who has worked with the best and knows what footballers are worth. 'You are grossly under-paid,' were his words to me, and he said his door was always open.'Just keep playing your game and you'll be fine. If you need any help, you know where I am,' he added. He patted me on the back and that was

SCANDALS

Me. On my way to the FAPL hearing. Nervous as hell but ready to clear my name.

THE CAST

Arsenal chairman Peter Hill-Wood, who got the ball rolling.

Arsenal vice-chairman David Dein – involved at every stage of the saga.

Left: Chelsea's Jose Mourinho and Peter Kenyon on the way to the FAPL enquiry. Their version of events didn't quite match mine…

My agent Jonathan Barnett. He had a lot to say at the inquiry. All worth listening to.

'Cole Dumped'. Dropped against Bolton in March 2005.
I'd like to say I took it like a real pro. Only I didn't.

November 2004. A 'friendly' against Spain: I almost
came to blows with their manager, Luis Aragones,
whose comments had whipped up a torrent of
racist abuse that swept across the entire stadium.
Sickening.

ASHLEY COLE

Ashley Cole & Masterstepz: An apology

ON 12 and 19 February
we published two sto-
ries concerning un-
named premiership
football players and a
music industry figure
taking part in a "gay
romp" in which a mo-
bile phone was used as
a "gay sex toy".

A photograph of the
England footballer,
Ashley Cole and
Choice FM DJ, Master-
stepz, appeared with
the 19 February story.
Although the photo-
graph was pixellated,
some readers have un-
derstood Mr Cole to be
one of the footballers
and Masterstepz to be
the DJ concerned.

We are happy to
make clear that Mr
Cole and Masterstepz
were not involved in
any such activities. We
apologise to them for
any distress caused
and we will be paying
them each a sum by
way of damages.

We wish Mr Cole the
very best of luck in to-
day's match against Ec-
uador.

MASTERSTEPZ

GERMANY 2006

Arsenal transfers. Tapping-up. Racism. Tabloid slurs. I put them all behind me. Cheryl and I and Buster had a World Cup to look forward to.

THE HIGHS   ## THE HEAT

Becks 'scores' against Paraguay in the opening minutes of our campaign. We're on our way.

And again against Ecuador. We're in the quarters.

Rio and I take on much needed liquid.

THE FANS

Mum and Mattie at the Sweden game.

STEVE DENNIS

Mum Cole and Mum Beckham giving their boys loud and excited support before the Portugal game.

STEVE DENNIS

BETWEEN MATCHES

STEVE DENNIS

Left: Cheryl, Mum, nephew Kenzie and me outside the England team hotel.

Below Left: Taking my mind off things in the hotel's games arcade. My head is steady… not sure about the back swing.

Below: Chilling in Baden-Baden with Cheryl and a smile for the paparazzi.

EMPICS

THE GAMES

Silky skills from the boss during the Ecuador game.

That block against Ecuador's Tenorio that kept us on track for the quarters.

There was no way Ronaldo was going to get past me. We stayed strong at the back and kept the Portuguese out…

COLORSPORT

…but with Wayne off we were up against it. I was down to take the fifth penalty…

…I wish I'd been needed. Over for another four years. But at least I did have something to look forward to…

GETTY IMAGES

GETTY IMAGES

that. He'll never know how much his words and belief lifted me at that time.

He's the most chilled manager I've come across. The man is almost horizontal. He's taken a lot of stick in his time and yet it rolls off him like water. Among many other things, he's been hammered for his lack of visible passion and animation on the touchline. Even in the middle of the World Cup, the media were at him; the *Daily Mirror* asked on 27 June, as we prepared for the quarter-finals: 'Passion? Energy? Does Eriksson even know what these words mean?'

Take it from a player who saw his passion behind the scenes and felt his energy in the dressing room, he knows exactly what those words mean. The fact he's not a hot-tempered, foot-stamping, air-punching screamer in the dug-out don't mean a thing. Only a writer or columnist who has never played the game could argue otherwise. What's the point in him shouting and screaming from the dug-out? The players can't hear him, it won't affect the outcome of the game and it's a waste of energy. His work is done with the team shape, tactics and team talks in the dressing room. Football has nothing to do with theatrics and melodrama on the touchline. What good is it to have a Scolari going nuts at every refereeing decision, foul or missed chance?! I know that's how Sven sees it. So it's wrong to judge him because the man is more focused than anyone I know. His belief – in himself and his team – was calm and solid. What do they say? Still waters run deep. That is Sven and he shouldn't be knocked for it.

On match days, he went round the dressing room before kick-off, and sometimes at half-time, and gave each player his individual attention, giving advice, being positive, urging them on. Like Arsene, his sole aim is to win, win and win again. As a result, he takes defeat as hard as anyone I know. He'll prepare like a perfectionist then put his plan into action. Once out on the pitch, it's over to us. But, once the match is done, he strikes me as the kind of man who'll go home or retire to his hotel room and *then* vent his frustration and worries.

In private, never in public: forever the private man. As players, we knew how much this World Cup meant to him, regardless of what the press said. Make no mistake, it mattered to him more than anything else in the world at that time.

I think his record as England coach speaks for itself. I don't give a toss how much stick or ridicule the media has given him, he was an excellent England manager in my book. England were down and out and heading nowhere when he took charge in 2001. We didn't even look capable of qualifying for the World Cup 2002.

That we went to Germany as one of the favourites, that the fans expected so much, speaks volumes for his reign, even if the tournament weren't his greatest hour. Germany was always the main aim for him, England and the FA; that was the target set when he was appointed. Along the way, he experimented with players and formations and took stick for it. But everything that he tried and tested was done with Germany in mind.

The stick dished out to him reached its height during the twists and turns of the qualifying route. We did the professional job that was required of us: we qualified and we qualified with something in hand. But, along the way, there were rash judgements made and press talk of 'shambles' and 'crisis' and 'disaster' as we narrowly beat Wales 1–0 then lost to Northern Ireland by the same margin, with those two results coming on the back of a 4–1 thumping from Denmark in a friendly in Copenhagen. We got battered and battered bad when the Danes scored three goals in seven minutes before finishing us off in injury time. We were awful. But it was the result at Windsor Park, Belfast, three weeks later, on 7 September 2005, that had the nation on our backs, and especially Sven's.

People had been saying that if we were to win the World Cup then we should coast to victory against the likes of Wales and Northern Ireland, thrashing them four, five or six nil. The talk was that another 5–1 versus Germany in Munich was on the cards. In some respects, that was a curse of a result for Sven – everyone expected us to roll over teams in the same fashion. But games against an underdog are like local derbies; they are battles and they're going to be hard. The underdog digs in deep, throws men behind the ball and raises its game 200 per cent, proving hard to break down at times. As Trinidad & Tobago would later prove in Germany.

We always knew Northern Ireland was going to be a tough one: small stadium, rubbish pitch, derby atmosphere and there was a lot of England lads not playing to form. As with Denmark, we had a bad day at the office, and were beaten by a David Healy strike on 74 minutes. It was our first defeat in a qualifier under Sven, and first to Northern Ireland since 1972. No-one in the team had been born then! The match was also remembered for Wazza losing his rag – he went crazy, crazy, crazy on the pitch and in the dressing room. His frustration boiled over, that's all. Just like the significance of the result, Wazza's moment at full-time was blown out of all proportion, and there were suggestions that he'd lost his rag with Becks. But the skipper was just trying to calm him down as the voice of experience.

Becks knows all about losing his head, and the repercussions of it. We all remember his lash-out against Argentina in France 98.

So he was trying to bring his experience to the fore. Like a true leader should. 'Calm down,' he said, assertively.

'I am fucking calm!' yelled Wazza, and he got all restless and agitated.

That kind of emotion and screaming takes place in dressing rooms up and down the country, week in, week out, and you'd be worried for the spirit of your team if it didn't. I'd like to have seen more of that in the Arsenal dressing room during the last season at Highbury, to be honest. Wazza is fiery by nature, but he's young and passionate and it comes as part of an immensely talented package. And before you say it, Germany 2006 and the Portugal match had nothing to do with his temperament. He didn't lose it. He didn't stamp on anyone and he didn't deserve to be sent off.

The World Cup seemed a long way off after that Northern Ireland match, but we didn't do much navel-gazing after it. We put the result in context as a one-off defeat. Our belief in ourselves ran deeper than the knee-jerk judgements of the press – and rash judgements served only to embarrass them in the end. Because we then tucked away 1–0 and 2–1 victories against Austria and Poland in the October to seal our place at the World Cup. We qualified by finishing top of Group 6. Then, in the November, came a friendly against Argentina. I was out injured and watched the match on television at the house of my friend Jon Fortune, the Charlton Athletic player. It was a hell of a game which we won 3–2. And, suddenly, England were heroes again. All talk of 'disaster', 'shambles' and 'crisis' were substituted with talk of 'an England team capable of winning the World Cup'. But if you looked closely at the game, we'd got battered and were trailing 2–1 after 54 minutes and not looking good. Then Argentina took off their best players – it was as much of an experiment for them as it was for us – and we took advantage, and Michael Owen scored two late goals in the 87th and 90th minutes; goals against a side weakened by their own substitutions. Once again, the players put the performance into context and just let the press get carried away.

People ask if the negative press gets to us. The answer is 'no' because sports journalists' reading of a game is hysterical at times which is why it lurches from the Northern Ireland 'shambles' to the Argentinian 'heroics'.

For me, what mattered was Sven's interpretation of a match, my own self-analysis, and chats with team-mates. Oh yes, and the opinion of the only pundit who matters: my mum.

We had three more international friendlies to come – Uruguay, Hungary and Jamaica – before that golden trophy beckoned us to Germany 2006 and the 18th FIFA World Cup finals. After many months and games of squad and tactical experimentation, the only question for the press left to ask was: 'Who would make Sven's 23?'

It was Thierry who had first spotted Sven hovering around the Arsenal training ground, in the first week of May. I was walking away from the dressing room with him, Sol and Arsene Wenger, heading across the sand and towards the pitch in our yellow bibs. That's when the Frenchman told us he'd seen the England coach. 'So what's he doing here again?' we all asked the boss out of curiosity.

'He's here keeping an eye on you two!!' joked Thierry. Then the boss piped up. 'Well, I told him to come.' It was one of those sudden interruptions that made us slow up in our march to the pitch. 'I've told him he should take Theo to the World Cup.'

It then became one of those moments that stopped us in our tracks.

Me, Sol and Thierry all looked at each other and started laughing. The boss kept walking.

This had to be one of his wind-ups, that 17-year-old Theo was going to get his chance in Germany, making his debut on the world stage for England *before* he had even made his debut for Arsenal.

'No, no . . . I'm serious,' said the boss, 'I'm very serious.'

'Oh come on boss, he's a hell of a talent but he's not even played a game for us yet,' I said.

We rejoined the amble to the pitch, hooked on the boss's every word. 'Yes, yes . . . that is a problem with experience but I think he's better than any of the other English strikers,' he said.

The boss was talking with the exception of Wayne Rooney. The 'curse of the metatarsal' had struck both him and the England team when he fractured his foot in a tackle during the Manchester United-Chelsea game at Stamford Bridge in April, and the doubts over his fitness had made Sven look for a back-up striker. That's when a call was clearly made between the boss and the coach. The Theo debate would ultimately dominate the thoughts of every football expert in the land.

But it took one Frenchman to ask what two Englishmen were thinking at that training ground.

'But do you really, really think he is ready for the World Cup?' asked Thierry.

The boss was emphatic. 'Yes, yes . . . with his pace and his talent, yes. If you put the ball over the top for him, he'll score.'

Now don't get me wrong. Theo is an exciting young player with a great talent. He has every chance of becoming world class. But potential is different to being proven, and he had not even played a first team game with Arsenal since his £12 million transfer from Southampton in January 2006. It was a gamble in anyone's book. In time, other national managers such as Bobby Robson would ask whether it was a reckless one. I first played for England aged 19 in a friendly against Albania in 2000. I also made my Champions League debut that same year. But would I have been ready for a World Cup? I'm not sure I would.

So Thierry decided to speak out and test Arsene's belief and wisdom. 'Okay boss,' he said. 'If he's *that* good, why has he not played for Arsenal?'

For once, there was no quick reply from the boss, so Thierry pressed him again.

'Alright, if you have so much faith in him to go to the World Cup, then play him in the Champions League final . . .'

The boss ummed for a bit but didn't really answer the question.

'Exactly!' said Thierry, and started laughing, knowing he had caught him out. We all ribbed the boss but there was no shaking his belief, and Sven was just as serious. Otherwise he wouldn't have been there. Afterwards, me and Sol started talking to the coach and he asked us about Theo. I remember my exact words: 'Really, really quick. Great player. Cool head on his shoulders. One for the future.' Sol nodded. Ever since his transfer from Southampton, I'd got used to seeing Theo on the training pitch and he was quick. Lightning quick. When through on goal, you'd back him to score with his pace and you do need speed at the highest level against the likes of Argentina and Brazil. Let's face it, he wouldn't be at Arsenal unless he was something special. He *is* something special, and he's up against top-class players every day in training. But London Colney is a world away from Germany.

Was he being rushed into the World Cup because of desperate measures caused by Wazza's injury? Would the burden be too much for Theo? And why was he good enough for the World Cup and not the Champions League final? Why weren't the boss prepared to take the same gamble as Sven? And who wouldn't make the squad if room was made for Theo? All those questions were going through my mind, in the interests of both Theo and England. Anyway, that's how we found out about the 'boy wonder' being part of the World Cup squad. Make no mistake, I couldn't have been happier for Theo. He is a sound lad with a great family behind him who would make sure his feet were kept on the ground. At his age, he'd not even know what fear was so maybe that was a good thing, too. The moment he was selected, the rest of the team were right behind him.

We all harboured reservations about whether it was too early but we also balanced that with the thought that he could be anything; England's dark horse. He could be Owen at France 98. Rooney at Euro 2004. Like the rest of England, we'd have to wait and see.

Sven announced his World Cup squad on 8 May. My name was up there on the big screen, sandwiched between John Terry and Sol Campbell. He'd also included some other exciting youngsters: Jermaine Jenas, Stewart Downing and Aaron Lennon. Pace seemed to be the binding quality they all shared.

Experience. Youth. Pace. Belief. All the key ingredients were in the mix for Germany.

The main reason for Theo Walcott's call-up was the injury to Wazza and although his name was still up there as part of Sven's selections, there was a massive question mark alongside it. It was like

David Beckham and the World Cup 2002 all over again: the prayer mats came out, one man's foot dominated conversation and the nation seemed to spend weeks asking itself: 'Will he or won't he?'

I was listening to the Manchester United-Chelsea match on BBC Radio Five Live when he got injured. I remember the boos at first as the crowd thought he was putting it on. Then I remember the silence – silence always stands out on radio – as Stamford Bridge realised this was a national injury, and then the commentator said something along the lines of 'Rooney is down and looks in real pain'.

As someone who had battled injury all season, I sensed it was serious by the tone of the commentator's voice and the silent reaction of the crowd. Not much silences Stamford Bridge, let me tell you. My heart went out to Wazza, especially when, the next morning, we all learned how serious it was: a broken metatarsal. To get crocked like that in the last two or three games of the season is every World Cup player's worst nightmare.

Over the following days and weeks, the media's reaction to his injury bordered on the hysterical. No longer was the World Cup about England. It was about how quickly Wazza's foot would mend and how fit he would be, as if we were a one-man team. It all became a distracting side-show, and a little annoying to be honest. Wazza is an exceptional talent and the England team is a better side with him in it. But to say, as some suggested, that our 'World Cup Dream Is Over' if he didn't recover in time was just bollocks when the team had other proven goal-scorers like Gerrard, Lampard, Beckham, Joe Cole, Crouch and Owen. Not to mention John Terry and Sol Campbell at set-pieces. The whole thing became silly and over-hyped.

While we all kept our fingers crossed for Wazza and hoped he'd make it, our confidence and belief weren't knocked by his injury. It was unfortunate but it weren't a disaster. It was an insult to the rest of the squad to suggest it was. We'd played eight internationals without Wazza before Germany, won seven of them and drawn one. With or without him, we felt we could win the World Cup. All the uncertainty was put to bed on 26 May when doctors cleared him to travel to Germany. **'ROONEY GOES TO WORLD CUP'** announced the *Evening Standard*. That was that sorted then, and Wazza was hungry to get back. In our prep for the tournament, we beat Hungary 3–1, thumped Jamaica 6–0 and met Prince William when he visited us during training. Crouchy even gave him a performance of his 'Robot' dance, and it got the Royal seal of approval. So we'd done the warm-up and all the positive PR. It was time to leave for Germany.

On the quick flight over there, I remember looking out of the window and thinking to myself: 'Champions League final and now the World Cup.'

I'm not sure I'll experience many better periods in my football career. I'll always remember the May and June of 2006.

The enormity of the World Cup hit me as soon as we stepped off the plane in the spa town of Baden-Baden, our base during the tournament. As soon as we touched down on German soil, the excitement shot through me. I was buzzing because at one stage in the season, with all my injuries, I wondered if I'd ever make it. I'd be lying if I said I was 100 per cent fit on arrival but I felt sharp enough. My only niggling worry was my thigh. It had gone again in the 6–0 drubbing of Jamaica, and I was substituted as a precaution. The truth was that I'd only know how it was once we started training and playing again. Thankfully, the media's fitness focus was elsewhere – on Wazza and Michael Owen – so I could keep my concerns to myself.

Once there, though, there was business to do and I couldn't wait to get started. We'd arrived suited and booted in Armani; there were loads of police at the airport plus a good gathering of fans. Then an oompah band played and some kids sang us a rap song when we arrived at our five-star team hotel, the Schlosshotel Buhlerhohe, set 3,000 feet up in the hills.

It was surrounded by dense forest and had views of the Rhine Valley – the kind of dream place and setting I'd like to have shared with Cheryl not 22 other England players. It was a world away from north London. In fact, its remoteness made the World Cup itself seem a world away. We were on our own secluded planet up there. It was so quiet you could hear your own mind ticking over. I remember the team coach chugging up the hilly road that twisted through the forest en route from the airport and I turned to Jermaine Jenas sat next to me and said: 'Please tell me we're not going to be doing this journey every day!' Sven *always* chose the hotels that were the furthest away from anywhere. Once we arrived, there were constant reminders of the job in hand and why we were there: St George's flags were pinned to the round balcony that overlooked the dome-like lobby, and there were life-size images of each player in action scattered at intervals down all the corridors; visual flashbacks to special moments and goal celebrations. There was Owen scoring a goal, Becks whipping in a free kick, Rio roaring on the defence, Sol rising to meet a header, Wazza screaming in celebration, me running down the left flank. With those images, Sven made sure the World Cup was kept in focus. Each player was given his own room and it was hard not to find it because there was a picture of your face in an England shirt on the door! No names, just a photo.

As feared, we were chugging up and down that road to our training camp – 20 minutes down the hill – nearly every day. It could have been worse – Sven could have made us run it.

It was at training that we got our first idea of the kind of heat we'd be up against during matches. It was always cooler in the mountains around our hotel so the heat didn't really bother us up there. It was when we trained, however, from mid-morning through to lunch at one o'clock, that we got a hint of how draining it was going to be.

Maybe that was why the practice sessions were never intense. Training was more tailored towards tactics than being put through the mill. Tactical awareness mattered more than physical stamina.

Everyone was already fit after a hard season in the Premiership so the bodies and fitness levels were finely tuned, even if the likes of me, Wazza and Michael Owen needed some extra sharpening after our injuries. What was more important was our tactical play, knowing the movement of each other, knowing where the runs would be made, and knowing the opposition. At club level, you tend to know the opponents already. With Arsenal, I'd have watched West Brom or Aston Villa ten times and pretty much know all about them. But with England, I'd seen the likes of Paraguay or Ecuador only once on a video. So we'd be made aware of their style of play and then get on the pitch to adapt and gel as a team. After an initial warm-up jog around the pitch, and some technical ball work, we'd do five versus twos, or seven versus twos. And Sven would also play 'Young England versus Old England', pitting experience against youth. So you had the likes of Robinson, Carragher, Jenas, Lennon, Wazza and Walcott lining up in a team against James, Gary Neville, Campbell, Ferdinand, Gerrard, Becks and me. Aged 25, I was classed as an oldie and I weren't happy! But that tells you a lot about the youth in the squad, and the positive signs for the future. I weren't happy with the results either because the young ones came out on top, winning most matches. None of us in the squad like losing and the young ones loved rubbing it in every time they turned us over.

The biggest downside to life in the England camp was the boredom factor, not helped by our location. Half the time, we seemed to be rattling around our luxury hotel wondering how to fill our time. We only got to see our wives/girlfriends once, sometimes twice, a week but, most of the time, we were all thrown together in what seemed like an isolation camp. The only way to escape the hotel was to go for a long walk through the forest but we were soon put off that idea when we heard one of the security guards patrolling the grounds was chased by a wild boar (although we all wished we'd seen it just for the entertainment value!).

One evening, all the families came to the hotel for a barbecue and that was a welcome break from routine.

As each player sat at separate tables with their partners and families, it was like a visiting day in prison; an FA luxury for good behaviour and good results.

But other than that one-off treat, it all got a bit mind-numbing. We did have a games room which was pretty cool, but even with that all the hanging around did my head in half the time. Via satellite, we had the main channels pumped into our rooms – BBC1, BBC2, ITV and Channel 4. I watched a lot of 'Big Brother' and MTV and kept up to speed with Wimbledon when it started. I'd also sit back and listen to some tunes on the iPod – some soul, jungle, garage and R&B.

All the main channels were broadcast on the big plasma in the massage room, too, and I'll never forget one funny moment on the eve of the World Cup opening ceremony. As this story proves, Sven is not only chilled but he also has a cool sense of humour – thankfully.

There was me, Rio, Wazza and two of the masseurs and we flicked on Channel 4. It was showing that piss-take programme, 'Sven: The Coach, The Cash and His Lovers'. It pretended to be one of those fly-on-the-wall documentaries, using look-a-likes. It had actors being Rio, Wazza and Becks all fighting over the mirror, kissing the World Cup trophy in the bath and Sven giving Wazza a foot massage to get him better. We were almost rolling off the beds laughing when 'Rio' came on the box with his plaited hair, and then 'Wayne' appeared looking like a right scruff-bag. We couldn't see the point in the programme but we almost couldn't see the screen through the tears of laughter.

Then, there was this scene showing 'Sven' having sex with some woman over a pool table. All of us started hooting with laughter: three players and two masseurs, belly-aching with laughter, roaring the place down.

'What is this?' said the Swedish voice from behind us.

That's when the laughter stopped dead.

The real Sven-Goran Eriksson had been behind us all the time. He'd walked in with Sammy Lee, Ray Clemence and Steve McLaren and they'd been watching us laughing our socks off at his expense. It was like your parents had just walked in and caught you watching a dirty movie or something.

Shit, I thought.

Shit. Shit. Shit. He's going to hate us. After all he's been through, he's going to hate us for laughing at him.

I looked at Rio. Rio looked at Wazza. We all looked at the floor.

Sven looked at us, started to smile and then, as calm as you like, laughed it off and said: 'My taste isn't that bad!'

It broke the silence and the ice, and everyone was laughing again. Sven because he was being funny, and us because we were so relieved! Like the rest of the lads, he was able to take the banter and have a laugh with us, despite his authority.

Without laughter, the days would have dragged even more in the hotel. There was a monotonous routine: wake around nine o'clock, leave for training at ten o'clock, lunch at one, chill in the afternoon, dinner at seven and then an hour or two to do our own thing, then a massage before bed at eleven.

The FA did its best to keep us entertained. One massive conference room was turned into an 'amusement palace', rammed with every kind of arcade game. There was a row of six rally racing screens against one wall, complete with steering wheels, gear sticks and bucket seats side by side; there was another two-man racing car console, a two-seat super-bike game, a Champion Football widescreen console for eight players, a Pacman, two Soprano pinball machines, a pool table, a table tennis and a golf simulator that allowed us to play a dozen 18-hole courses around the world. Plus table football, arcade golf and a shooting game. When Mum came one night with my seven-year-old nephew Kenzie, she said it looked like something straight from Southend-on-Sea. Although, to be fair, our set-up put Southend in the shade. In the player comment book, Wazza wrote that it was 'a boss games room but where's the burger bar?' and Jamie Carragher wrote 'Not as good as mine at home!' Stevie Gerrard cracked us all up when he scribbled 'What a pile of shite'.

I played the golf simulator a lot with Jermaine Jenas, Wazza and Wayne Bridge. Jermaine was having himself for hitting the longest drive of the tournament. Rio was having himself because he was shit-hot at table tennis. And Crouchy was having himself because he beat all-comers on the tennis courts. Crouchy's that good at tennis, he could have played at Wimbledon as well as the World Cup! If not at the same time. A gang of us spent ages playing the Champion Football arcade. I used to be shit-hot because me and Jermaine Pennant used to play Pro Evolution Soccer on PlayStation in our spare time. I used to be the king of arcade soccer in the England camp but my crown seemed to have slipped in Baden-Baden. The lads kept ribbing me because the team I selected as my colours was Chelsea not Arsenal. Maybe my sub-conscious was trying to tell me something! The problem was that I kept getting battered by the likes of Wazza, Aaron, Jermaine and JT. I hate losing – even on the computer. As does Wazza. That boy's got the same fierce face playing arcade soccer as he does when he's chasing a ball that's been put over the top for him. One night, he got the right hump when we held a 'Question of Sport' quiz. There were three teams of four: me, Bridge, Lamps and Rod the masseur; Rio, Wazza, JT and Bill the masseur; Carragher, Stevie G, Stewart Downing and Steve the masseur.

My team kicked their arses that night which was good because we beat Carragher, and he has the best sporting knowledge of the entire squad. It all came down to the last question, and it was Wazza's team to answer. They had to guess the stadium from the photo on the big screen. We needed them to get the question wrong so it could come back to us. So we sucked in Bill the masseur.

'Come on Bill, you massaged there – you must know this one!'

Quick as a flash, he takes the bluff and shouts out: 'HAMPDEN PARK! IT'S HAMPDEN PARK!'

Wrong answer. Question gets passed to us and we get it right – Pride Park. And we won the quiz.

Wazza was up on his feet, 'He didn't say it . . . he didn't say it . . . that weren't our final answer!'

You should have seen his face, it was so funny. He was going mad. He's so easily wound up and his loathing of defeat over *anything* reminds me of Thierry at Arsenal but, let's face it, that competitive spirit and hunger to win at everything and anything is what makes them the top-class strikers they are. The other player who cracked me up all the time was Carragher. I'm glad we had people like him in the camp because he was so entertaining. He looks really serious half the time but he's so funny and is always coming out with wisecracks. Sometimes, just the sound of his voice had me in stitches. It must be his and Wazza's thick Scouse accent that sets me off – the both of them just come across as comics. We also found a ready-made stand-up comic in our new masseur Bill Blood. He might be crap at 'Question of Sport' but he was such a joker and had more gags up his sleeve than anyone. What a top bloke he was. Half the lads went to the massage room just to hear his routine!

It's unusual for players to be thrown together for such a long period of time so it's good when everyone gets on. It's odd when you think about it. With their clubs, players may spend a maximum of two or three days together for an away fixture or a Champions League match. It's only for the World Cup or Euro Championships that a team has to get used to 'living' together. Of course, everyone has the independent space of their own rooms if we're getting on top of one another but the upside to it all is that the players get the chance to bond, people's characters come out a lot more and a better rapport is built between us all; gelling back at the hotel is almost as important as gelling on the pitch, and our time together as a unit in Baden-Baden served to strengthen 'the family' behind the England team. The closer you get, the better you know one another and the better the team spirit. I suppose that's the upside of boredom – it makes you talk more and get to know each other better. I came away from Germany knowing more about Stevie Gerrard, Wazza and Lamps than I ever did and I had a good time hanging out with Rio, Jermaine and Aaron. All of us were itching for the World Cup to start. We were in Group B, and couldn't wait to get our first match – and first win – under our belts.

11

Sweat and Tears

'Jesus, we're going to melt out here', I thought during the pre-match warm-up.

The heat on the pitch in Frankfurt was something else, and all the lads looked at each other and thought the same thing: 90 minutes at 90 miles an hour in this cauldron and we'll be cooked. It drained me even as I jogged. It was about 35 degrees inside the Waldstadion. It was like Japan and South Korea all over again.

When the sun smothered you, it rinsed you dry.

It was an absolute killer. We'd only trained mid-mornings so we'd not known how intense it would be. We'd guessed but guessing was no preparation – it was the sort of heat that made you want to run and hide. The only way I can describe it is to imagine being in a sauna when someone flashes up the heat and it hits you, tightening the stomach. It was like that out there. Only we couldn't sit there in a towel and sweat it off. We had 90 minutes of World Cup football versus Paraguay ahead of us. My whole body, my head, shoulders and feet became so hot even in the warm-up; the feet are probably the worst thing in those conditions. It feels like they're on fire within your boots, and they're sliding around in the socks with all that sweat, and the blisters become chronic. Even the lads on the bench said the heat was unbearable – and they were just sitting there!

It weren't just the heat that worried me, though. During the warm-up, I felt my thigh tighten just as it had done in the Jamaica game. I was thinking to myself, 'Why now? Why now?' I weren't going to tell the gaffer. It was only the warm-up. Maybe it just needed loosening up and I'd be alright once I was playing. I'm not one to give in that easily.

Back in the dressing room, all the lads mentioned the heat. The South Americans would be used to it but we weren't and that probably heightened the anxiousness everyone was feeling at the time. It was England versus Paraguay *and* the heat. But that's the World Cup. It's part of the battle.

I'd had my usual text messages from Mum and Cheryl before the game. 'Good luck, have a good one xx' from Mum and 'Good luck for the match. I'm nervous for you. Hope you win babes x' from Cheryl. We always played music in the dressing room before a game, and turned it up loud. Each player chose a song to put on the iPod speakers. I chose Chris Brown and 'Poppin'' but the one we always played before every match was a garage number chosen by Michael Carrick. I can't remember for the life of me what it was called but it sounded good and the boys loved it. I was sat in between Gary Neville and Stevie Gerrard as kick-off neared. Sven was walking round, reminding each player of his tactics and danger men. People often ask what it's like in the dressing room before a big game like that. No-one's head-butting walls or jumping up and down or anything like that. There's more of a quiet focus with this England team. You can tell everyone is in their own heads, mentally gearing themselves up – deep breaths, doing stretches, downing water, just thinking. When we walked out on the pitch, the atmosphere was just amazing; the kind that reached down and lifted you off your feet, and tingled the old spine. I remember the huge video display cube that was suspended by steel cables high above the centre-circle, and it cast a giant spider's web shadow across the entire pitch. There was a lot of hype before the game, and I'd done an interview for ITV, about how we hadn't won a World Cup opener in twelve years, so there was added pressure. Paraguay, who had also beaten Argentina in the run-up to the finals, were going to be no push-overs but everyone expected us to turn them over by three, four or five goals. We'd have to get used to that ton-weight of expectation going into other games like Trinidad & Tobago and Ecuador. Privately, among the players, we knew that if we didn't at least reach the World Cup final on 9 July, we'd have had a disappointing tournament.

All the lads linked arms for the national anthem. Flags of St George were everywhere I looked. What a sight that was. England here, there and everywhere. There were apparently 35,000 of our fans out of the 48,000 capacity. 'Eng-er-land . . . Eng-er-land . . . Eng-er-land!' they chanted. We really do have the best and loudest fans in the world.

They had something to cheer about on three minutes when Becks delivered another one of his free-kick missiles that zipped into the box and went in off their defender Carlos Gamarra. Three minutes later, their keeper Villar went off injured. Something told us it was going to be our day. Our first half was a professional job and we were always on top going into a 1–0 half-time lead.

We got into the dressing room after that first 45 minutes and everyone was saying the same thing: 'Seriously, my legs are dead.' We lapped up water like dogs left in the back of a car on a hot day. Some lads had an ice-bath for ten minutes. Some of us sat there with cold towels draped over our heads. It was silent in that dressing room. We were all just trying to cool down, get our energy back. No other games would be as tough as the heat we faced versus Paraguay so this was as bad as it got, but that first half killed us. In the second half, we kept dropping deeper and deeper and that gave them more space in midfield, and a chance to thread more balls through. I was also struggling with my thigh. If I'm honest, I think it hindered me through the first game because it made me a bit wary, so some match commentators were right when they said I weren't at my sharpest. But I knew I'd get better, fitter and stronger with every game. As much as we fought fatigue, we felt in control. Paraguay were pressing us without actually posing a real danger. What a relief it was when the final whistle went. I felt like crawling down that tunnel. I was knackered. No-one had the strength to be jubilant. It was job done and time for an ice-bath. Later in the day, Trinidad & Tobago held Sweden to a 0–0 draw so the day couldn't have gone better. We beat Paraguay, won our first World Cup opener in years and were two points clear of the rest in Group B. But the press still battered us, knocking our performance, saying it was 'a stuttering start' and our 'flaws had been exposed'. There's just no pleasing those boys who work up a sweat while sat on their arses behind their lap-tops in the press benches.

Newspapers were kept away from us at the team hotel. We'd learned our lesson from the Euro Championships 2004 and the World Cup 2002 when the press battered us for fun. We'd only get angry when we should be focused. Of course, word did get through, via friends and family, that the newspapers were giving us a hard time. And some sports writers were giving our families a rough ride at the Brenner's Park Hotel where the wives, girlfriends and families stayed in the centre of Baden-Baden. One 'writer' deliberately wound up my mum and a few others one night, saying there were 'no world-class players in the England team' and he'd rather see 'England play well, lose and go home than play badly and still win' – the kind of crap you'd never see him write in his own newspaper. Then he started hammering Becks in front of his family. You see, this is the side of the media the fans don't see –

the arrogance and the stirring behind the scenes. And if any family reacted, it would have made bad headlines. Thankfully, the families were better than that and didn't rise to the bait.

What's rich is that the press made a meal of the wives and girlfriends, and their 'behaviour'. There was a lot of media attention on the so-called 'WAGs'. It became silly. Despite what the papers said, they were never a distraction to the team because we weren't seeing the headlines or photographs. All we noticed as players, especially at the Sweden and Ecuador games, was that we'd come out for training and this huddle of green-bibbed photographers would have their backs to us, ignoring the business on the pitch because they were more interested in who was in the stands. There was always about thirty photographers, all with their bird-watcher lenses trained on the wives and girlfriends. It was a joke. Me, Rio and Gary Neville were warming up near the corner flag once and we couldn't believe it. 'What is that all about??' I said. I didn't get it and weren't interested, and neither was Cheryl. As far as we were concerned, she was there to watch me play football in the same way I'd supported her during concerts. She came to support me and England, not be part of a media-made circus, and she did all her cheering and singing when and where it mattered – in the stadiums where we could hear them.

Cheryl is not a WAG – she's a recording artist and a name in her own right. She had her image long before I came along and weren't in Germany to be recognised or make a name as a 'footballer's wife'. She knew what the focus of everyone's attention should be and it weren't Cheryl Tweedy in a bar in Baden-Baden. For me, all that WAG stuff was a creation of the media to give *them* a distraction, to give *them* something to write about. I bet the wives and girlfriends of other teams went out in different towns but just didn't have the press blowing it up. Cheryl hung out a lot of the time with Victoria Beckham and was happy chilling at their hotel. We both live the quiet life at home so it didn't surprise me. What was important to the players was having our families close by. If you know your loved ones are close at hand, you won't miss them and you'll stay focused.

I'd see Cheryl and my mum the day after games, and that allowed me to escape the isolation camp of the team hotel. We looked forward to those days after being cooped up as a team. But Baden-Baden the town was mad; it was overrun with reporters and photographers from across Europe. Half the locals looked bemused by it all. It was hard to chill when every walk down the street was shadowed by half a dozen photographers. But we only had to face it once a week. The wives and girlfriends had it every single time they stepped out of the door.

There was one night the press never found out about – the night Sven secretly allowed me out. He's normally strict with the players' curfew but it was Mum's 50th birthday so he made an exception. 'I'd have been up there myself having a word had he not let you come down!' said Cheryl. So it's a good job the coach agreed, then. For his sake.

Cheryl had told Mum that it was just them two going for a quiet dinner. But when she turned up at this wine cellar restaurant, all the wives, girlfriends and families were there to throw a surprise party. It was like a mini-wedding reception down there, with '50' banners strewn all over the place. Mum thought that was the end of her surprises. She had no idea I was walking down the road in my England training kit, unnoticed by the photographers, sneaking under their noses. Gary's dad, Neville Neville, was on his feet raising a toast when I walked in, carrying her birthday cake. As soon as she saw me, she burst into tears.

'Happy birthday, Mum,' I said, and she started crying again.

It was great having Mum and Cheryl, and my brother Mattie and his son Kenzie, out there cheering me on in Germany. I'd always look for them in the stadiums, just like I did at Arsenal, and give them a wave during the warm-up. They all lived and breathed that tournament with me. So it was good to share that surprise with them. I was only allowed to stay at the party for half an hour but it was a good night, made even better because the press missed it all.

Our second group game was against Trinidad & Tobago in the Frankenstadion, Nuremberg. It was hot but cloudy and nowhere near as stifling as Paraguay, so that was a relief. I remember the fans belting out 'Three Lions'. 'It's comin' home . . . it's comin' home . . . IT'S COMIN' . . . ' You can't beat that sound when it's bouncing around all sides of a stadium.

I couldn't have felt better myself. My thigh problem had gone away – not even a niggle – and that's why you saw me pressing forward a lot more, linking up with and overlapping Joe Cole. We combined early on to give Crouchy a good chance but the keeper saved it. I've had a good understanding down the left with Joe ever since the qualifiers. My problem in the match was the right-winger I was marking – he didn't track me.

I'd go forward and he'd stay up so on one of their counter-attacks all it needed was one quick ball over the top. Good job I've got the engine to get up and down.

We had the upper-hand in the first half without breaking through. On 41 minutes, both me and Joe went for the same Stevie Gerrard cross to the back post. Joe snatched at it just as I felt it might have been falling to me. Then Crouchy missed a good chance about a minute later. There was one scary moment when JT cleared off the line just before half-time. That's what defenders do. But I think that moment unnerved the fans. They saw it as a wobble in what was a poor first half for us. Next thing, the entire ground seemed to be chanting 'ROOOOO-neeeee . . . ROOOOO-neeeee'. He was on the bench after the medical experts had given him the all-clear that morning, so the chant was more of a demand to Sven. We'd seen him banging the chances away in training and the man is amazing – the skills he does, the strength he has.

I could understand the fans' frustration because we'd been playing shit but didn't need reminding. We're on the pitch in the thick of it, knowing things aren't working. But like I've said before, teams with nothing to lose can make it hard; throwing men behind the ball. Trinidad & Tobago were a pace and power side but they don't know how to out-play or out-skill us, so they set out to frustrate us. There weren't much to say at half-time. We all knew we couldn't get worse than what we'd just played.

Ten minutes into the second half, substitutes Wazza and Aaron Lennon came on, and seemed to have the right impact. Our game took on more urgency and we started creating more chances. We just couldn't kill them off. It's frustrating being a defender when it's 0–0 and time is slipping away. You feel helpless. You know your job is to keep a clean sheet but you also see the struggle and frustrations ahead and you want to get forward to help score.

I knew we'd win, though. All the time I kept thinking, 'Keep banging on the door, we'll get through.' And on 82 minutes we did, when Crouchy met a perfect cross from Becks, and then Stevie Gerrard followed up with one of his bullets in the 90th minute. It meant we'd qualified for the knock-out stages.

Becks was the architect of our first goal for the second game running. He'll always carve something out; a set-piece, a free kick, a killer cross. So the stick he started getting over his performances was a disgrace. They were caning him – it was like he was being singled out when none of us were at our best. Maybe it was because he was captain. It was unfair because his input on the pitch had been massive and decisive. The good thing was that he'd end up having the last laugh.

I wrote earlier about how Sven was horizontally chilled, but I don't think I've seen him as jumpy as he was before and during the Sweden game in Cologne. He'd shown more aggression in his instructions on the training pitch, he was restless and more forceful before kick-off and, during the game, I got the odd glimpse of him banging the side of the dug-out in frustration with his fist. He weren't being that cool in the humidity of the Koln Stadium for our evening kick-off. It was our last group match, we wanted to finish top of the table with nine points and wanted to stuff our international bogey-team who we hadn't turned over for I don't know how many years.

In the first half, we played our best football of the tournament, and Joe Cole scored one of its best goals. Before that we'd suffered an early blow one minute into the game when Michael Owen went down. He'd just passed me the ball, I passed it to Joe, looked back and saw Michael crawling to the touchline. I knew then it was serious. We later found out that his right cruciate ligament had gone. It was a tragedy for his World Cup but our sympathies had to wait another 89 minutes as we looked for top gear.

With Crouchy and Rooney up front, Owen Hargreaves as our midfield linchpin, Lamps finding his range, and Joe Cole on fire, we seemed to swamp Sweden. We were inventive and slick. Chances came thick and fast: Lamps on three minutes, Joe on 21, Wazza denied on 25, and Crouchy soon after. Then came the brilliant Joe Cole goal on 34: chest down and bang – a dipping 30-yarder that went in off the post.

Then Lamps shaved the bar about five minutes later.

This is it. This is more like it.

I was up and down that left flank, overlapping and finding space; the way we were playing, I could even get a goal here, I thought. Everyone was pumped up as we went into half-time 1–0 to the good. Everything, for the first time in Germany, had gone to plan.

Then it all went wrong. Don't ask me how or why but that thing called 'second-half syndrome' sucked something out of us. From being dominant in one half, we suddenly found ourselves on the back foot in the second. As we lost our grip, we lost our confidence, and Sweden got back in the game on 54 minutes. Our defending at set-pieces became poor. I was on the back post covering a corner when their man, Allback, rose and flicked a backward header that came at me high and fast on the line. I nearly handballed it – that's how quick it came at me – as I flung myself in the air, jerking my head at it. But it was a bullet that skimmed off my head and flew in. Sweden kept coming at us, and then hit the crossbar. And then again.

'What the fuck is happening to us?' I thought. We roared encouragement to each other, spurred each other on, tried to find our rhythm again. Sven tried to shake things up. Off came Wazza and Rio. On went Stevie Gerrard and Sol Campbell. Crouchy was alone up front but we weren't keeping the ball, let alone getting it to him or Joe. Back at our end, Sol threw down his body to block a Larsson shot. Stevie cleared off the line a bit later. I'd also made a crucial block just inside the box.

Dig deep. We're not on the ropes yet. Come on!

We dug in and kept chipping away and, five minutes from the end, Stevie turned super-sub and headed home a Joe Cole cross. I punched the air just inside the Swedish half, and the entire stadium roared with relief. I looked at Sven. He was blowing his cheeks. It was against the run of play but we'd done it. Or so we thought. Until we got undone at a set-piece again.

We'd been told in training that 35 per cent of goals come from set-pieces, and we're normally organised and tight. But in the last minute, we let in the softest goal. I was on the back post again. In came the ball from a throw-in. Bounced into the penalty area. Bounced into the six-yard box. No-one got it. Larsson poked it home for 2–2. We were gutted. Sat in the dressing room afterwards, you'd never have guessed we'd finished top of the group with seven points. There was complete dejection. We'd lurched from a great first-half performance to a bad second half. We discussed the game a bit. There was a lot of determination to put things right; an eagerness to get back to training and sort it out. Especially our organisation at set-pieces.

Later on, I was watching TV and a soccer programme was on. Next thing I know, I'm getting blamed for *both* goals. I was sat there watching an ex-professional footballer, Peter Beagrie – Manchester City, Bradford City and Scunthorpe United – blaming me. I got so angry. He said I should have got to that first bullet header. As a defender, I had to cover and stick to my post. It's not my job to cover the *whole* line. There was nothing I could do about the height and pace of that flick-on. Maybe if I'd had a head as big as Beagrie, I'd have stopped it. The second goal was something of a collective blame so why he singled me out, I've no idea. It was bad enough having the media on our backs without ex-professionals jumping on the bandwagon. Good job Mark Lawrenson wrote good things about me in his newspaper column to correct the balance. He backed me to the hilt; defender understanding defender.

Look, we knew we had to get better. We knew where we'd done wrong. Swedish lesson learned.

Let's face it, we weren't the only team struggling. France – who went on to be finalists – were having a stinker in the group stages and struggled against the likes of Toga. Brazil weren't too hot either, and they should have lost some of their games with the chances teams had against them. No team was really caning anyone.

For me, it weren't a high-quality World Cup and no one team stood out. But we knew the press were on us. The bad vibes filtered through the player press conferences. One newspaper's headline after the Sweden game was '2ND HALF, 2ND RATE'. Our form and tactics were being hammered.

There was a lot of stuff written about Sven being tactically uncertain and messing with formations but, as players, we had to adapt and be versatile, and there were no complaints from us. We'd grown used to working with different shapes during qualifying and training. It didn't affect my game whether he went 4–4–2 or 4–5–1. The latter was good because it meant there was either an Owen Hargreaves or

Michael Carrick as the holding man in front of the back four, filling the hole in the middle, protecting us in front and doing his job to stop the threat of the opposition play-maker. But for me, 4–5–1 didn't best suit Wazza and I think he needed a striker up there with him so he had the licence to go do his thing. I think with players like him, he's got to be allowed to play his game. Half the time, it's about striking a balance between what suits a player and what's best for the team but Sven's tactics can't have been far off the mark – those two goals against Sweden were the only ones we conceded throughout the entire tournament. We were solid. Tactics weren't the issue. The problem was a team not firing on all cylinders.

There were times when a few of us asked ourselves 'What *is* going wrong?' but no-one could put their finger on it. We were having a bad tournament. No need to turn it inside out. But we were still getting the results, still winning.

In the Premiership, you can have a run of five or six mediocre games, grind out results, and still win the championship. But on the World Cup stage, five or six mediocre performances can cost you, so we knew the score. We kept saying to each other that we can play better, we have to take our time and the goals will come. We had to be honest, though, and recognise something was amiss in the second halves. We just didn't know what. We knew the problem but not the cause. Sven was also frustrated that he weren't getting the best from us.

The gamble of taking Theo Walcott didn't pay off. When it came down to it, I don't think Sven shared the same conviction as Arsene Wenger. Theo has all the attributes to be world class but he weren't ready. But I'd stack my mortgage on him taking the world by storm in a few years. His age and lack of experience isn't his fault and he will have learned a lot from his time in Germany. I felt sorry for him because his introduction to the squad was, in the end, premature and I think it's put an unnecessary expectation and pressure on his young shoulders. But he's got a big future ahead of him.

I thought we missed the likes of Darren Bent and Jermain Defoe, Sven made a mistake not taking them along. Going into a World Cup, you need proven strikers, all day long. We needed someone in the 4–5–1 formation like Darren because he always runs behind the defence and we didn't have no-one like that. Crouchy comes to the ball. Wazza comes to the ball. Michael Owen weren't 100 per cent fit and then got injured. We had a great squad but I think someone like Darren or Defoe would have added that extra dimension.

Up front, I think Crouchy was one of the great stories of the summer. He discovered his goal-scoring touch. There's much more to his game than just his aerial threat. Even back in our youth team days, when I was with Arsenal and him with Spurs, he was big and long but could still play with his feet. He holds up a ball and distributes it well – as he would prove in the Portugal match. He's surprised a few people, shut up a few critics and grabbed a cult following along the way with his dancing. I was dead pleased for him. What with Lamps, Stevie Gerrard, Joe Cole and Becks backing up Crouchy and Wazza, England had the players. It was a matter of time before it all clicked for 90 minutes. That's what we told ourselves going into the must-win game against Ecuador.

We'd reached the stage of no second chances.

'ASHKNEE COLE' is how the *Sun* described it with a headline across two pages. 'This is the moment Ashley Cole saved England from World Cup disaster,' it said. And the *Daily Mail* ran a sequence of photographs, frame by frame, asking how I'd managed to pull it off.

It was my best moment of the World Cup, and it happened 11 minutes into the Ecuador match inside the Gottlieb-Daimler-Stadion, Stuttgart – and it was a good way to celebrate my 50th cap.

Ecuador had punted the ball high in the air down their left, JT's gone for it but was caught off balance and his header shot backwards into the path of Carlos Tenorio. I've set off running just as JT has started falling backwards. I was out wide on their right, with about 20 yards to make up in a matter of seconds. 'Shit,' I'm thinking, 'they're going to score.' I'm running like mad for the sake of it.

If Tenorio had a little more confidence, he'd have scored. But he hesitated, and I'm closing down the gap with every stride, running into the box.

Then he's ready. He brings back his right boot and I knew there was nothing else to do but hurl myself, full speed and full stretch, into his shot. We were so close to goal, Robbo's gone the wrong way, the ball's heading high right and their guy's sure to score. The ball missed my trailing left leg but skimmed the top of my right knee and thigh.

And clipped the bar.

It all happened so quick: the frantic running, the desperate lunge, the shot, the bar, and then I was lying there, looking up, not quite believing it hadn't gone in. As a defender, stopping a certain goal like that felt as good as scoring one. I knew what I'd done and was buzzing inside. I didn't want to smile too much because I was playing it all serious but I felt like celebrating. But you can't. Not as a defender. Robbo came up to me: 'Great tackle Ash' and slapped me on the back. I had JT saying it, Rio saying it, Becks saying it, Stevie saying it. And Sven was a happy man at half-time, too. Back at the team hotel that night, I was playing chess with Jermaine Jenas and Rio and the match highlights came on TV and masseur Rod Thornley and Wazza were watching it. Neither of them thought the ball had touched me until they'd seen it on the box, and they came up to me and asked: 'How the hell did you cover all that ground?!' It's good to know my injury year hadn't affected my speed.

It would have been an uphill struggle for us had that goal gone in because Ecuador were hard to break down. People underestimated them, talking about them being 39th best in the world, as if rankings are everything. Germany had only battered them because Ecuador rested five players in preparation for our match. They were a fair side and in cat-and-mouse games like that, anyone who'd have conceded one goal would have been up against it from then on. So I was happy. I think it was my best-ever block. I'd done one similar at West Ham a few seasons back – denying Kanoute when he took it round Seaman and slotted home, only to find me hooking it off the line. But the Ecuador block was more crucial. I felt I'd given something back to the team because, in previous games, I didn't feel I'd played my best.

We had to grind out a result against Ecuador. That one-on-one I blocked was a rare chance for them but we weren't at our best once more. It was that man Becks who rose to the occasion, and answered his critics yet again – tucking in one of his precise free kicks from 20 yards out on the hour mark. I was the first player to jump round his shoulders in celebration. The look on our faces says it all. I was so happy for him. All the lads were. We knew he'd been under pressure, and I think the media stick got to him. I knew he'd been down before the match but, like he said, just give him the ball, let his feet do the talking. Becks has been a good mate and a great England captain, and someone with his skill can change a game. In three of our games – Paraguay, Trinidad & Tobago and then Ecuador – it was him who'd made the breakthrough. It makes rubbish of the criticism he was getting. Shortly after his goal, he was sick on the pitch. I didn't realise until we got in the dressing room. The man was spent – he'd given everything and a little bit more. And he'd put us through to the quarter-finals.

After the game, I was giving a little chat to a reporter and said: 'We're happy, we've won and we're through to the last eight.'

'Yeah, but you didn't play well again,' he replied.

'Yeah, but we're through!! You hammer us when we go through, you'd have hammered us if we went out!'

Imagine what it's like for a minute: you've just played your socks off as a team, given it 100 per cent in another hot stadium, you've done the job, you've won 1–0 and you're in the quarter-finals of the World Cup and then you're faced with all that negativity. Sometimes, some positivity, respect and recognition might not go amiss in the English press; moaning all the time and finding fault – it pisses me off.

After the match, I learned of another victory – against the *News of the World* and the *Sun*. There had been justice in my case over the rubbish about a 'gay sex orgy' and a mobile phone. Their fun and games with my life, relationship and reputation had been exposed as nothing but a pile of crap; the Rav Singh story fell on its arse. The newspapers made what they call 'an offer of amends' on 21 April and agreed to apologise and pay both me and Masterstepz substantial damages. They dragged their heels but the apology eventually came on the morning of the Ecuador match. No-one had wanted to distract me with it before the game but the *News of the World* printed this on page three: 'We are happy to make clear that Mr Cole and Masterstepz were not involved in any such activities. We apologise to them for any distress caused and we will be paying them each a sum in the way of damages. We wish Mr Cole the very best of luck in today's match against Ecuador.' The *Sun* made its grovelling apology the next day – and wished me luck in the quarter-final match versus Portugal.

I didn't feel like celebrating or nothing because the article shouldn't have been printed in the first place. I felt cleared of suspicion and relief that it was over. More than anything, I felt there was, at last, some justice coming my way. The FA Premier League had made me question whether justice existed.

Every one of the players knew what was ahead of us versus Portugal on 1 July. We weren't getting big-headed but with no Deco and no Constinha, our opponents weren't at full strength. We were also better than them. Miles better. Whatever the press had heaped on us, our confidence swelled as we arrived at the WM-Stadion in Gelsenkirchen. We couldn't wait to get out there and avenge our Euro Championship 2004 defeat in a penalty shoot-out. We all remembered how bad that felt.

Not this time. Not now.

Before kick-off, Sven said his piece. He knew – we knew – how close we were. He spoke calmly but the belief was there. It went something like this: 'Our aim was to get here, and we're here now. Our aim was to qualify and we qualified. Our aim was to finish top of the group and we did that. We're now in the quarter-finals. We're not ready to go home yet because our aim is to win the World Cup – and *we can win this World Cup!*'

I can't speak for the rest of the lads but I was buzzing after hearing that.

It was always going to be a huge game, with a bit of needle.

We knew that in their earlier ill-tempered game, Portugal had two sent off and Holland had two sent off. We weren't up against a team of sporting gents. In the first half, we had the upper hand. Wazza had a good chance blocked on two minutes, and fired in a shot on nine, and Lamps went close twice. We had Joe Cole as the source of many of our attacking moves and Owen Hargreaves was a colossus on the day; he had a brilliant game. As a defence, we reduced Portugal to a few long-range pot-shots. I couldn't believe we didn't score in that first half.

In the second, Becks twisted his knee and had to go off, and Aaron Lennon came on and almost had an immediate impact, turning their boys inside out before putting one in the box, but Joe fired over. Lamps also missed a good chance in front of goal. So it weren't as if we weren't attacking and carving out opportunities. For me, it was only a matter of time before we scored.

Then came the turning point on 62 minutes. Wazza was right in front of me, running just outside the centre circle with the ball. He had Chelsea's Carvalho and Petit around him, and he was getting his arms and shirt pulled from every angle. I was thinking to myself, 'Blow the whistle ref . . . blow the whistle.' If Wazza had been wearing a Portugal shirt, he'd have thrown himself to the floor. But he stood up and fought for the ball while trying to keep his balance in a tangle which had seen

Carvalho slide in from behind. So Wazza's half bent over with his right foot forward, and he puts his left foot back, and it's that boot that connects with Carvalho's upper thigh/groin area. I heard the whistle that should have been blown seconds earlier for the foul on our man. But it's for a foul on Carvalho. He was there rolling around and dying Hollywood-style. I say that because, in my mind, he *wasn't* stamped in the nuts. I've seen it on TV. It was accidental. But the Portugal players went mad. That's when Ronaldo came steaming over, got in the face of the Argentinian referee and started screaming: 'He stamped on him . . . he stamped on him!' I heard it. I was right near Wazza and he looked at his Man United team-mate and couldn't believe his ears. 'Oi Ronnie, what you fucking doing!' he said, and pushed him gently away, 'I'm your team-mate . . . what you doing?!'

In that melee, there was a bad vibe in the air. I saw the Portuguese reactions. I saw the look of authority on the ref's face. And he stepped in front of Wazza and held his red card in the air. What a sickener. Me and JT just stood there with our mouths open, lost for words while the whole stadium seemed to groan. Look at the pictures of that moment and you can see Wazza closing his eyes in disbelief, and me gawping. I had to have a word with the ref: 'What about their foul on him! What you going to do about that?'

But he didn't understand me, and waved me away.

I could tell Wazza wanted to go mad. He was on the verge of losing it because it was such an injustice. But he had to walk. It's then that I went up to Ronaldo myself. 'Come on Ronnie, what you playing at?' I weren't in his face or nothing but I was letting him know that he was out of order.

'He stamped on his balls . . . I saw him,' he said.

'He never, and what about the foul before, eh?'

'You can't stamp on someone's balls,' and that's all he said before he went to wink at his dug-out. What gets me is the inconsistency of it all. Wazza was having his arms pulled off and that tangle should never have happened because it should have been our foul.

We'd had meetings with FIFA officials twice at our team hotel – once before the tournament and once during – and they'd told us the rules were tougher: any pulling of a shirt or player was an immediate yellow.

No second chances. We were also told deliberate diving was a yellow, but Portugal got away with *Swan Lake* in virtually every match. They must use diving boards in training or something. Ronaldo is among the worst in my view. He's a skilled player but he lets himself down with all that throwing himself around. He don't need to do it – he's a brilliant footballer.

With the sending-off, we had to sacrifice Joe Cole to make way for Crouchy. Suddenly, we were down to ten men, with no Wazza, Becks or Joe.

But the team effort after that was nothing short of heroic. Hargreaves was superb, Crouchy was amazing, and we all battled and battled and gave everything. On 78 minutes, a Lamps free kick was parried by their keeper and I was convinced Aaron was going to bang away the follow-up but it lacked pace. JT shot just over in the final minute of normal time. Our ten men had run Portugal ragged. In extra-time, we kept going – Crouchy and Aaron getting into the danger areas and going close.

Cramp was getting to a lot of us but we kept running and running, desperate for a way through. The longer the game went on though, the more the thought of penalties crept into my head. We'd had to defend more since the sending-off and the balance of play had tilted against us. When Aaron was substituted to make way for Jamie Carragher, I knew we were preparing for penalties. It was going to be a repeat of 2004. You can't practise a penalty. It don't work like that. You can't practise what it's like in that stadium, at that moment, with that pressure. So, yes, we banged them away in training but it's not the same. Penalties are a one-off moment. Dancers practise dance routines. Cheryl can rehearse a song. Get it right in rehearsals, get it right on the day. But not penalties. Practice don't make perfect penalty-taking.

I sat down on the pitch as we took in loads of water. There was a roaming TV camera on my shoulder and one of the masseurs was massaging my legs. They were heavy. I was knackered. We just needed one final push. I was sat there trying to block out all other emotions. Of course, you can't help but think about Southgate, Batty, Pearce, Beckham and Waddle and all those penalty nightmare misses of old. It lurks in your mind somewhere, adding more pressure and a little bit of fear.

I knew Cheryl and Mum would have been watching me. Cheryl told me later that she was thinking, 'Don't put yourself up for a penalty . . . just don't.' I think she was more worried than me. But I was always going to be one of the chosen penalty-takers.

'Keep your head Ash . . . keep your head,' said Gary Neville, as I laid out on the grass. To my left, there was a team huddle but I wanted to be on my own, in my own head, mentally preparing. When they came round to take the order, I said: 'I'll go number five.'

The stadium's loudspeakers played a song: *'Que Sera Sera . . .* whatever will be, will be . . .'

I took off my socks because they were getting baggy. I pulled them back on snug round my feet. I tied my shoelaces tight. Everything needed to be just right. I tried to forget about the last day in training when I'd taken two penalties and they'd both been saved by David James.

The week before, I couldn't miss; him and Robbo couldn't get nowhere near them. So I kept thinking about that week; kept thinking positive. Becks came up to me: 'Stay focused, stay positive!' As the keepers headed towards goal, we lined up as a team and linked arms in the centre circle, facing the goal that would become one long, slow walk away in the distance. We psyched ourselves up, shouting out to each other. 'THIS IS OUR TIME!', 'WE'RE GOING TO DO IT!', 'COME ON . . . WE'RE GOING THROUGH!' Owen Hargreaves was to my left,

Rio to my right. None of us could keep our feet still as we were standing there, nervous and restless but confident and believing.

We believed even when they scored and then Lamps had his shot saved.

Because then Viana missed for them, hitting the post, and the stadium went crazy. I wanted to scream with relief. Owen Hargreaves, the man who could do no wrong that night, stepped up and capped his performance by slotting home. 1–1.

Then they missed again. Surely, this time, in this place, it was ours. After all those other heart-breaking losses, now was our time. Score the next one and we're 2–1 up. Up stepped Stevie Gerrard. And missed. I started begging in my own head, 'Please don't let us lose this . . . please don't let us lose this.' Postiga scored their next. JT obviously felt some shoulders slump in the line. 'THIS IS OUR TIME LADS . . . WE'RE GOING TO DO IT!' He was still saying it. Or maybe, like a lot of us, he just weren't prepared to accept that it was all going tits up.

Then it was Jamie Carragher's turn. In training, he'd been the coolest penalty-taker ever. He didn't miss one. Not one. But he was up against it the moment he had to re-take. With his first, I knew the ref hadn't blown, and then you had to worry for him. Psychologically, the goal got smaller. I almost couldn't look. Up he goes, one more time. Saved. That's when our heads went down – just as Ronaldo walked up, knowing all he had to do was score. I was willing him to miss. Most of the stadium was willing him to miss. And 30 million people back home were, too. 'Miss it and let me take mine, let me have a go,' I thought. I would have been next. Miss it. Miss it. Miss it.

He scored, and there was a sickening eruption of cheers from the pocket of Portugal fans as a mass of redcurrant shirts rushed towards their keeper. It hurt so much. Everyone saw the devastation of the lads in the centre circle. Words cannot describe how bad it felt, or the shocked silence in the dressing room afterwards.

We should have beaten Portugal. With a little more luck and a referee that knew the difference between a stamp and getting entangled, we'd have done it. Even in extra-time with ten men, we still had good chances. We were two games away from being in the final. It's scary when I think about it now, and it gets me angry: two games away from being in the final, and we went out like we did. On our day, without doubt, we're better than them, France, Germany and Italy. The World Cup had our name written all over it, and it should have been our time. We should have won it. But we didn't play well enough and squandered a golden opportunity. We know we did. That's what made it so hard to take.

It was also hard to hear the odd moron chanting, 'WE'RE SHIT AND WE KNOW WE ARE . . . WE'RE SHIT AND WE KNOW WE ARE . . .' as we walked around the pitch, thanking the fans. It was more of a trudge. I did it in my white socks and then threw my red boots to a more appreciative fan. We hadn't been shit. Not in the quarter-final. But I was too numb to feel bothered. Normally, I'd look for Mum and Cheryl in the stand but I didn't want to find them this time; I was too close to tears. I just wanted to get to the dressing room and sit with a cold towel over my head.

Wazza was in his seat, already changed, when we got in there. A lot of the lads told him not to be hard on himself. A bit later, I was sat eating a Pot Noodle on the massage table when he came over to me. 'It's a joke what happened out there. I didn't mean it. I didn't do anything. Where was I supposed to put my foot?' he said.

'I know,' I said to him, 'but Ronnie was out of order – he's supposed to be your team-mate and he's doing that to you. It's a disgrace.'

For me, it was like Thierry trying to do one on me. Wazza and Ronaldo are good mates at Old Trafford. They get on. Which makes it even more of a disgrace, and the fact he winked at his bench afterwards makes it ten times worse.

To his credit though, Wazza was calm in the circumstances. He'd had more than an hour to himself to get the anger and injustice out of his system. He was gutted but calm.

On the coach to the airport, I was sat with him and we spoke a bit more. He was sorry, he said. Not that he was blaming himself but he knew we'd have had a better chance of winning with 11 men. It made him feel guilty but I told him it weren't his fault. I felt for him. I said Ronaldo was the one out of order. He was the one who should be saying sorry, I told him.

He was going to knock him out next time he saw him if he didn't say sorry, he said.

He felt let down by Ronaldo more than anything. He was pissed off. So was I. But he weren't baying for his blood or anything like that – although I reckon there could be some juicy tackles going in at the Manchester United training ground this season! Wazza isn't going to let it fester. Even on the coach, he started being peace-maker. I know the media would like to imagine it as a Rooney-Ronaldo war but the truth is different.

Wazza got out his mobile and tapped out a text to his Man United team-mate. By the look on his face, he was doing it through gritted teeth but he sent it. He texted something like:

'Well done Ron!' like he was being sarcastic or something, 'All the best in the next round.'

Far from issuing threats, Wazza congratulated him that night. I'm not sure if he got a reply though.

As we arrived at the team hotel back in Baden-Baden, all the staff started clapping us as we walked into the lobby. We weren't expecting that but it was a nice touch.

Before dinner, we were all asked to get together in one of the meeting rooms. That's when Sven said his goodbye. After five years, it was hard to believe he'd managed his last game for us. There was a lot of respect and sadness in that room as we all stood there, listening to him one final time.

He said he'd never known such a great bunch of lads, such a good

England team, and he felt sure we'd win a big tournament under our new manager, Steve McLaren. He said we were going home too early. You could tell he was hurt. It was all over his face. Then, with his voice cracking, he ended by saying: 'I would like to thank you all. Me and Tord [his assistant] have had the time of our lives and we wish you all good luck for the future.' The applause for him probably echoed down the Rhine Valley, and it showed how popular he was.

Then Steve McLaren stepped up. He said that when Sven joined, the England team was going nowhere, uncertain of World Cup qualification for 2002. But then he created a team that qualified three times – for that tournament, the European Championships 2004 and the World Cup 2006 – and there had been some memorable results. 'And Sven,' he said, 'I am going to be honoured and privileged to work with this team after you.' We all started clapping again. It was emotionally charged in that room. So many different feelings from a mad day. We were all pleased Steve was the new man in charge, picking up the baton, but sad to be losing Sven. When he went to bed that night, about an hour after dinner, he said goodnight to each player and member of the FA staff. It was a quiet exit in the end.

The whole squad then went to the bar, unable to sleep, all sat around one big table, drinking beers. Becks went to his room. We didn't know it at the time but it was to draft his resignation speech as captain. But he's still got so much to give to the team as a player, and he'll always be someone to look up to no matter whether he's wearing the armband or not.

It was the end of an era on so many fronts, and a time for new beginnings. I still had no idea where I'd be playing the 2006–07 season but I couldn't think too much about that because there was a new life as a married man to focus on. The biggest fixture and event of the year, the wedding, was two weeks away.

12

New Futures

After the Sweden match I was tired and achy when I linked up with Cheryl. We were sat on the bed in the hotel, chilling with the TV on when I went to her: 'I think I've done something to my neck . . .'

'What's the matter with it?' she asked.

'Just got a sore neck . . . can you have a look at it?'

'Well, before I do, you better have a look at my neck first . . .'

She sat up, half-turned away from me, lifted up her hair and there it was – a new tattoo with the words, inked in italics, saying 'Mrs C'.

They'd done a good job with it, it was a nice touch. I'm going to get a similar one done. Just don't know yet what it will say. Cheryl had returned to London in the middle of the World Cup to do a photo shoot for Girls Aloud before our final group match, and she'd nipped into her favourite tattoo parlour. She was 'Miss T' at the time but was planning ahead, and it was a little surprise for me. It weren't that premature. I've had her name stored in my phone as 'WIFE' for ages. The 'Mrs C' tattoo was one of a million things Cheryl had been planning ahead of the big day. Looking back, it makes you wonder where she got the time what with her own UK tour, the World Cup and us moving house and everything. I don't know how she managed it all.

We'd moved in May into what would become our new marital home; we needed a house with a garden not a flat, and we love it there. It backs onto a golf course, and it's a great place to come home and chill.

Our wedding was Saturday 15 July 2006 – six days after Italy had been crowned world champions. I'm taking none of the credit for sorting the day. It was Cheryl's hard work and vision that made it happen, together with the wedding planner Katie Mash and Banana Split. Cheryl knew exactly what she wanted, and Katie knew exactly how to make the dream happen. And Cheryl even had the carriage, pulled by two white horses, just as she'd imagined it back in Dubai when we'd got engaged.

All I did was try on the gear and join in the food-tasting sessions. The details, ideas and inspirations were Cheryl's. She tried to persuade me to wear a top hat but I weren't having it, so that was the only time I dug in my heels!

For legal reasons over licences, we'd married the day before, the Friday, at Sopwell House Hotel. It was an informal, private ceremony and I'm going to keep it that way, witnessed by close family. But it weren't *the* wedding, or *the* main event. Our dream occasion, and the big day Cheryl had put her heart and soul into, was reserved for Wrotham Park, Hertfordshire, where friends shared in our celebration. It couldn't have gone better.

All the media was still convinced the venue was Highclere Castle. It was funny because the papers had been full of it all week, showing photos of Highclere, and telling everyone THIS was the 'secret' venue. We laughed when we saw the *Evening Standard* printed a big photo of the castle with a headline: 'On Saturday, she marries Ashley Cole at this enormous castle . . .' and all the nationals followed suit the next day. As predicted, every piece mentioned the same thing – that we'd chosen 'where Jordan and Peter Andre had got married'. So we were right to switch venues.

The press only found out about Wrotham Park on the morning of the wedding, and went mad, apparently, reckoning they'd been made to look like right idiots. But they'd got other stuff wrong, too. Like Victoria Beckham had given Cheryl advice on what dress to wear, and what designer to use while they were out in Baden-Baden – as if she'd not got her dress designed and ready by then! They said we'd paid the owners of Highclere to put up a massive marquee to throw the media off the scent but the marquee was for another party that had nothing to do with us. All we'd done was ask Highclere to say nothing. Then they reckoned our dog Buster had a special sequin outfit made for him by Girls Aloud and was to attend the wedding, but that was rubbish. People wrote madness half the time, and it's the reason why we chose to do a deal with *OK!* to make sure our wedding was told in our words, and the facts were correct.

I'd been chilled up until the big day. I'd gone to Marbella immediately after Germany with Jermaine Jenas and Rio and we'd seen Joe Cole and Michael Carrick out there. Everyone called it a stag do but it was nothing but a break to be honest. After coming back from the World Cup absolutely gutted, I needed to get away; an escape from reality for a bit. I needed to get a clear head for the wedding. World Cup then straight to Marbella – I'd rather that than be at home, having time to get nervous. I switched off poolside and did nothing but chill with the lads. By the time I got back, I only had five days to think about my nerves. I suppose reality hit me on the Monday before the Saturday when our home was wedding prep headquarters: there was a stylist measuring my head for the top hat I'd never wear, and asking me about shoes and trouser sizes, there was a hairdresser putting foil in Cheryl's hair, there was Girls Aloud trying on their bridesmaid dresses, and there were table plans scattered around the place.

I'd prepared for Paris and Barcelona. I'd prepared for Germany and the World Cup. But the build-up nerves to Hertfordshire and our wedding was something different. Just thinking about my speech gave me the jitters. For Cheryl, just thinking about the day made her cry.

On the Friday night, we did the traditional thing and stayed in separate hotels. I used a hotel the England team use now and again – The Grove. It's about a 20-minute drive from Wrotham Park and the nearby chapel we'd chosen for the wedding.

Come the big day, the weather was gorgeous, and I'd soon have a chance to moan about the heat again; it was as hot in my Roberto Cavalli tailcoat suit as it was in the Waldstadion for the Paraguay match! And my room was as packed and busy as any football dressing room, with shoe boxes and suit carriers strewn everywhere.

There was a photographer and his assistant from *OK!*, my writer friend Steve Dennis, best man Mattie, and groomsmen Jermaine Wynters, Paulo Vernazza, Jon Fortune, and Cecil Talian, all getting into their specially-made suits. And the hotel manager John Cole kept popping in to make sure everything was going smooth. 'Soccer AM' was on Sky to keep the boys occupied while I sat on the bed rehearsing my speech, over and over.

I timed myself. Three minutes. Shit – it weren't meant to be that long.

'It's all in the delivery,' said Wynters, 'you can't just read it out you know, you've got to get the tone right.' As if I didn't have enough to worry about. I read it again, and again, and again – getting the 'delivery' right. Soon enough, as we started getting changed, the boys had their own issues to fret about: fiddling with their cuff-links, failing to fit the button-hole roses, clueless how to do Windsor tie knots, and worrying about the sweat showing through their extra-thin cream shirts. It was hot, and we were all sweating before we even got outside. 'Look at my pits!' they were all saying.

I'd only ever seen Thierry Henry fuss about his appearance more!

I stood in the window, near the dressing table, to practise my speech one more time in my head. On the table, there were the his and hers wedding rings in their burgundy Stephen Webster presentation boxes. When the boys weren't looking, I opened up Cheryl's box for one last look, and her eight-carat heart-shaped yellow diamond dazzled back at me. She's going to look gorgeous, I thought.

'Are you sure you're going to be okay looking after the rings?' I asked brother Mattie. He told me to chill.

'I'm not sure about him and those rings,' I said to Wynters, 'and where's my speech . . . who's got my speech?'

There was a girl from hotel reception in the room. She'd answered our SOS on the button-hole front. 'The cars have arrived!' someone shouted 'and we're already late. The bride's supposed to be late, not the groom!'

'Mattie, have you *got* the rings?' I asked him as we went to the door.

'Yeah, look . . .' and as he brought them out, one of the presentation box lids fell open and my ring dropped out, and rolled across the wooden floor and under the bed. He picked it up – then dropped it again.

'Wynters, look after the rings until we get to the chapel!' I said.

I had the best brother to be best man and his speech would turn out to be spot on, but trusting him with the rings was too much for my nerves. We all piled down a fire-exit to avoid the press. I'd not told the boys that two Rolls-Royce Phantoms would be taking us to the chapel; they thought they were wicked.

'Right,' said Jon Fortune, 'let's go start the rest of your life.'

*

'Keep looking straight ahead, and I'll be fine,' I was thinking, over and over.

I was standing at the altar with Reverend Keri Eynon in front of me in his robes; Mum ahead of me to the left with other relatives; Cheryl's mum to the right with her family; and the seven-strong, white-suited Gospel Choir straight ahead beneath the arched stained glass window. Behind me, every pew was packed and there was that quiet murmur of people whispering as we waited for the bride. The groomsmen were sitting on the front pew behind me to the right, trying to distract me with some banter, trying to keep me laughing. Maybe they noticed I was swallowing hard.

Outside the chapel, it had been madness with the press. I'd fought through a scrum with the groomsmen just to get from car to chapel door. I kept thinking about Cheryl arriving in her horse-drawn carriage and getting through that lot. She was late, but she's always late. Kick-off should have been 5 p.m. It was more like 5.30. Then I heard the shuffling of feet, people shifting on the pews.

She's here, she's here. I looked round and saw the seven brides-maids, all in matching 1950s-style knee-length dresses, reddy-pink in colour. Cheryl tells me it was coral. I saw her band-mate Kimberley Walsh with a tissue in her hand, all teary-eyed, and then I had to look away. The Gospel Choir started up, singing Alicia Keys' 'If I Ain't Got You'. Then I started to go, almost. Cheryl had chosen all the songs for the ceremony. The moment she joined me to my right at the altar, I could tell she was looking at me. I turned to look at her. She just looked so amazing – like a little princess. That's when I did cry. I'm not talking a full-on Gazza cry. I'm talking a few tears. But it was emotional. And then Cheryl started. And that was almost a full-on Gazza. Her dress was out of this world. Now, I've got Cheryl to help with this next description – to get it right. Because it's not enough to say she looked beautiful in a stunning dress. I've got to describe it. Women are best at those things so, it's like Cheryl says, it was a Roberto Cavalli number with sequins, beads and diamanté, and silk sleeves edged with pearl buttons, and the back of the dress had a train trimmed with tiny bows. As soon as I saw her, I thought, 'Wow!'

When it came to the 'exchange of promises', we stood facing each other, holding each other by both hands. Just before the reverend did his piece, I leaned forward and whispered to her how amazing she looked. The reverend thought I was going in for the kiss. 'I've not said you may kiss the bride yet!' he joked. The laughter rescued Cheryl from a full on blub.

'Ashley, do you take Cheryl to be your wife in marriage?' he asked, and Cheryl gripped my hands, and looked up to the roof, letting out deep breaths, trying to compose herself as I said 'I do'.

'Cheryl, do you take Ashley to be your husband in marriage?' he asked her, and she'd recovered and was beaming. 'I do,' she said. The Gospel Choir sang 'Ain't No Mountain High Enough'. Then we made our vows, calling upon all those people present to witness us say 'to have and to hold, for better for worse, for richer for poorer, in sickness and in health' and all that. Cheryl had joked that she'd wanted 'for fatter for thinner' but she couldn't have everything! We exchanged rings, our families lit candles to symbolise unity, and the reverend 'pronounced' us as husband and wife. And then the Gospel Choir sang 'Oh Happy Day'. Then me and Mrs Cole led the way to the reception, a short ride away, at Wrotham Park where the marquee and the tables for the wedding breakfast looked belting. We couldn't have found a better location. And this was Cheryl's unique day; where 'Ashley Cole and Cheryl Tweedy got married'. No-one else. Our location. Our day.

Cheryl's dad Garry was first up with the speeches. Half the marquee was full of Geordies from Cheryl's side of the family so when he whipped out a Newcastle United No. 3 shirt with 'Cole' on the back, it got the loudest cheer of the day. Then Mattie did a nice – and harmless – best-man's speech. Then it was my turn. I'd wanted to make it serious not funny and, instead of trying to describe it, this is the speech in full. I'll let you imagine the silence and my nerves but this sums it all up for me:

> First of all, I'd like to thank everyone for joining me and Cheryl – or should I say Mrs Cole – in this celebration of our marriage. It is a special day for us both, and it's important that so many friends and family are here to share it with us.
>
> We're also a bit relieved to see that you all made it. We were starting to worry that you'd believe everything you read in the newspapers and end up in the middle of Berkshire asking for directions to Highclere Castle. I'm not one for great speeches. I had one all planned out in my head when I proposed to Cheryl on the sand dunes in Dubai. But I went to pieces the moment I went down on one knee.
>
> But I'd like to say that I feel like the luckiest, happiest man around today, and I'm proud to call myself Cheryl's husband, and Cheryl as my wife.
>
> Ever since we met near the tennis courts at our old flat, I knew she'd end up marrying me. She played hard to get for a while and tried to play it cool but, like Arsene Wenger taught me, always keep tight to your man and they'll never get away. And I was never going to let Cheryl get away, and I knew she was having me from day one . . .
>
> Seriously, Cheryl is my biggest support, my best friend and now my wife and I'm proud to stand in front of you all and declare how much I love her, and how happy she makes me. And, as everyone can see, she makes a beautiful bride. The rest of Girls Aloud don't look too bad either . . . and I'd like to thank them, the other gorgeous bridesmaids and my brilliant ushers for doing such a good job today.
>
> Cheryl is also the reason today has happened. Her input and signature is all over this wedding, and she has shaped and visualised

this whole occasion from day one. I may have looked at the plans, nodded in the right places and done as I was told . . . but she has put her heart and soul into today and I'd like to thank her and Katie Mash at Banana Split and everyone here at Wrotham Park for working so hard to make this day extra special when there was also one World Cup, one 'Chemistry' tour, and one house move to think about.

Apart from Cheryl, there are also two other very special women here today – our mums Sue and Joan. I don't think either of us know where we would be without your love and support, and we can't thank you enough for all that you do for us both. You've been behind us from day one in our careers and during our relationship, and we're lucky to have mums like you cheering us on . . .

I'd like to thank you all again for sharing this day, and I know some of you have travelled far to be here. We hope you'll have a memorable day with us.

And then I made a toast to 'my beautiful bride, my wife . . . Cheryl'.

I got through it okay in the end, and I relaxed after that. But Cheryl had one last surprise for me up her silk sleeve. She led me to the floor for the first dance and then the toastmaster announced on the mike that, specially for me, she had flown in from America John Legend. I couldn't believe it as this circular stage slowly revolved round, and there he was – the legend himself – sat at his piano. It was an unbelievable moment to add to so many other unbelievable moments on an unforgettable day. Once John Legend played his brilliant numbers, we then had a surprise for the other guests. Two doors either side of the stage slid open to reveal 'Ashley & Cheryl's Nightclub' with Masterstepz on the decks, and everyone drifted through and had a belting time, partying through till two in the morning. For us, it was great to see so many dancing, so many people enjoying themselves, and sharing it all with us.

We spoke about the day all the way to our honeymoon in the Seychelles. Everything had gone perfect from start to finish.

I never for a minute expected to return to Arsenal's training ground for the 2006–07 season. I'd made it clear to the boss I'd be leaving, I'd said my goodbyes, emptied my locker, and spoken to team-mates during the close season. 'The Final Salute' had been a whispered goodbye to the fans – and it felt like a farewell not many would have been bothered about anyway.

Back at our meeting in May, the boss had asked if I'd thought of a club I wanted to join. He floated some names: Real Madrid? Barcelona? Chelsea?

Yes, *he* mentioned Chelsea.

So we spoke about those clubs and that's when he said Chelsea shouldn't be ruled out. As much as he didn't want me to join them, if they paid the right money and I wanted to go, he said 'the club wouldn't stand in my way'. Those very words would become important later on.

I told him I hadn't given Chelsea much thought because, in all the tapping-up saga, they'd made it clear they weren't interested. There was also a lot of talk at the time about Roberto Carlos joining them so what was the point? 'If I'm honest, boss, I'm still dealing with my decision to leave. I just want to concentrate on the World Cup but, if anywhere, I'd say Madrid . . .' I told him.

That's when he said G14 – the group of elite clubs in Europe – was meeting at the end of May, and Mr Dein would speak to Real Madrid. I left for Germany with the belief that Arsenal would have already started talks. Everyone's minds seemed made-up. The boss had even told me that he was going to start looking for a new left-back.

By the time I came home from honeymoon, I expected a virtual done deal, as swift as Patrick's with Juventus. I'm not sure whether Arsenal thought I weren't that serious or whether I'd change my mind but nothing had been sorted when I returned home. It was a million miles away from being sorted. Arsenal were late to open up negotiations, Madrid were nowhere, and all the paper talk was about Chelsea. And what with all the recent history, it was never going to be a smooth passage from then on.

I'd sensed trouble even before I arrived home – I'd read something in the paper while in the Seychelles with Cheryl. And when I say 'paper' I literally mean an A4 sheet – the daily newsletter of world headlines dropped into our villa. What the British papers started calling 'the most controversial transfer in Premiership history' was even making news in the Indian Ocean. I read that Arsenal had put a price of £30 million on my head.

'That can't be true,' I said to Cheryl, sure the papers had it wrong, and we both laughed about it.

Only it seemed to be true, according to the newspapers I saw when I got back. Chelsea had, apparently, held 'civil' talks with Arsenal. Peter Kenyon made a £16 million offer but David Dein wanted £30 million; the same man who had told the FAPL inquiry that my value was between £15 and £20 million. And why should Chelsea pay £10 million over the odds, regardless of how financially sound the club may be?

Lots of figures were being thrown around but nothing seemed to get sorted, and progress was slow and frustrating. I felt like a bargaining chip, with the stakes too high. I didn't know whether I'd be playing in red, white or blue, and all I kept reading about was a £30 million barrier to progress or realism. It felt to me that Arsenal had done nothing to keep me last season, and now it seemed obstacles were piling up at the exit door. Even the papers picked up on it, with one article observing: 'Arsenal are doing everything they can to spike the guns of both Cole and Chelsea.'

Arsenal did not want me to write this book, too, withdrawing permission for me to use official club photographs which did nothing more than capture great memories from my time at Highbury. There'd been all sorts of stories about Arsenal demanding to change chapters in this book. 'GUNNERS THROW BOOK AT ASHLEY' said the *Sun*, but it weren't true. The club asked to see a copy of the book before publication but we refused.

Its behaviour puzzled me to be honest. Once again, in relation to my transfer, it seemed intent on turning a molehill into a mountain. Another saga was played out in the newspapers, and it made them look silly in my view – trying to keep a player who made it clear he didn't want to stay. By dragging things out, it allowed my uncertain future to overshadow a pre-season tour to Austria and the opening fixtures in the new Premiership and Champions League season.

The media noted Arsene Wenger's frustration over the distraction and I'm like screaming in my head, saying, 'Well get it sorted and stop mucking around with Chelsea then!!!'

And all I could do was watch it unfold in the reports on TV and in print almost every morning. Arsenal seemed to be flexing its muscles, wanting to look like they were doing all they could to keep me. Chelsea stood firm. Arsenal wouldn't budge. Chelsea backed away. The deal was on, then off.

Talks broke down, then got going again. And all the time, I was stuck at home, observing everything get jammed with mounting despair. It got to the stage where I wanted everyone to cut the crap, stop the posturing and just get the deal done. I wanted to phone Mr Abramovich myself and tell him how much I wanted to leave – just to make it clear, in case he was hearing something different. It all dragged on through July and August, right up to the transfer window deadline at midnight on 31 August. It felt like Arsenal were toying with Chelsea, toying with my future. I've heard people talk in the past about 'player power' but I've never felt so powerless in my life. It's the clubs themselves that have to sort the deals out. All I could do was watch and wait.

Leo Spall in the *Evening Standard* weren't wrong when he wrote:

'The Ashley Cole transfer saga has had more twists and turns than a fortnight of *EastEnders*.'

The one episode that intrigued the media was my reported meeting with Mr Dein on Monday 31 July, three days after returning from honeymoon. It wasn't a meeting I'd expected to have because I'd been laid up on the Sunday with a pounding head, sickness and a gut that was hanging. I'd called physio Gary Lewin and told the club doctor all about it because the first day of pre-season training was the Monday. With the rest of the squad still in Austria on a pre-season tour, they told me to rest up and not to worry.

But come Monday, when I felt even worse, I got a call from my agent Jonathan. 'Look,' he said, 'you're going to have to go in. All the television cameras are there, David Dein is there, all eyes are on you, and he reckons you're trying to mug him off in front of the media.'

I was too ill to drive myself so Cheryl took me in, and waited in the car park. 'You shouldn't be going in this state. What's he expect you to do when you're ill?' she said.

The first face I saw in reception at London Colney was Sean O'Connor, who runs the training ground. He told me Mr Dein was waiting in the boss's office. I felt too rough to care. The media went on to describe our meeting as 'an angry showdown' but it was nothing of the sort. It was civil for the hour we met. Mr Dein, suited and booted as usual, was all smiles and charm and good with words. I was dressed in tracksuit and flip-flops, and just told him straight what I thought. I sat on the sofa. He pulled up a chair, and sat there with his notepad and pen. I felt a bit inferior again, just like the time at his house.

We got the small talk out of the way: the wedding, the honeymoon, and the Seychelles. And all the time, I'm thinking, 'Just hurry up . . . hurry up . . . or I'm going to throw up.'

Then he told me that, whatever I thought of him, I was wrong; wrong to leave Arsenal, wrong to write the book, and that he didn't think that I meant half of what I'd said about him.

'No, seriously, I mean what I've said, Mr Dein. I'm allowed an opinion, and I've just told the story from my point of view.'

He then said I owed Arsenal because it had made me the player I am but I weren't having that. 'I've made myself Mr Dein,' I told him. He shook his head, unable to agree. 'What makes players like me is fight, spirit, determination and ambition to be a winner,' I added.

When we eventually got down to the transfer talk, I told him: 'You're taking the piss by asking for £30 million, because I thought you only rated me at £20 million.'

And he was like frowning, looking puzzled, and saying, 'No, no, no', disagreeing again. So I reminded him about his value of me at the inquiry. 'But not once have I felt like you've treated me like a £20 million player – I still feel I'm treated like a kid. And then you're asking for £30 million. It don't stack up.'

'Well, Chelsea *have* to pay more,' he said, and he went on about Michael Essien signing for £24 million, Didier Drogba joining them for £24 million, Shaun Wright-Phillips for £21 million, and Shevchenko for £30 million, in order, I guess, to back up his argument that I was worth £30 million to Chelsea.

'So, you're going to kill all our chances of sorting out this mess by holding to that valuation?' It was my one chance to make my feelings known, not via an agent.

He went on to explain that Arsenal were losing one of their best players, one of their best assets and, as a result, were making Chelsea better. I actually think he said '*them* better' but it was clear who he meant. If they wanted me that much, they'd have to pay, he explained.

'Well whose fault is it that you're losing me? It's not my fault, it's your fault!' and we traced old circles.

But I wanted him to know that I weren't happy with the handling of negotiations with Chelsea. 'You're asking too much, you know they're not going to pay it,' I said, knowing the boss had earlier said the club wouldn't stand in my way. He disagreed – again – and said Chelsea will pay.

'What happens if they don't, Mr Dein?' I asked, fighting another wave of sickness.

And that's when he said that I'd have to stay at Arsenal and see out the two years left on my contract. I felt too lousy to feel anger but decided to spell it out for him. 'I've told you I don't want to play here no more. It's not fair on anyone if I stay, not me, not the manager, not the players, not the fans. Because if I make a mistake or don't have a brilliant match, I'll get the blame. I don't want to go into every game with all the pressure on my shoulders again. So now what?'

'Would you consider playing for any other clubs in England? What about Manchester United, Newcastle or Liverpool? Do you want me to call them for you?' he asked.

He made it clear that he'd sell me quicker than he could click his fingers if it was Real Madrid or Barcelona. 'But I don't want to go abroad any more,' I told him.

'Oh, so you've changed your entire argument about wanting to go abroad now?'

What he didn't realise was that me and Cheryl had spoken a lot on our honeymoon about a life in Madrid. I know that she'd discussed it with Victoria Beckham in Germany and, going into the World Cup, I'd have said there was a 75 per cent chance of me moving to Spain. But Real Madrid's Fabio Capello hadn't come in for me, Roberto Carlos had seemed set to stay on at the Bernabeu and I didn't want to go there as second choice, and so we'd done some serious rethinking. We're newly married, we love our new house, Cheryl's career is in the UK and I had to ask myself if I really fancied moving to a different country and being alone for long spells. When you put it all into the melting pot, and it all becomes real, you tend to think differently. The upshot was that we both agreed to shelve dreams of playing in Europe. Ask any player or agent, a dream move can suddenly not look so attractive when the personal situation is considered. Cheryl and me being just married, happy and settled in London was a decisive factor. I'm happy, so why mess with it?

We'd also discussed Chelsea after the boss told me not to rule them out. Somehow, while lazing in the sun in the Indian Ocean, the switch from north to west London didn't seem so bad.

'I'll get hammered if I go there, the Arsenal fans will never forgive me,' I said to Cheryl one evening.

It took her to point out the blinding obvious: 'They've hammered you anyway, and they've never forgiven you for the past eighteen months . . . so what's the difference!' Mrs Cole had a point. She said it was like the jealous husband who forever falsely accused the wife of cheating. In the end, so fed up with the accusations, she just goes and does it anyway because the grief couldn't get any worse. I couldn't have put it better myself. That's what we'd discussed and that's what I explained to Mr Dein.

I also needed to remind him why we were here in the first place. 'You ask the fans,' I said, 'and all this is *my* fault. I'm "greedy", "disloyal", I "forgot my roots" and I'm "a traitor". I'm "scum" – and that's all because of how the events of the last eighteen months have been portrayed. The impression given was that I was greedy. And, to be honest, I don't feel that Arsenal ever once publicly backed me.'

I was feeling so ill. But my argument was slick. And, so he could be sure not to blame agents, I reminded him of something else as well. 'Regardless of whether it was you or someone else on the board, one of you didn't want me to re-sign for Arsenal. I didn't ask for ninety grand a week. I didn't even ask for the same wages as other players. I asked for sixty grand!'

Then it all came out: his take-it-or-leave-it offer, the £55k a week offer, the decision to risk me for £5,000.

'Maybe it was both our faults,' he said, and I think he'd sensed my injustice.

But I couldn't share the blame. 'No, Arsenal started all this, and it didn't have to be like this!'

After an hour of non-stop talking, it was clear there was no future for me at the club. He even invited me to get Peter Kenyon on the phone, get us all in a room together and 'we can have this sorted in an hour'.

Then he said he wanted to sort a swap deal with Chelsea. 'Well who you asking for? Shaun Wright-Phillips?' I asked.

'No, we want Gallas.' It was a timely wish because William Gallas had just failed to show for Chelsea's pre-season tour of the United States. I think Mr Dein was resigned to losing me on that final day in July. So why it took another 31 pointless, agonising days, I've no idea.

'Have you heard anything?' asked Arsene Wenger during training as time ticked by without any news.

'Erm . . . shouldn't I be asking you that question boss?' I said.

I'd been left out of the official team photograph because he 'felt something could happen in the next few days', but nothing did. By mid-August, the scary thought crept into my mind that I'd have to walk back across a broken bridge, and stay at Arsenal. The thought depressed me, and it probably didn't do much for the boss either. I sensed he was sick and tired of the speculation that had dogged the previous season and was now overshadowing a new one. I think the whole thing affected our relationship to be honest, made us both a bit wary and it all got a bit awkward between us for a bit. That was sad because I'd never had a problem with the boss, the fans or the staff. But I suddenly felt like an outsider, an outcast – even though Arsenal kept reminding everyone I was still one of them. Every day became the same: go early into London Colney, do training and then leave. And as every day passed without progress, I felt chained to Arsenal.

I remember the last week of August for how bleak everything looked. Chelsea had seemed to walk away, refusing to pay the 'ransom money' as some people were referring to the price tag. Arsenal's chairman Peter Hill-Wood had started talking about how I 'needed to get my head right' for the new season. And Betfair slashed my odds of staying from 8–1 to 11/10. Somebody, somewhere seemed to know something.

By Wednesday 30 August, I was with the England squad in Manchester, preparing for our first Euro Championship 2008 qualifier versus Andorra. In the back of my mind, I was mentally gearing myself up for sticking out another season at Arsenal. It seemed like the personal nightmare was going to continue. If they couldn't sort out an agreement in six weeks, what hope did they have in the 24 hours before the transfer window deadline? I went to bed wondering how it had all gone wrong, angry that Arsenal's negotiating tactics seemed to have blocked my move.

It was just before training with the England squad the following day that my mobile rang. 'Both clubs are talking again,' said my agent Jonathan, 'so keep your phone on and stand by.'

I'd been lazing on my hotel bed but, after that phone call, I started pacing the room, unable to settle. I was like a wasp at training, buzzing everywhere: excited, anxious, worried, pumped-up. I looked at JT and Lamps and Shaun Wright-Phillips, and wanted to be their club, as well as international, team-mate. 'You heard anything yet?' they asked. 'Nothing,' I said, as my mind counted down the minutes that turned into hours.

Then, back at the hotel, the phone rings. It's Jonathan. Both clubs had reached an agreement. The deal was a straight swap with William Gallas plus £5 million. And a medical had been lined up for me at a hospital in Rochdale. When I heard that, I'd never moved so fast; faster even than when sprinting to make that block in the World Cup against Ecuador.

The doctors gave the thumbs-up to Chelsea, and I'd signed the papers to become a Chelsea player by 10 o'clock that night. By the time all the paperwork had been completed in London, the deal was done with minutes to spare before the transfer deadline doors shut. Talk about cutting it fine!

I was so happy, I couldn't begin to explain. I rang Cheryl. I rang Mum. And then lay back, mentally drained, on my bed, knowing I could now concentrate and get back to playing – and enjoying – my football.

'I knew it'd be alright in the end!' said Rio over breakfast before the Andorra match the next day.

'I'm glad you were confident – because I bloody weren't!' I said.

It was after the Andorra game – which we won 5–0 – when I was really able to think about it all for the first time. I'd only ever known one club since the age of nine so it felt weird to be thinking about Stamford Bridge as my new home. But the quiet elation I also felt told me that it was the right move. I know from JT, Lamps and Joe Cole what a great club Chelsea is, and what a great spirit there is. I need to be at a club where I can feel that kind of spirit again, and I feel I'll better myself for being there. It's a fresh start.

Of course, I'll get absolutely caned by the Arsenal fans and that's something I've got to deal with. In the same professional manner that Sol dealt with his move from Tottenham to Arsenal, and how Emmanuel Petit dealt with his move from Arsenal to Chelsea. The Arsenal fans will think I'm disloyal but it's my life, and I weren't happy there no more. I'd given it a year to see if the situation improved and it hadn't. It was a miserable, forgettable year for me – apart from the Champions League final.

I never thought I'd see the day when I'd actually leave Arsenal. I just hope the fans understand where I've come from, the reasons for leaving and the reasons for doing this book. I'm not asking for sympathy – just an awareness of what's gone on, how I didn't want to leave, and how I feel the board messed things up. Not me.

This situation couldn't have just been my fault. I'm not disloyal. I'm a loyal and honest person and I've got principles. I can wake up in the morning and look at myself in the mirror knowing that I've done no wrong. I tried to be fair. I tried to be decent. I wonder if the Arsenal board could say the same?

I'd only ever worn red and white all my life – from childhood through to first team football. But now blue is the colour. It'll take some getting used to and that first moment when I pulled a blue shirt over my head was weird but thrilling. I've rediscovered real excitement for being at a club again, and rediscovered a happiness without hassle and grief weighing me down. I look back to Arsenal and regret only that the dream turned sour. I don't regret all those wonderful years there. I don't regret leaving. For things to turn round at the Emirates Stadium, in my view the board will need to put its money where its mouth is, and invest in the team just like it promised Thierry it would do. I've not seen much evidence of what I think is needed by way of investment in the recent transfer window and, however shrewd Arsene Wenger is, Arsenal needs to build a new team and a new future not just a new stadium. Or it will be letting down its players and fans.

With England, life already looks good under new coach Steve McClaren. We're upbeat again but we know we've got a lot of hard work ahead of us. The European Championships 2008 is next up in Austria and Switzerland, and the qualifiers have already started in our qualifying group, Group E, where we'll come up against Croatia, Russia, Israel, Estonia, Macedonia and Andorra. We've got to fancy our chances. But first, my eyes are on the new Premiership campaign, and a new era with Chelsea. It's going to be a challenge in itself, but I'm relishing it.

I look back to January 2005 and can't get my head round what has happened, and how much has changed. One Champions League final, one World Cup, two legal battles, one house move, one dream wedding. And a transfer from north to west London.

I'm glad I've written it all down because it's given me the chance to review it and take it all in. If you'd have told me at the start of 2005 that

I'd be wearing a blue shirt and running out for home fixtures at Stamford Bridge this season, I'd have laughed in your face. But here I am. Some would say that's life. I'd say 'that's football'.

But that was then. This is now. I've got my memories and medals from Arsenal; they will always be special. I'll treasure them. They're one part of Arsenal and Highbury that will be with me forever, and no amount of stick or boos from the fans can tarnish them.

But I've had enough of looking back for the time being. I've put my side of the story across. It's now time to look forward; a time for new futures with Cheryl, Chelsea and England.

Co-writer acknowledgements

When Ashley hobbled in to our first meeting in the winter of 2005, his belief in this book, and the reasons for writing it, were as obvious as his passion for the game, and it's been a blast working alongside him. So my thanks firstly go to him and Cheryl for making this book such a joy to work on, for your hospitality, co-operation, endless patience, and fun company. Thanks for everything – including the spag bol and the golf.

Big thanks also to: Ashley's mum, Sue, for your invaluable input and showing me how to go nuts at a match; Cheryl's mum, Joan, for your endless refreshments; and all of Ashley's mates – especially Jermaine Wynters and Steve 'Winky' Jacobs – who've not only made me feel welcome but have chipped in with advice, stories and drinks along the way.

Without the vision and encouragement of Ashley's agent, Jonathan

Barnett, this book would never have happened, and I'm indebted to him and everyone else at Stellar Group – especially David Manesseh, Johnny Whitmore and Zara Parness – for your help and support. Thank you to my agent Ali Gunn, of Gunn Media, for hauling me off the bench and selecting me as part of this team.

Huge thanks also to: everyone at Headline, including managing editor Lorraine Jerram, Rhea Halford, Sarah Kellard, Rachel Geere, Wendy McCance, Sarah Thomson, Caitlin Raynor and Georgina Moore but most especially sports publisher David 'High Fidelity' Wilson who, despite being a Partick Thistle fan, actually has sound judgement and his faith in this book kept driving me and Ashley forward.

Ashley's lawyers Graham Shear and Alison Green for your time and guidance; 'Gooner' Alan Edwards for your insight; Simon Townsend and Stephen White for your crucial 'assists', and Katie Mash at Banana Split for helping me polish the wedding details.

Special thanks are reserved to my twin brother Ian Dennis – your Five Live football wisdom and anorak knowledge was always there to be relied on. Thanks kid. And my heartfelt thanks, as ever, to Mum and Dad, Cliff and Shirl, and big sis Nic for your endless love and support.

And finally, thank you to the England players' families who helped make Baden-Baden such a memorable occasion, not forgetting the unsung heroines of organisation at the FA – Carol Day and Kelly Brown.

Steve Dennis
August 2006

MY DEFENCE